Conquest and Catastrophe

CONQUEST
and
CATASTROPHE

Changing Rio Grande Pueblo
Settlement Patterns in the
Sixteenth and Seventeenth Centuries

ELINORE M. BARRETT

UNIVERSITY OF NEW MEXICO PRESS

ALBUQUERQUE

© 2002 by the University of New Mexico Press
All rights reserved.
First edition

First paperbound printing, 2009
Paperbound ISBN: 978-0-8263-2412-2

15 14 13 12 11 10 09   1 2 3 4 5 6 7

Library of Congress Cataloging-in-Publication Data:

Barrett, Elinore M.
Conquest and catastrophe : changing Rio Grande pueblo settlement patterns
in the sixteenth and seventeenth centuries / Elinore M. Barrett. —1st ed.
p.   cm.
Includes bibliographical references and index.
ISBN 0-8263-2411-8
1. Pueblo Indians—Rio Grande Valley.
2. Pueblo Indians—Land tenure—Rio Grande Valley.
3. Pueblo Indians—Relocation.
4. Land settlement patterns—Rio Grande Valley—History.
5. Pueblo Revolt, 1680. 6. Mexico—History—Spanish colony, 1540–1810.
7. New Mexico—History—To 1848. I. Title.
E99.P9 B355 2002
978.9'01—dc21

2001005020

DESIGN: Mina Yamashita

To Robert D. Campbell

Contents

List of Illustrations

Maps

Tables·

Appendix Tables

Abbreviations

ARMS refers to the Archaeological Records Management System, the data base of primary materials on all archeological sites in the State of New Mexico. It is managed by the Laboratory of Anthropology (LA), a division of the Museum of New Mexico, which assigns identification numbers to all archeological sites in the state.

Acknowledgments

I wish to thank the many people whose advice has helped me overcome the myriad problems that have arisen in the writing of this book. The following archeologists have kindly shared their expertise: Jan V. Biella, Richard C. Chapman, Michael L. Elliott, Jeremy Kulisheck, Michael P. Marshall, Stewart Peckham, Ann F. Ramenofsky, Kathryn Sargeant, Curtis F. Schaafsma, the late Albert H. Schroeder, David H. Snow, and Richard P. Watson. Paleoclimatologists Julio Betancourt, Jeffrey S. Dean, Henri D. Grissino-Mayer, Matthew W. Salzer, and Louis A. Scuderi have generously provided advice and data. Richard Flint, John L. Kessell, Carroll L. Riley, and Joe S. Sando have given of their time to critically review parts of the manuscript. My thanks also go to Laura Holt, librarian at the Laboratory of Anthropology and to Rosemary Talley and Lou Hecker, respectively the former and present persons in charge of the Laboratory's site files. Their aid was invaluable in obtaining needed materials. Maps 1 and 3 were made by Kerri Mich, who recently completed an M.A. degree in the Department of Geography, University of New Mexico. I also wish to acknowledge the support the Department of Geography has afforded me. Map 2 is the property of the University of New Mexico, which has granted me permission to use it in this volume. I especially wish to recognize the long-term support of my mentor, the late James J. Parsons. I feel grateful to all listed above as well as to the many others unmentioned for the help they have given me, but I alone am responsible for any errors or omissions in this work.

INTRODUCTION

Scholarly and popular interest in the Pueblo settlements of the American Southwest has persisted for well over a century and has given rise to innumerable studies carried out to satisfy these interests. The present study, focused on the theme of settlement geography, attempts to identify the pueblos of the Rio Grande Pueblo Region that were occupied during the critical years when two very different cultures were confronting each other. These years begin with the period of Spanish exploration of the region—1540–1598 (Part One)—and continue through the period of early Spanish settlement—1598–1680 (Part Two)—followed by the period of Pueblo revolt, Spanish reconquest, and subsequent Pueblo resettlement (Part Three). The purpose here is to provide a baseline settlement location pattern for the whole of the Rio Grande Pueblo Region and to document the changes in that pattern that took place during a timeframe that extended over more than 160 years. In taking a more holistic approach than has been previously attempted, using both historical and archeological materials despite the shortcomings of each, it has been possible to construct a credible settlement geography of the Rio Grande Pueblo Region during the sixteenth and seventeenth centuries.

At the time of initial Spanish contact, the Rio Grande Pueblo Region extended some 215 miles along the Rio Grande rift valley and to outlying areas to the east and west (map 1). At that time there were probably some one hundred settlements (pueblos) grouped linguistically into loose clusters that occupied specific drainage areas within the region. Most of the Pueblo peoples spoke languages related to the Tanoan family. In the Far North subregion were two Northern Tiwa pueblos, Taos and Picuris. People who spoke Southern Tiwa occupied the Albuquerque-Belen Basin. Between these two subregions were the Tewa speakers in the Española Basin and their linguistic cousins the Tanos in the Galisteo Basin. To the south the Piro people were established in the Socorro Basin, and to the east were the Tompiros in the Estancia Basin. Towa speakers occupied pueblos in the Jemez Mountains to the west of the Rio Grande and Pecos Pueblo to the east. Keres people, whose language belongs to a distinct family, had come to inhabit pueblos in the Santo Domingo Basin and along the adjacent lower Jemez River as well as farther west at Acoma.

As happened everywhere in the Americas with the coming of Europeans, native peoples and their cultures suffered great losses. The Pueblo peoples of the Rio Grande Pueblo Region were no exception. Throughout the Americas much of the demographic loss was caused by epidemics of diseases brought by Europeans. Although no evidence of such epidemics in the Rio Grande region prior to the 1630s has yet been discovered, elsewhere most such disasters began near the time of contact, and it is likely Puebloans suffered a similar fate. Thus, loss of Pueblo lives and possibly abandonment of some of their pueblos could have taken place during the contact period, but, because specific information is lacking, discussion of Pueblo settlements in that period (part I) cannot include any concrete effects of epidemics. However, the great decline in population and number of pueblos that took place by the 1640s, discussed in part II, could imply that the Pueblo population had been previously weakened by exposure to European diseases. After four decades of Spanish colonization and missionization, the Rio Grande Pueblo Region suffered its greatest loss of people and settlements in historic times. Between 1598/1602 and 1641 the population was reduced by a possible 74 percent, and some 44 or 54 percent of the pueblos were abandoned, with the greatest losses incurred in the southern subregions. Further decline was experienced in the 1670s with the abandonment of the Estancia Basin pueblos and with them the first substantial reduction in the territory of the Rio Grande Pueblo Region. Between about 1600 when Spanish settlement began and 1680 when the Spaniards were driven from New Mexico, the Pueblo peoples lost 62 percent of their settlements and about 78 percent of their population. Further losses related to the Pueblo revolt and Spanish reconquest are recounted in part III. During that period and its aftermath, the twelve years of freedom from Spanish rule (1680–92) cost the Pueblo peoples dearly. Their population was probably reduced by another 38 percent and the number of settlements by an additional 35 percent, in addition to further loss of territory.

PART
ONE

Rio Grande Pueblos and

Spanish Exploration,

1540–1598

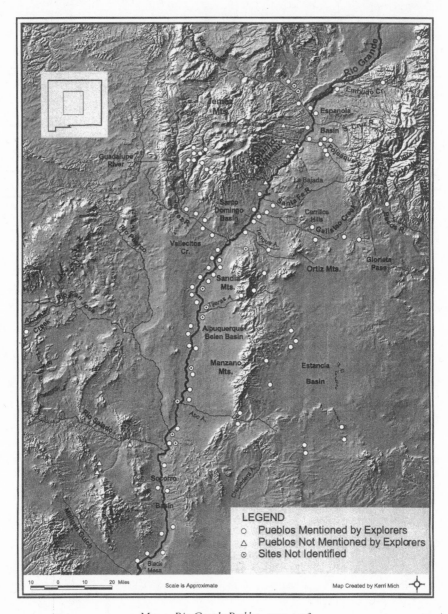

Map 1. Rio Grande Pueblos, 1540–1598.

Introduction

Previous works concerned with Pueblo settlement during the period of Spanish exploration of New Mexico in the sixteenth century have only dealt with parts of the Rio Grande Pueblo Region or with the reports of a single exploratory expedition. Part I therefore presents an overview of Pueblo settlement in the entire Rio Grande Pueblo Region in the 1540–98 contact period. By integrating all of the chronicles of the sixteenth-century Spanish explorers with the work of archeologists who have reported on the pueblos of the protohistoric period in this region, it has been possible to work out an approximation of the Pueblo settlement pattern during the contact period.[1] The area of the Rio Grande Pueblo Region is shown on map 1.

Greatly exaggerated reports received by Spanish authorities in Mexico City about the settled agricultural villages in what came to be known as New Mexico led them to launch a full-scale expedition to explore the area. This expedition, headed by Francisco Vázquez de Coronado, was the first to penetrate Rio Grande Pueblo territory and was followed by six others in the ensuing fifty-eight years (table 1).

Table 1. Spanish Expeditions to New Mexico, 1540-1598

Expedition	Period in New Mexico		Number of Spanish Men
Coronado	7/1540-4/1542	21 mos.	350*[1]
Chamuscado	8/1581-1/1582	5 mos.	12[2]
Espejo	2/1583-7/1583	5 mos.	16[3]
Castaño	12/1590-6/1591	7 mos.	**[4]
Morlete	3/1591-6/1591	4 mos.	43[5]
Levya-Humaña	1593	1 year	n.d[6]
Oñate	5/1598	...	129[7]

Sources:
[1] Hammond and Rey, *Narratives,* 7, 9, 103; Riley, *Rio del Norte,* 155, 296.
[2] Hammond and Rey, *The Rediscovery,* 8, 69.
[3] Ibid., 18-19, 154-155.
[4] Ibid., 36, 39, 269, 294; Schroeder and Matson, *A Colony on the Move,* 11.
[5] Hammond and Rey, 1966:43-46.
[6] Hammond and Rey, *The Rediscovery,* 49, 323.
[7] Hammond and Rey, *Don Juan,* 14, 16, 289-300, 390.

* estimated.
** 160-170 estimated total including men, women, and children.

Reports with useful information about settlements were produced by members of all except the Morlete and Leyva-Humaña expeditions. Failure to find new sources of wealth and a disabling accident that befell Coronado brought an end to his expedition and, apparently, to Spanish interest in New Mexico; but knowledge of a numerous settled population remained, offering an opportunity for spreading Christianity. This challenge was taken up forty years later when an expedition jointly led by Fray Agustín Rodríguez and Captain Francisco Sánchez Chamuscado engaged in both proselytizing and exploration. Growing hostility by local people who resented their demands for food prompted withdrawal after a few months, although Rodríguez and another priest insisted on remaining behind. Investigation of reports that they had been killed was the reason for sending another expedition to New Mexico. A small party under the leadership of Antonio de Espejo reached Pueblo country a year later, following the same route up the Rio Grande. After confirming that the priests had been killed and unsuccessfully exploring the region for mines, his party returned to New Spain via the Pecos River.

Despite such disappointments, the perception of New Mexico as an attractive place persisted and seven years later lured a group of colonists, who had become discontented with the poverty of resources in their province of Nuevo León, to set out for New Mexico, although they did not have permission from authorities in Mexico City. The leader, Gaspar Castaño de Sosa, and a small advance party were able to explore part of the region before they were arrested by Juan Morlete, who had been sent to apprehend the colonists and return them to New Spain. This arrest did not deter Captain Francisco Levya de Bonilla and Antonio Gutiérrez de Humaña from making another unauthorized entrada two years later. A Mexican survivor of this expedition reported later to Juan de Oñate that they had spent about a year exploring Pueblo country, making their headquarters at San Ildefonso Pueblo. While exploring the eastern plains, all members of this expedition were killed except Oñate's informant, eliminating the possibility of a report that could have added much valuable information about Pueblo settlements. Finally, five years later, in 1598, an authorized colonizing expedition arrived in New Mexico. The initial exploration of the region carried out by its leader, Juan de Oñate, provides additional settlement data, as do the lists of pueblos to which he assigned priests and the lists of pueblos from which he obtained pledges of loyalty. One of his soldiers, Juan Rodríguez, returned to Mexico City in 1602 and provided the cosmographer Enrico Martínez with information for a map of New Mexico for use by the

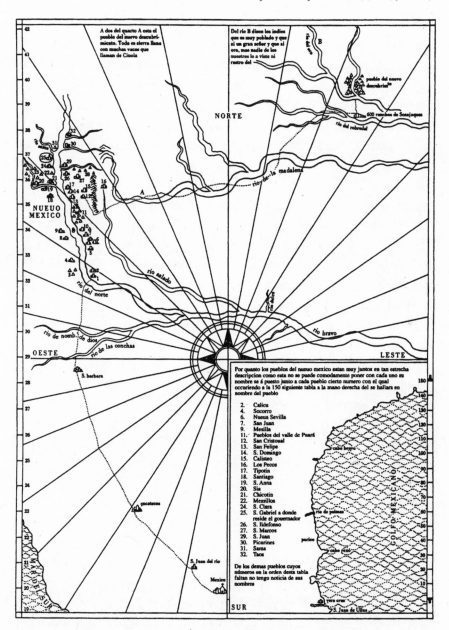

Map 2. New Mexico in 1602. Based on the Enrico Martínez map of 1602.

viceroy. A redrawn version of this map, map 2 of this study, will be referred to as the 1602 map.[2]

Although the Spanish explorers did not find the fabulous cities initially sought, they were favorably impressed with the Pueblo settlements, especially as they contrasted them to those of the nomadic and seminomadic peoples of surrounding areas. What the Spaniards encountered in the Rio Grande Pueblo Region was a type of sedentary society composed of a number of linguistically distinct peoples who shared some basic characteristics. They lived in villages, in substantial, well-built houses, and sustained themselves principally by the crops they grew in their fields. They clothed themselves with cloth woven from the cotton they raised. They made fine pottery as well as utility types in which to store the surpluses of maize (corn) and other foods they produced. Many aspects of their way of life were derived from the cultures of the Anasazi people of the San Juan Basin to the northwest and the Mogollon people to the southwest, who, in turn, were influenced by the Mesoamerican civilization of central Mexico.

At the time they were first contacted by Spaniards, the Pueblo peoples of the Rio Grande region were experiencing an era of cultural florescence, according to scholars who named the period—which began about 1300/1325—the Classic Period.[3] They lived in clusters of terraced multistory roomblocks separated by plazas that contained subterranean religious structures called kivas. Some of the largest pueblos contained more than one thousand ground-floor rooms. These large pueblos, surrounded by extensive areas of garden plots and numerous small, seasonally occupied field houses, were distinctive features of Classic Period settlements by the early fifteenth century. They rarely occupied defensive sites, but were typically located on the margins of river floodplains where conditions were more favorable for agriculture than in previous upland locations. Such large pueblos were the result not only of population growth but of a trend toward abandoning smaller pueblos and aggregating into larger communities. The implication is that methods of food production, trade networks, and techniques of social integration were adequate to maintain such population concentrations. However, some settlement instability within the region continued. A number of areas were abandoned after the mid-fifteenth century, and elsewhere even large pueblos were frequently deserted, with some partially reoccupied later. Of the 295 pueblos established in the Rio Grande Pueblo Region at various times during the Classic Period (1300–1600), 93, and possibly 102, were occupied at some time during the contact period.[4]

It was this late Classic Period society that Spanish explorers encountered, adding their own element of instability—although their impact on the overall Pueblo settlement pattern was slight. Major change did not come until permanent Spanish colonization was initiated in 1598.

CHAPTER ONE
General Regional Settlement Pattern

By the sixteenth century the greatest concentration of settled farming villages in the American Southwest was in the Rio Grande Pueblo Region. Some ninety-three pueblos were located in an area that stretched 215 miles along the Rio Grande rift valley from Taos Pueblo on the north to Senecu on the south, in addition to outlying areas to the east and west (map 1).[1] Forty-four of these contact-period pueblos were located along the margins of the Rio Grande floodplain in the several structural basins through which the river flows. The majority of these riverine pueblos were in the central and southern parts of the region—in the Albuquerque-Belen and Socorro Basins. North of the Albuquerque-Belen Basin most of the pueblos—some twenty-eight—were located along tributary streams that drain the slopes of the southernmost ranges of the Rocky Mountains: the Sangre de Cristo Mountains on the east and the Jemez Mountains on the west. Some fifty miles to the west of the Rio Grande, one lone pueblo, Acoma, was still occupied in the contact period. The remaining twenty were located east of the Rio Grande: fifteen in the Galisteo and Estancia Basins, four on the periphery of the Sandia Mountains, and one—Pecos—forty miles east of the Rio Grande.

An additional nine pueblos might have been occupied at some time during the contact period but are not mentioned by any of the explorers. Archeological evidence supports the possibility that on the Pajarito Plateau, on the eastern side of the Jemez Mountains, as many as six pueblos continued to be occupied, in addition to three in the Rio Salado drainage west of the Socorro Basin. Also within the Rio Grande Pueblo Region were several "empty" areas where substantial and lengthy Pueblo settlement had come to an end prior to 1540. They include the Rio Puerco Valley, Las Huertas Canyon, Santa Fe River Valley, Santa Cruz River Valley, and possibly the Chupadera Basin. The numerous pueblos in the Chama Basin have been considered abandoned by the end of the fifteenth century, but the explorers provide some limited evidence that such was not entirely true.

Within the Rio Grande Pueblo Region the general settlement pattern consisted of loose groupings of linguistically related pueblos that occupied specific drainage areas. The pueblos reported by the explorers fall into ten such subregions in addition to the isolated pueblos of Acoma and Pecos. Whether the settlement pattern during the contact period included field houses that were occupied seasonally is not certain, although the work of archeologists has established that they were a common part of the precontact landscape.[2] Salvage work done prior to construction of the Cochiti Dam (on the Rio Grande in the Santo Domingo Basin) reveals that in an area where three pueblos were found—two of them occupied as late as 1525 and 1539—there were also fifteen one-room, fourteen two-room, and two three-room structures that have been interpreted as places for use in the summer season.[3] Spanish documents of the contact period are, however, virtually silent about field houses. Pedro de Castañeda, chronicler of the Coronado expedition, in summing up the population of the Pueblo provinces visited, notes that his figure is all-inclusive because between the pueblos there were no houses (caserías) or other buildings (habitaciónes).[4] Although this observation could be interpreted to mean that there were no field houses, it could also mean that he ignored them because their occupants were counted at their main residence in the larger pueblo. When the Espejo expedition was travelling north through the Piro subregion, its recorder, Diego Pérez de Luxán, notes that all the land along the Rio Grande was bordered by sown fields, but he does not mention any field houses.[5] He does, however, mention them when the expedition passed through the Rio Grande–Rio Conchas confluence area south of the Rio Grande Pueblo Region, and he may have felt it unnecessary to do so again.[6] There he notes that the people lived in pueblos but they also had flat-roofed houses in their fields where they resided during harvest time. Later, when the expedition was in the vicinity of Acoma, its leader, Antonio de Espejo, reports fields planted along what must have been the Rio San Jose four leagues (twelve miles) from Acoma Pueblo, so located because the river provided the only reliable source of water in the area.[7] He does not mention field houses, but Baltasar de Obregón, who later interviewed some of his men, writes: "Each Indian has a shack on his field where they gather their harvests."[8] Given the need to tend and guard crops in fields located at a distance from the pueblo, it is reasonable to assume that the practice of using field houses continued during the contact period despite the fact that the explorers paid so little attention to them.

A question naturally arises about the number of people who occupied the Rio Grande pueblos during the period. This question is more difficult to answer than the one pertaining to the number of pueblos because the archeological and historical data are much more inadequate as a source of demographic data. Typically, deteriorated rooms in a pueblo were abandoned and used to deposit trash, while new rooms were added or pueblos that were abandoned at one time might be re-occupied and new sections constructed. As a result of such practices the number of occupied rooms at a given time at each site is not known at present, and, therefore, the number of rooms or overall size of a site cannot serve as a reliable basis for estimating the number of its inhabitants. Historical data are not helpful either because they consist of a few highly generalized estimates that are incomplete because the explorers, with the exception of Oñate, did not visit all parts of the Rio Grande Pueblo Region. Pedro de Castañeda estimates a population of twenty thousand men in the Pueblo country visited by Coronado's expedition, which included the Zuni and Hopi pueblos but not the Tompiro of the Estancia Basin, the Tewa of the Pojoaque drainage, nor the Northern Tiwa pueblo of Picuris.[9] Excluding the figure of three to four thousand men for both the Zuni and Hopi would leave a total for the Rio Grande pueblos of sixteen to seventeen thousand men. To this total, however, would have to be added a figure for the pueblos not visited, which would probably be as great if not greater than the sum subtracted, thus giving a total of possibly more than twenty thousand.[10] As a rough estimate, if each man represented four people, there might have been eighty thousand or more people in the Rio Grande Pueblo Region in 1540.

About forty years later the recorder of the Chamuscado expedition, Hernán Gallegos, does not hazard an overall population estimate, but gives the number of houses and number of stories per house for each pueblo they passed through—but they did not visit the Northern Tiwa pueblos of Taos and Picuris nor the Tewa pueblos of the Española Basin.[11] Furthermore, the clues to how many people lived in each house give such widely varied results that his data cannot be used as a basis for estimating population. Antonio de Espejo, whose expedition followed a year later, does provide population estimates for the provinces he visited, but he too failed to reach the pueblos of the Northern Tiwa and the Tewa and does not provide figures for the Southern Tiwa of the Middle Rio Grande subregion or for Pecos.[12] Even so, he comes up with a total of 183,000 for the remaining Rio Grande areas, a figure that is probably excessive.[13] Gaspar Castaño de Sosa, whose expedition entered New Mexico in 1591, provides no population data to speak of.

The only population data to compare with those given in the Coronado documents are those from the Oñate period at the end of the century. Oñate estimates a total of sixty thousand Indians for all of the pueblos, including the Zuni and Hopi, although in another instance he mentions forty to fifty thousand Indians.[14] A figure of sixty thousand is supported by a witness at the 1601 Mexico City investigation of Oñate's tenure as governor of New Mexico, conducted by Francisco de Valverde. He claims there were fifty to sixty thousand Indians.[15] Two Valverde witnesses in 1602 mention twenty-five thousand and thirty thousand able-bodied men in the Pueblo population, figures that would indicate something greater than sixty thousand.[16] Testimony given by loyal colonists in New Mexico all agrees to the proposition put to them that there were sixty thousand or more people in the pueblos.[17] However, other Valverde witnesses and several clergymen give lower figures ranging from twelve to thirty thousand Indians.[18]

It would appear that the Rio Grande Pueblo population had declined from Coronado's time, especially if the Zuni and Hopi population could be excluded from the end-of-the-century figures, but it should be kept in mind that the reliability of all population estimates in the contact period is in doubt. The lack of any appreciable decline in the number of Rio Grande pueblos during this period and the absence of any documentary evidence of epidemic disease events could argue for a stable population, but it is difficult to believe that the Rio Grande Pueblo population escaped the fate of other populations in the western hemisphere when contacted by Europeans who carried diseases to which they had no immunity. It would have been unusual indeed if no one in the seven expeditions that entered New Mexico between 1540 and 1598 carried such pathogens.[19] Nevertheless, the poor quality of the limited data makes it difficult to know with any confidence the size of the Rio Grande Pueblo population either at the beginning or the end of the contact period.

The explorers' journals do provide some idea of the distribution of population within the Rio Grande Pueblo Region. The subregions were comprised of varying numbers of pueblos that were characterized by differing degrees of concentration. The largest and densest grouping consisted of the twelve to thirteen Southern Tiwa pueblos established along a fourteen-mile stretch on both sides of the Rio Grande in the northern part of the Albuquerque-Belen Basin. The Jemez people occupied nine or perhaps as many as fifteen pueblos located one to three miles apart in direct linear distance in the canyons and on the high mesas of the southwestern flank of the Jemez massif. The Tewa pueblos were another important group consisting of about eleven settlements somewhat more widely distributed in the Española Basin and adjacent areas. The most scattered pueblos were those east of the Rio Grande in the

Estancia and Galisteo Basins where sources of water were fewer. For the most part, population data for these and other subregions is either not available or unreliable. The best that can be said is that the pueblos of the Rio Grande Pueblo Region were smaller and less populous in the southern subregions and increased in size northward.

As far back as Coronado's time it is noted that in the southern part of the Albuquerque-Belen Basin (his "Tutahaco" province) the pueblos were, with two exceptions, small in contrast to those in the northern part of the basin ("Tiguex" province).[20] Gallegos, coming up the Rio Grande with the Chamuscado expedition from the El Paso area, observes that the pueblos were larger and the population more numerous as they travelled north, and his data on the number of houses per pueblo bear this out.[21] Espejo also notes that the Southern Tiwa pueblos were larger than those of the Piro in the Socorro Basin farther south.[22] Pedro de Bustamante of the Chamuscado expedition reports that, among the Keres pueblos to the north, the pueblos and houses were better constructed than those of the Piro and Southern Tiwa, also noting the four to five stories of Keres houses in contrast to the three-story Southern Tiwa houses and the two stories of the Piro houses.[23] Pueblo houses were components of roomblocks that were terraced, with each story set back from the one beneath. The roomblocks were grouped around one or more plazas, which contained the subterranean ceremonial structures called "kivas." Comments in the Coronado documents indicate that a pueblo with two hundred houses would be considered large, and that smaller ones would range down to thirty houses.[24] Gallegos's data would agree with this description, although he mentions several pueblos with more than two hundred houses. In the Oñate documents several people state that the smallest pueblos contained thirty to forty houses, generally with two stories, and the largest, four hundred houses with four to five stories.[25] Occasionally some explorers also give figures for the number of people living in the pueblos. Castañeda states that most pueblos had about two hundred inhabitants and the few large ones up to eight hundred or one thousand occupants.[26] Unfortunately, the data on the number of people and the number of houses are sufficiently patchy and variable from one reporter to another that these figures are not useful in deriving a generally applicable rate that could be used to convert the number of houses to a population figure.

Whether reported in terms of the number of houses, warriors, or persons, a few pueblos stood out to the extent that they especially attracted the attention of the explorers who visited them. They were Taos, Pecos, Zia, and Acoma. Information about Taos comes from the Coronado documents, which state that it was the largest of all the pueblos with a population of fifteen thousand souls, houses five to six stories high, and the largest ceremonial chambers.[27] These same sources describe Pecos as very strong, with five hundred warriors, five hundred houses four to five stories high, and eight large plazas.[28] Sources from the Chamuscado expedition agree with the number and size of houses at Pecos, but a year later Luxán claims there were two thousand warriors.[29] Castaño de Sosa adds that it was very large, containing five plazas and sixteen kivas.[30] Oñate refers to it as the "great" pueblo of Pecos.[31] Jaramillo of the Coronado expedition classes Zia with Taos and Pecos as "well worth seeing," and Castañeda describes it as a fine village with many people.[32] Gallegos saw it as a large pueblo with two hundred houses, but a year later Luxán reports one thousand houses, five large plazas and many smaller ones, and four thousand men—numbers with which Espejo agrees, adding that the houses were three to four stories high.[33] Although Coronado describes Acoma as a small city, members of his expedition, besides noting its strong position atop a small, steep-sided mesa, mention that it had two hundred three- to four-story houses and two hundred warriors.[34] Gallegos mentions five hundred houses, as many as he reported for Pecos, and Espejo says it had six thousand souls.[35] Oñate describes Acoma as having five hundred houses and about three thousand Indians.[36] In a bloody battle with the Acoma, it was reported that his men killed six hundred and took prisoner another six hundred, an indication of large size.[37]

Despite the scanty population data available for individual pueblos, the data do convey a sense that there were other large pueblos, and that in each subregion there was at least one pueblo that was larger than the others. Much of this data comes from Gallegos's house counts, which, unfortunately, do not give a complete picture because he did not visit all of the pueblos. In the large cluster of Southern Tiwa pueblos at the northern end of the Albuquerque-Belen Basin, he lists a pueblo with 230 houses that he calls "Torre de la Medina," which might possibly have been Kuaua.[38] In the Jemez cluster he gives data for only two pueblos, one of which—"Puerto Frio"—had three hundred houses and might have been Nanishagi in San Diego Canyon; but Oñate visited what he called the "great pueblo" of the Jemez, which was located on a steep-sided mesa, indicating that there might have been an even larger Jemez pueblo.[39] As for the important group of Tewa pueblos, Gallegos did not reach far enough north to visit them, and Castaño de Sosa, who did visit them, does not give any concrete information about their size.

Oñate initially established his headquarters near San Juan Pueblo because it might have been the largest of the Tewa pueblos. Gallegos did visit the Keres pueblos in the Santo Domingo Basin, where three of the six pueblos had two hundred houses: "Castildabid" (Katishtya), "Castilblanco" (Gipuy), and "Buena Vista" (Tunque).[40] Farther east, in the Galisteo Basin, the largest pueblo was his "Piedrahita" (possibly San Cristóbal), with three hundred houses.[41] This pueblo was probably the same one Luxán calls "Pocos" and describes as large, with houses four to five stories high and fifteen hundred warriors.[42] Among the five pueblos clustered along the east side of the Manzano Mountains, the largest, with two hundred houses, was "Ruiseco" (possibly LA 371).[43] Gallegos and his party did not travel farther into the Estancia Basin, but they were informed of three large pueblos to the south. One of these was probably Las Humanas Pueblo, which was undoubtedly the one Oñate refers to later as the largest of the three and comparable to Zia.[44] The largest Piro pueblo was not large compared to those mentioned above, but the one Gallegos called "Piña," with eighty-five two-story houses, stood out as almost twice the size of the next largest in that subregion.[45] Piña was probably the pueblo Luxán called "El Gallo," for which he reports one hundred houses and eight hundred souls.[46] It is interesting to note that, among the largest pueblos, many were located on the frontiers of the Rio Grande Pueblo Region: Acoma, Taos, Pecos, San Cristobal, and Las Humanas.

The Chamuscado and Espejo expeditions of the early 1580s visited the Rio Grande Pueblo Region at the height of a major drought that affected most of western North America. It occurred within a longer period of below-normal precipitation that extended from about 1400 to 1790 and was considered the severest drought of less than fifty years duration to have occurred within the last two thousand years.[47] This drought was also within the timeframe of the Little Ice Age, a global event occurring from about 1450 to 1850 that was characterized by cooler, drier conditions.[48] Climate reconstructions for New Mexico show that, beginning in the 1560s and increasing after the early 1570s, there was a substantial decline in precipitation in an already dry climate, culminating in severe conditions during the years 1579–85. Drought conditions of a lesser degree continued into the early 1590s—the time when Castaño de Sosa's expedition arrived. Drier than normal conditions emerged again (prevailing from about 1598 to 1602) when Oñate's large expedition entered New Mexico. Only Coronado's two-year stay in New Mexico coincided with relatively wet years, but the approximately two thousand people in his expedition put a strain on the Puebloans' food supply despite any larger than normal surplus they might have produced in those years. Under drought conditions the Pueblo peoples were even more stressed.[49] Appendix tables A, B, C, D, and E provide data that indicate moisture conditions in New Mexico in the sixteenth century.

Despite the severity of the drought, the explorers of the 1580s and 1590s do not mention it. Having travelled over a thousand miles through the arid lands of north-central Mexico to reach the Rio Grande Pueblo Region, they probably considered the dryness they encountered normal. The only comment is made by Luxán, who reports in July 1583 that they were refused provisions at Pocos Pueblo (San Cristóbal Pueblo in the Galisteo Basin) by the occupants, who claimed that because there had been no rain they had no food to give and were uncertain about a harvest that year.[50] It is not until the end of the century that further reports about climate are forthcoming, when some of Oñate's clergy and settlers report on the poverty of resources in New Mexico. In October 1601 the custodian Fray Juan de Escalona writes to the viceroy that frost had scorched the Indians' maize fields (milpas) and that in previous years shortage of rain had caused the greater portion of their fields to dry up. He also reveals the Spaniards' inability to harvest crops when he reports that they had consumed in their three years in New Mexico what maize the Puebloans had been able to save during the previous six years.[51] Captain Luis de Velasco reports to the viceroy from San Gabriel in March 1601 that the country lacked rain and the summer heat was oppressive, while later in November Captain Alonso Sánchez testifies that the land was without food because there was no rain that year.[52] That same year a treasury official in Mexico City, Francisco de Valverde, was charged with questioning some of the people who had returned from New Mexico about the situation there. A number of them state that there was little rain in the May to August growing season, and one notes that although some fields were irrigated, others depended on seasonal rain.[53]

In contrast, the explorers often comment about the winter climate, describing it as bitterly cold with frequent heavy snows and frosts, and prolonged from October through March.[54] Such comments were particularly frequent during the two winters the Coronado expedition spent in New Mexico, when there were also reports of the Rio Grande freezing over—even to the extent that mounted horsemen and loaded carts could cross it.[55] Temperature reconstructions based on tree-ring data from the San Francisco Peaks area of northern Arizona show low values for the early 1540s but even lower ones in the early 1580s, when the Chamuscado and

Espejo expeditions visited the Rio Grande Pueblo Region (appendix table G). Castaño de Sosa mentions two frozen rivers, one of which might have been the Rio Grande and the other the Santa Fe River, while some of Valverde's witnesses claim that the Rio Grande froze over in the winter, an indication that comparable cold temperatures extended to the end of the century.[56] Valverde's witnesses also note that snowmelt, which began mainly in May, provided an important source of moisture to the soil and enhanced stream flow—somewhat offsetting the scarcity of summer rain but not to any great extent, given the prevailing drought.[57]

The picture of summer and winter climate in the Rio Grande Pueblo Region in the sixteenth century that can be gleaned from historical and paleoclimate sources shows a severe climate regime, one that was particularly difficult during most of the contact period because of the extreme drought conditions that prevailed. The presence of outsiders who depended to a large degree on the food stores they mostly coerced from the Puebloans added to the latter's burden of surviving under these conditions.

CHAPTER TWO
Settlement Patterns within the Region

T he pattern of settlement in each subregion is discussed in the following sections. Tables 2 through 10 show the pueblos reported by each explorer and those shown on the 1602 map. These tables also reveal which areas were not visited by individual explorers and, to some extent, when during the contact period the pueblos were occupied, including which were inhabited throughout the period.

Southern Rio Grande

This southernmost subregion of Rio Grande pueblos was occupied by Piro people who lived in nine pueblos located along a fifty-seven-mile stretch of the river centered on the Socorro Basin (table 2).

Table 2. Pueblos Reported by Sixteenth-Century Spanish Explorers: Southern Rio Grande Subregion

Pueblo Name	LA No.[a]	Coronado 1540-1542	Chamuscado 1581-1582	Espejo 1583	Castaño 1591	Oñate 1598	1602 Map
?			La Pedrosa	T. de Puala			Unnamed
Sevilleta	774		El Oso	T. de Puala		N. Sevilla	N. Sevilla
Alamillo	---		Elota	Unnamed			Unnamed
?				Ruin			
El Barro	283			Ruin			
Pilabo	791			Ruin			
Teypama	282			Ruin		Socorro	Socorro
Las Cañas	755		Piña	El Gallo			
Qualacu	757		Piastla	Unnamed		Qualacu	Calicu
N. Señora	19266		San Juan	Unnamed			Unnamed
S. Pascual	487		Santiago	Unnamed		Unnamed	Unnamed
Tiffany	244		S. Miguel	Unnamed			Unnamed
Senecu	---		S. Felipe	S. Felipe		Tzenequel	Unnamed
Milligan	597		Ruin	Ruin			
TOTAL		4[b]	9	[10][c]	n.d.	Incomplete	9

[a] New Mexico State Laboratory of Anthropology site number.
[b] Incomplete. Reported by one of Coronado's officers who visited only the northern part of the Piro province.
[c] Espejo claims there were ten Piro pueblos, but his chronicler Luxán mentions only nine.
[ ] Total number of pueblos reported.

Coronado, who initially reached the Rio Grande farther north, sent one of his officers into what was probably Piro territory, but this foray produced no information that would help identify Piro pueblos.[1] The full extent of the subregion was first explored some forty years later by the Chamuscado expedition, which moved north through it in August 1581.[2] Eighteen months later, in February 1583, the Espejo expedition covered the same route.[3] Reports from these two expeditions provide the best historical information about the Piro pueblos. Hernán Gallegos of the former and Diego Pérez de Luxán of the latter both kept diaries of their journeys, each providing somewhat different types of information that together help identify the nine Piro pueblos occupied at that time.[4] Gallegos names the pueblos encountered by the Chamuscado expedition, giving the number of houses in each, the side of the river on which they were located, and the site characteristics of some. He does not give distances between pueblos, but that information is, in most instances, supplied by Luxán.

Both expeditions encountered the first inhabited pueblo, which each called "San Felipe," at the Senecu site on the west side of the Rio Grande above its junction with Milligan Gulch.[5] Both had previously passed a ruined pueblo two leagues (six miles) to the south at Milligan Gulch (LA 597), and Luxán notes another three leagues below that near a place he calls "El Malpaís."[6] From Senecu, Espejo and his party spent the next three days travelling north along the river they called the "Río del Norte," passing five pueblos and naming the last and largest one El Gallo.[7] El Gallo may well be the pueblo Gallegos calls "Piña," the one that he also notes was the largest in this area. He says it was located on the east side of the Rio Grande, which he called the "Guadalquivir," in a large meadow formed by the river—a description that fits the Las Cañas site.[8] The four unnamed pueblos that Luxán mentions between his San Felipe (Senecu) and El Gallo (Las Cañas) probably occupied sites that conform to the sides of the river on which Gallegos also places four pueblos. They were Tiffany and Nuestra Señora on the west side and San Pascual and Qualacu on the east side. Espejo's party moved quickly north from the Las Cañas site past four large ruined pueblos and a small inhabited one before stopping to camp, a distance of five leagues (fifteen miles) that would have brought them to the vicinity of the Alamillo Pueblo site.[9] Gallegos does not mention any ruined pueblos above his Piña Pueblo, but notes that farther up, on the side of the "Sierra Morena" (Manzano Mountains), was a small pueblo he called "Elota," one that could have been at the Alamillo site. The best candidates for the ruined pueblos are Teypama, Pilabo, and El Barro, all west-side pueblos, but a fourth site cannot be identified.

Leaving his camp above Alamillo, Espejo led his expedition north three leagues (nine miles) to a campsite he called "El Término de Puala." It was located between two masonry pueblos, one midsize and one small, that were two "harquebus shots" apart. Given the distance upriver, this place was likely close to the Sevilleta site near the confluence of the Rio Grande and the Rio Puerco and marked the frontier between Piro territory and that of the Southern Tiwa to the north.[10] Puala refers to Puaray, the name of an important Tiwa pueblo and the name sometimes also given to the Tiwa province as a whole. Identification of the second pueblo near El Término de Puala cannot be made, but there is good correlation with the pueblos Gallegos lists north of his Elota (Alamillo site). Espejo's two are also on the east side and located near each other: one medium-sized on a high hill ("El Oso") and the other small and in a bend in the river ("La Pedrosa"). The former could fit the description of Sevilleta, with the smaller unidentifiable.

Fifteen years later, when Oñate and his advance party travelled upriver through Piro territory, the first landmark he mentions is Black Mesa, his "Mesa de Guinea," located on the east side of the Rio Grande, which he called the "Río del Norte."[11] He continued up that side of the river, passing by one pueblo before stopping to camp near a second he called "Qualacu." The first pueblo was undoubtedly San Pascual.[12] He then went on, mentioning that his party camped opposite a west-side pueblo (Teypama) whose inhabitants brought them provisions, an action for which their pueblo gained the name "Socorro."[13] They next camped in a small pueblo they called "Nueva Sevilla," which, like many of the Piro pueblos they had passed, was deserted—the inhabitants having fled when Spaniards appeared.[14] Although Oñate does not mention all of the pueblos along his route, documents associated with his expedition indicate that most of the pueblos occupied in the 1580s were still occupied in 1598. Oñate's list of forty-four "Atzigues" (Piro) pueblos is not very helpful because it contains many duplications and mistakes, but it does confirm that Senecu was occupied.[15] The pueblo "Tzenaquel de la Mesilla," noted as the southernmost settlement, is a clear reference to Senecu, whose Piro name was Tzen-no-cue.[16]

The 1602 map, based on a report by one of Oñate's men who returned to New Spain that year, gives a more complete accounting of Piro pueblos. On the west side of the Rio Grande are three pueblo symbols that could well indicate Senecu, Tiffany, and Nuestra Señora, and above them Oñate's Socorro (Teypama) is named. On the east side of the river one of the southernmost pueblos is named "Calicu" and the other below it is most certainly San Pascual. There is a considerable gap north of these two before reaching Nueva Sevilla (Sevilleta) and two other unnamed pueblos. The one to the south might be Alamillo and the other the unidentifiable pueblo close to Sevilleta. Seemingly, the only changes from the settlement pattern of the 1580s took place in the central part of Piro territory with the reoccupation of Teypama and abandonment of Las Cañas. Settlement in this mostly uninhabited part of the subregion with its four large ruined pueblos appears to have been quite unstable compared with areas to the north and south, except in the extreme south where ruined pueblos were also noted. There has been speculation that abandonment of these pueblos might have been caused by epidemics of European diseases that reached the area even before the Spaniards arrived or by the depredations of non-Pueblo peoples.[17]

In contrast to the nine Piro pueblos contacted by the various Spanish expeditions, the Piros themselves claimed that their nation consisted of twenty-odd pueblos.[18] Although this number might have included some unoccupied pueblos, it raises the question of where the additional pueblos were located. A clue is provided by Espejo, who, besides reporting ten inhabited pueblos located close to the river on both sides, says there were others off the beaten track.[19] Presumably this would mean away from the river, and possibly some of the twenty-plus pueblos claimed by the Piros were so located. Sites in the Rio Salado drainage area to the west and the Chupadera Basin to the east might have been included in their figure. No settlements in these areas were reported by Spaniards, but archeological evidence suggests that in the former drainage area three pueblos were inhabited in the contact period: Magdalena, Bear Mountain, and Silver Creek.[20] Because ceramic evidence is less clear for the Chupadera Basin pueblos, it cannot be known with any certainty if any pueblos were occupied in the contact period, but there is the possibility that five might have been inhabited at some time during that period.[21] If they were not, the basin would be one of a number of areas with significant Pueblo settlement that had been abandoned before the Spanish entradas.

Estancia Basin

East of the Rio Grande and its bordering Sandia-Manzano Mountains lies an extensive basin of internal drainage, an old Pleistocene lake bed that contains large salt flats. Around its western and southern margins Spanish explorers found eleven pueblos (table 3).

Table 3. Pueblos Reported by Sixteenth-Century Spanish Explorers:
Estancia Basin Subregion

Pueblo Name	LA No.[a]	Coronado 1540-1542	Chamuscado 1581-1583	Espejo 1583	Castaño 1591	Oñate 1598	1602 Map
Chilili	874	Unnamed	Zacatula			First salinas	
---	371	Unnamed	Ruiseco				
---	372	Unnamed	La Mesa				
Tajique	381	Unnamed	La Joya				
Quarai	95		Francavilla			Last salinas	
Abo	97		Unnamed	Unnamed		Abbo	
Tenabo	200		Unnamed	Unnamed		Second Abbo	
Las Hum.	120		Unnamed			Cueloze	
Pardo	83		Unnamed				
Blanco	51		Unnamed			Xenopuy	
Colorado	476		Unnamed			Patasci	
TOTAL		incomplete[b]	11[c]	[11][d]	n.d.	incomplete	n.d.

[a] New Mexico State Laboratory of Anthropology site number.
[b] Four of the seven pueblos Coronado associates with the "snowy mountains" but did not visit.
  See Table 7 for the three other pueblos.
[c] These eleven pueblos in addition to Paa-ko and San Antonio were the thirteen reported in the area
  south of the Galisteo Basin.
[d] Espejo reports eleven pueblos in his "Magrias" province, two of which he visited.
[ ] Total number of pueblos reported.

Although no member of the Coronado expedition seems to have visited these
pueblos, four of the seven pueblos Coronado associates with his "snowy mountains"
(Sandia–Manzano Mountains)—those he also describes as "on the plain"—might
have been the Estancia Basin pueblos located east of the Manzanos: Chilili, Tajique,
and the two somewhat smaller unnamed pueblos located between them (LA 371
and LA 372).[22] Quarai, the fifth pueblo in this area, might not have been occupied
in the 1540s. Archeological evidence indicates that it was inhabited only intermit-
tently during the sixteenth century.[23] The pueblos at the southern end of the basin
apparently escaped the notice of Coronado, although this seems odd in view of the
extensive exploration he carried out in the Rio Grande Pueblo Region and beyond
during the two years his expedition was in the Southwest.

The first Spaniards who actually came to the Estancia Basin were members of
the Chamuscado expedition. They travelled "behind the Sierra Morena" (Manzano
Mountains) to investigate the salt deposits and while in the vicinity visited and
named five pueblos.[24] These were probably the four pueblos Coronado referred
to as "on the plain," with the fifth being Quarai, which at this time was apparently reoccupied.[25] At Quarai in December they were informed about three very

large pueblos farther south, but they did not go on to contact them because it was snowing heavily.[26] These pueblos were likely Las Humanas, Pueblo Blanco, and Pueblo Colorado.[27]

Two other very large contemporaneous pueblos, Abo and Tenabo, were seemingly ignored by the informants at Quarai. Another settlement, Pueblo Pardo, located just south of Las Humanas, was probably occupied at that time also. That there were eleven pueblos in the Estancia Basin at the time of Chamuscado's visit is reinforced by information he received earlier, when he was told about thirteen pueblos that lay three days' travel up the river and to the south.[28] Because he had previously accounted for pueblos along the Rio Grande and in the Galisteo Basin, it is likely that these thirteen pueblos were located east of the Sandia and Manzano ranges. Two were probably east of the Sandias and outside the Estancia Basin: Paa-ko and San Antonio; the remaining eleven were the pueblos of the Estancia Basin.

A year and a half later Espejo broke his journey northward at Término de Puala to visit pueblos in the Estancia Basin. Travelling ten leagues (thirty miles) from his camp on the Rio Grande, he reached a pueblo that was probably Abo. On his return trip the next day he stopped at another that was undoubtedly Tenabo.[29] He reports that the province, which he calls "Maguas/Magrias," consisted of eleven pueblos, a number that accords with the information Chamuscado obtained as well as with the archeological evidence.[30] The Castaño de Sosa expedition did not visit or report on the Estancia Basin. Oñate entered it from the north, passing through the pueblos east of the Manzanos, which he called the "salinas" pueblos, before reaching Abo and then going on to three other pueblos that were probably Las Humanas, Pueblo Blanco, and Pueblo Colorado.[31] Apparently the smaller Pueblo Pardo was again ignored by the Spaniards.[32] Oñate named the three pueblos, one of which he describes as very large, "Cueloze/Quellotezei," "Xenopue/Genobey," and "Patasci/Pataotze."[33] Because it was at Cueloze that he received the oath of loyalty from pueblos in the area, it must have been the largest and, therefore, Las Humanas. The 1602 map does not show any pueblos in the area of the Estancia Basin, a major omission on what is otherwise a reasonably accurate map.

Middle Rio Grande

Spanish explorers found the largest number of inhabited pueblos in this centrally located part of the Rio Grande Pueblo Region, the Albuquerque-Belen Basin. Within the basin, the largest in the Rio Grande rift system, twenty to twenty-two pueblos were located along a sixty-mile stretch of the river between the Rio Puerco confluence on the south and the Jemez River junction on the north. Within this territory of the Southern Tiwa people, twelve to thirteen pueblos were clustered within a fourteen-mile distance at its northern end, with the other eight or nine spaced irregularly over the southern two thirds (table 4).[34]

Table 4. Pueblos Reported by Sixteenth-Century Spanish Explorers:
Middle Rio Grande Subregion

Pueblo Name	LA No.[a]	Coronado 1540-1542	Chamuscado 1581-1582	Espejo 1583	Castaño 1591	Oñate 1598	1602 Map
North							
Kuaua	187		Med. Torre	Poguana			
Santiago	326	Alcanfor	Palomares	Comise			Santiago
Watche	677		Campos	Achine	Unnamed		
Sandia	294		Cáceres	Guagua	Unnamed		
Corrales	288		La Palma	Gagose			
Puaray	717		Malpaís	Simasse	Unnamed	Puarai	
Maigua	716		Nompe	Suyte	Unnamed		
?			Cempoala	Nococe			
Alameda	421		Villarrasa	Hacala	Unnamed		
Chamisal	22766		Culiacan	Tiara	Unnamed		
Calabacillas	289		Analco	Taycios			
P.Marcadas	290		San Pedro	Casa	Unnamed		
?			Puaray	Puala			
SUBTOTAL		[12-13]	13	13[b]	[15]	incomplete[c]	[12][d]
South							
?			San Mateo				
Pur-e Tu-ay	489						Mesilla
Isleta	724		S. Catalina	Guaj'otes			Unnamed
Bei-juiTu-ay	81		Taxumulco	Unnamed			Unnamed
Valencia	953		Tomatlán				Unnamed
?				Despob.			
Lad.delSur[e]			Mexi'cingo	Despob.			Unnamed
Casa Colo.[f]				Unnamed		S. Juan B.	S. Juan
?			Piqui'tengo				
Abo Confl.	50241		Caxtole	El Corv.			Unnamed
S.Francisco	778		P. Nuevo	Unnamed			
?			Ponsitlán	Unnamed			
SUBTOTAL		[8]	9	8	n.d.	incomplete[c]	7

[a] New Mexico State Laboratory of Anthropology site number.
[b] A list of thirteen names is given but no location information.
[c] Of his list of ten pueblo names in the Middle Rio Grande Subregion, only "Puarai" and "San Juan Bautista" can be matched to sites.
[d] Eleven pueblo symbols designated "Valle de Purá" are shown without regard to specific locations.
[e] Ladera del Sur is LA 50257 and nearby Ladera Pueblo is LA 50259.
[f] LA 50249 is the earlier and LA 50261 the later component of this site.
[ ] Total number of pueblos reported.

Coronado's people were the first Spaniards to enter the Southern Tiwa area and they differentiated between these two groupings by giving them names as separate provinces: "Tiguex" on the north and "Tutahaco" on the south. They had arrived in Pueblo country at the Zuñi pueblos (his "Cíbola" province) about 125 miles due west of the Rio Grande, and it was from there that Coronado sent out advance parties to explore the new lands. Captain Hernando de Álvarado was the first to travel east to the Rio Grande, which he called the "Nuestra Señora."[35] His party, which included a delegation from Pecos Pueblo that had come to Cíbola to greet the Spaniards, travelled five days to Acoma Pueblo and another three to the Rio Grande. Because they were headed for Pecos Pueblo, which lay to the northeast, they reached the river at Tiguex province in the northern part of the Albuquerque–Belen Basin.[36]

Coronado himself later led a party to the Rio Grande, also in eight days, arriving at Tutahaco province.[37] Although he indicated that Tutahaco was south of Tiguex, his route to the Rio Grande is so vaguely described that the only clues as to how far south he went are the distance, which could not have been greatly different from that covered by Alvarado because the number of days is the same, and the likelihood that his Zuni guides would not have taken the party to a destination that was inconvenient for their own return. It is therefore probable that Tutahaco was located in the southern part of the Albuquerque–Belen Basin and not farther south in the Socorro Basin as has been suggested.[38] Coronado's chronicler, Castañeda, reports a total of twelve pueblos in Tiguex and eight in Tutahaco but mentions few individual pueblos. Those mentioned were the ones involved in what has come to be called the Tiguex War, information about which is drawn from Castañeda's chronicle and the documents related to the 1544 investigation of Coronado's expedition.[39] In the latter some witnesses from the expedition stated that there were thirteen Tiguex pueblos.

The series of attacks comprising the Tiguex War, which extended from about late December 1540 to late March 1541, began at a pueblo called "Arenal" that was located anywhere from one half to three leagues (one to eight miles) from the pueblo the Spaniards took over for their quarters, one called "Alcanfor," "Coofor," or "Coofer." The Tiguex people, forced to accommodate Coronado's large expedition, were further aggravated when forced to hand over clothing to the Spaniards. The people of Arenal, who suffered an additional outrage when a Spaniard molested one of their women and went unpunished, retaliated by stampeding a herd of the Spaniards' horses, killing some of them. Arenal was besieged for two days during which Coronado and his maestre de campo García López de Cárdenas met at a pueblo called "Alameda," located between Arenal and Alcanfor, a quarter league from the latter. It was deserted as were most of the other Tiguex pueblos, many of the residents having fled the area or taken refuge in two large pueblos. One of these pueblos, the largest in the province, was called "Moho," "Pueblo del Cerco," or "Tiguex" and was located three to four or possibly five leagues (eight to ten or thirteen miles) from Alcanfor. It was then attacked and besieged for at least fifty days, during which a second pueblo, described as a half league beyond Moho and possibly the one called "Pueblo de la Cruz," was also attacked and burned.

Scholars have puzzled over the identity of these five pueblos for many years, but divergent views remain.[40] It is generally assumed that most, if not all, of these pueblos were located on the west side of the Rio Grande, the direction from which the Coronado expedition approached Tiguex province.[41] No mention is made of whether they were north or south of each other, but visits between the Spaniards and the Keres of "Chia" (Zia) Pueblo on the lower Jemez River suggest that the others were north of Alcanfor. One possible reconstruction locates the latter quite far south at Bei-jui Tu-ay, with Arenal at Isleta and Moho at the Corrales site.[42] Alcanfor is correlated with Bei-jui Tu-ay on the basis of its Southern Tiwa name, which means "stolen pueblo." Another reconstruction locates Alcanfor farther north at Piedras Marcadas, with Alameda at Calabacillas, Arenal at Corrales, Moho at Santiago, and Pueblo de la Cruz at Kuaua.[43] For many years Kuaua was thought to have been the pueblo occupied by Coronado's army, and in 1935 it was named Coronado State Monument, but failure to find artifacts of that era casts doubt on this designation. Excavation of Santiago has yielded artifacts associated with Coronado's army such as crossbow boltheads, making this site the one most commonly agreed upon as Alcanfor.[44] The discovery in 1987 of a campsite (LA 54147) just four hundred meters west of Santiago that contains Spanish artifacts such as nails, a plate from an armored vest, and a Mexican obsidian blade has been interpreted as the possible encampment of Coronado's several hundred Mexican auxiliaries and gives further credence to Santiago as Alcanfor.[45]

If Alcanfor was at the Santiago site, where were the other four pueblos involved in the Tiguex War located? A recent proposal that emphasizes the defensible nature of the Moho site would extend the limits of Tiguex province northward to include that part of Santa Ana Mesa at the confluence of the Rio Grande and the Jemez River. It is stated in the Coronado documents that Moho was located on a height, one close enough to the Rio Grande that its inhabitants tried to cross it as they fled the pueblo at the end of the siege.[46] It is argued that no other Tiguex pueblo meets this description nor could any other one have withstood a siege by Coronado's large army for at least fifty days. A pueblo on Santa Ana Mesa in the confluence area, Canjillon Pueblo (LA 2049), and one about four miles north, Basalt Point (LA 2047), are suggested as Moho and the pueblo a half league beyond. They are very defensible sites—and the twelve-mile distance between Santiago (Alcanfor) and Pueblo Canjillon is about right—but their surface remains have been interpreted as late seventeenth-century refuges. Until further investigation yields evidence that these sites were larger and occupied earlier, their correlation with Coronado's siege pueblos remains speculative. But other pueblos identified as Moho remain suspect because they lack its site characteristics, and so the matter remains unsettled for the present. Besides the besieged pueblos, a number of other Tiguex pueblos were burned, but all were repaired and reoccupied by the time the next Spanish expedition arrived forty years later. It reports thirteen pueblos in the area of the old Tiguex province south of the Rio Grande–Jemez River junction, with Keres people in possession of the confluence area and Santa Ana Mesa.

The reports of the 1580s give a more complete picture of the Tiwa settlements in the Middle Rio Grande subregion. Starting from the Piro-Tiwa frontier, Gallegos mentions a total of twenty-two pueblos north to the Tiwa-Keres border, while Luxán notes at least twenty-one, both listing thirteen in the cluster at the north end of the Albuquerque-Belen Basin, the figure some of Coronado's men also mention.[47] Although there is some similarity in the number and location of the pueblos they report in the southern Albuquerque-Belen Basin, there is also considerable discordance despite the lapse of only a year and a half between the visits of the Chamuscado and Espejo expeditions.[48] At one time an uninhabited frontier zone was thought to exist between the Piro and Southern Tiwa, largely because there were no known sites in the area and because it was considered a buffer zone between two hostile peoples, but some sites have been identified in this area and, although statements by explorers indicate there was conflict, Espejo notes that only a half league (1.5 miles) separated the Piro and Tiwa provinces.[49] Gallegos's and Luxán's lists of Piro and Southern Tiwa pueblos further reinforce the likelihood that there was no significant no-man's-land in the frontier area.

After Espejo returned from visiting his Magrias pueblos in the Estancia Basin, the expedition decamped from Término de Puala and travelled four leagues (twelve miles) along the Rio Grande to a pueblo they named "El Corvillo," passing some small pueblos and many deserted ones along the way. One of these small pueblos might have been at the San Francisco site, located four miles north of Término de Puala (Sevilleta).[50] This site might also have been Gallegos's "Ponsitlán" or his "Pueblo Nuevo," both of which were located in this area. A distance of four leagues would have put El Corvillo in the vicinity of Abo Arroyo where there was a small pueblo, Abo Confluence, that could possibly have been occupied at that time.[51] This east-side pueblo could also have been Gallegos's very small "Caxtole."

As Espejo's people continued north they observed that all of the pueblos were deserted, the inhabitants having fled the Spaniards' approach. It was known that the Tiwa people were responsible for the deaths of the two priests from the Chamuscado expedition who had insisted on staying behind when that expedition returned to New Spain. They called their next campsite, four leagues north of El Corvillo, "Los Despoblados." It was between two pueblos, one very large that, given the distance, would have been near the Ladera del Sur site. Ladera del Sur is not a large site, but Ladera Pueblo, located 150 meters away, is.[52] Archeological evidence does not indicate that the latter was occupied in the contact period, but the site is badly damaged and such evidence could have been destroyed. It seems reasonable that, if Luxán could observe that both pueblos were deserted, the two pueblos would have been in sight of each other. There are no other pueblo sites that fit the information Luxán gives. A pueblo they encountered along the way might have been at the Casa Colorado site, which was also on the east side of the Rio Grande.

It is here that matching Luxán's and Gallegos's pueblos becomes especially difficult. Gallegos mentions a large west-side pueblo he calls "Piquinaguatengo," opposite Caxtole at Abo Arroyo. But there is no such site at that location, and Luxán does not mention a comparable pueblo.[53] Gallegos's next pueblo, "Mexicalcingo," was on the east side, but whether it occupied the site at Casa Colorado or at Ladera del Sur cannot be known because he does not give the distance. Above Mexicalcingo was his "Tomatlán" and across the river opposite it on the west side was "Taxumulco." These pueblos fit the sites of Valencia and Bei-jui Tu-ay, respectively, and are not likely the same as the two pueblos near Luxán's Despoblados camp because the latter were presumably on the same side of the Rio Grande.[54]

From Los Despoblados the Espejo expedition covered five leagues (fifteen miles) to a pueblo called "Los Guajolotes." This distance would have brought them to the Isleta site, which is located on the west side of the Rio Grande. Luxán notes another deserted pueblo along the way, one that could have been either Valencia or Bei-jui Tu-ay. That he does not mention both, when it is very likely that these were the sites of Gallegos's Tomatlán and Taxumulco, further brings out just how speculative is the reconstruction of the settlement pattern in this area. Espejo had been travelling along the east side of the Rio Grande, but at some point, perhaps at Valencia, his party must have crossed the river (although Luxán does not mention it), because they actually entered Los Guajolotes, noting its abundant provisions, including turkeys. Here, at the Isleta site, there again seems to be a correspondence with Gallegos's west-side "Santa Catalina" Pueblo. Above Isleta lay the first pueblo of the northern cluster, called "Puaray" by Gallegos and "Puala" by Luxán. Luxán gives the distance as three leagues (nine miles) and mentions no pueblos along the way, whereas Gallegos notes one, "San Mateo," placing both it and Puaray on the east side.

Both Gallegos and Luxán list twelve pueblos above Puaray/Puala (table 4).[55] Unfortunately Luxán does not continue to mention each pueblo encountered as Espejo's expedition moved north through the northern cluster of Tiwa pueblos (Coronado's Tiguex province), but later, when he named the pueblos in this area, Puala is the thirteenth and last on his list, reinforcing its location as the southernmost of these pueblos.[56] It cannot be said that the other pueblos on his list are in any geographic order, but Gallegos does supply this order. Above Puaray he notes five pueblos on the east side of the Rio Grande: "Cempoala," "Nompe," "Malpaís," "Cáceres," and "Campos."[57] Above Cempoala, the sites to which they could correspond are respectively Maigua, Puaray, Sandia, and Watche, although occupation of the latter during the contact period is questionable.[58] A bigger question surrounds Cempoala, for which no site has been found. Two other contact-period sites that today are on the east side of the Rio Grande, Alameda and Chamisal, were located on the west side of the river at that time.[59] Gallegos's west-side pueblos were "San Pedro," "Analco," "Culiacán," "Villarasa," "La Palma," "Palomares," and "Medina de la Torre," beyond which lay the Keres pueblos. The west-side sites to which they correspond are probably Piedras Marcadas, Calabacillas, Chamisal, Alameda, Corrales, Santiago, and Kuaua.

The location of Puaray in the 1580s remains a puzzle. It was at this pueblo that members of the Chamuscado expedition took leave of the two priests who insisted on staying behind, and it was there that the latter were probably killed.[60] When the Espejo expedition, whose purpose it was to learn the fate of the priests, arrived, they named the pueblo "Puala de los Mártires."[61] Gallegos locates it on the east side of the Rio Grande and Luxán puts it three leagues (nine miles) north of Isleta. Luxán also mentions that when they were camped near Puala they were visited by a delegation that had come from eight to ten leagues (twenty-four to thirty miles) upriver, making it likely they were Keres people from San Felipe Pueblo.[62] If the distance were ten leagues, it would have brought them to that site three leagues north of Isleta where Luxán located Puala. That site would have been two miles above the Rio Grande–Tijeras Arroyo junction (or just south of Albuquerque in the general vicinity of the Rio Bravo Boulevard and Highway 47 intersection), an area where there are no known pueblo sites. It would also have been about ten miles south of the other twelve closely spaced pueblos of the northern cluster.

A location somewhat farther north would seem more likely for Puaray, and consensus among modern scholars does place Puaray in the midst of Coronado's Tiguex pueblos on the east side at the LA 717 site (Fisher site #13), which is about seven leagues north of Isleta. This location also accords with information provided by Castaño de Sosa in 1591 and Oñate in 1598.[63] Castaño de Sosa gives the distance from the first Southern Tiwa pueblo he encountered to his main camp at Santo Domingo as five or six leagues.[64] Six leagues, or twenty-four miles (at four miles to the league), would be roughly the distance from Santo Domingo to the LA 717 site, an indication that his first pueblo might have been Puaray or a pueblo close to it. Oñate also establishes the location of Puaray in the vicinity of LA 717, and not farther south, when he too states that it was six leagues from Santo Domingo.[65] While at Puaray, one of his men, Gaspar Pérez de Villagrá, claimed he saw on a wall inside one of the houses a mural depicting the death of the two priests, but the scene had been painted over with whitewash and it is doubtful its contents could have been clearly discerned.[66] Oñate does not report it, and scholars have tended to treat it as apocryphal.[67] Even if it were true, it does not prove that the pueblo where the killings took place was LA 717. Residents of Luxán's Puala de los Mártires could have painted the scene in a different pueblo.

A possible explanation of the discrepancy between the reports of Gallegos and Luxán and those of Castaño de Sosa and Oñate might be that there were two Puarays: the one of the 1580s and the one of the 1590s. After the Espejo expedition left Pueblo country, the people of Puaray/Puala, wishing to disassociate themselves from the place where the killings had taken place and where Espejo's men viciously attacked them for refusing to give food, might have destroyed their pueblo and moved to the one at LA 717, giving it the same name.[68] Perhaps Gallegos's San Mateo and Cempoala, located respectively south and north of his Puaray, were destroyed at that time as well, leaving the area devoid of identifiable sites.

Which other pueblos of the northern cluster were still inhabited in the 1590s cannot be fully determined from either the Castaño de Sosa or Oñate reports. Castaño de Sosa visited pueblos on both sides of the river, which he called the "Río Grande," claiming there were a total of fifteen, but he did not name any of them.[69] Because he probably approached the area through Tijeras Canyon from the east side of the Sandias, the first pueblo he would have encountered was the most southerly on the east side.[70] He found this pueblo deserted and was told that the people had fled because it was they who had killed the priests, but inhabitants fled from the other pueblos as well, so it is difficult to know if that particular pueblo was Puaray. It probably was not, because from that first pueblo Castaño de Sosa proceeded up the east side of the Rio Grande, visiting four other pueblos before crossing to the west side. Above Puaray (LA 717) the only sites are Sandia and Watche and, as mentioned, there is some doubt about the latter's occupancy during the contact period.[71] Below it was Maigua, which is less than a mile south of Puaray. Identity of the fourth pueblo is still in question. Possibly it could have been Gallegos's Cempoala, if that pueblo had not been destroyed previously. In this area of intense urban settlement it would not be surprising if this site has been lost.

On the west side Castaño de Sosa's pueblos are even more difficult to link to known sites, but it is possible that the pueblo across the river from the first one he encountered on the east side was Alameda and the other near it was Chamisal. The southernmost, which he describes as very large, might have been Piedras Marcadas.[72] Oñate gives a list of "Tigua" (Tiwa) pueblos, but the only recognizable name is Puaray.[73] The 1602 map shows twelve pueblos. Unfortunately, eleven are placed without regard to location, designated together as "Pueblos del valle de Puará," but the twelfth, Santiago, is correctly placed at the north end of the west side. This later location might well be the site of Coronado's headquarters (Alcanfor/Coofer), indicating that it continued to be occupied.

As for the southern part of the Albuquerque-Belen Basin, the explorers who came after Chamuscado and Espejo have little to add. Castaño de Sosa did not visit the area, and Oñate moved through it quickly, mentioning only newly built "San Juan Bautista" four leagues (sixteen miles) above Sevilleta, which would have put it at the Casa Colorado site (LA 50261).[74] The 1602 map, based on information from a member of Oñate's expedition, is more helpful. The arrangement of symbols indicates that the pueblo sites could have been Abo Confluence, Casa Colorado (named "San Juan"), Ladera del Sur, and Valencia on the east side of the Rio Grande; Bei-jui Tu-ay and Pur-e Tu-ay on the west side; and Isleta on an island in the river (actually, a volcanic outcrop in the western floodplain). The northernmost pueblo on the west side is named "Mesilla," a name that would fit the Pur-e Tu-ay site, which is on a small butte. Although its late ceramics leave open the possibility that Pur-e Tu-ay was established after the end of the contact period, they do not preclude the possibility of occupation at the time of Oñate's arrival.[75]

Rio Puerco–Rio San Jose

North of the Southern Tiwa settlements in the Albuquerque-Belen Basin lay the pueblos of the Keres people, whose territory extended up the Rio Grande in the Santo Domingo Basin, along the lower reaches of the tributary Jemez River, and to isolated Acoma Pueblo, located about fifty miles west of the Rio Grande. Acoma was the survivor of an earlier phase of Keres settlement in the Rio Puerco–Rio San Jose area.[76] Located in highly dissected plateau country, it occupied a spectacular site atop a small, steep-sided mesa 357 feet above the surrounding surface, bounded on the west by a broad wash created by ephemeral Acoma Creek, a tributary of the Rio San Jose that flows via the Rio Puerco to the Rio Grande. There is no doubt that Acoma was inhabited throughout the contact period. It was visited by most of the explorers, all of whom comment on its unique, fortress-like site.[77] The Espejo expedition, travelling west from the lower Jemez River to Zuni, stopped at Acoma en route and mention the latter's irrigated fields four leagues (twelve miles) away along what must have been the Rio San Jose, the only dependable water source in the area.[78] Between Acoma and the Rio Grande Valley lies the valley of the Rio Puerco. Although it contained substantial Pueblo settlement earlier, and a few pueblos were occupied as late as the early sixteenth century, it was an unoccupied area during the contact period.[79]

Lower Jemez River

During the contact period there were five pueblos along the lower twenty miles of the Jemez River. All of the Spanish explorers except Castaño de Sosa mention these Keres settlements, generally treating them as a group separate from those in the Santo Domingo Basin (table 5).

**Table 5. Pueblos Reported by Sixteenth-Century Spanish Explorers:
Lower Jemez Subregion**

Pueblo Name	LA No.[a]	Coronado 1540-1542	Chamuscado 1581-1582	Espejo 1583	Castaño 1591	Oñate 1598	1602 Map
Sta. Ana	[b]		Guatitlán			Tamaya	S. Anna
Chackham	374		La Guarda				
Zia	28	Chia	Valladolid	Ziaquebos		Tzia	Sia
Old Zia	384		La Rincón.				
C.C. Zia	241						
TOTAL		1	4	[5][c]	n.d.	5[d]	2

[a] New Mexico State Laboratory of Anthropology site number.
[b] Sixteenth-century site unknown.
[c] Espejo reports five pueblos in "Punames" province.
[d] Oñate lists names of five lower Jemez pueblos, but only two of these names can be linked to sites.
[] Total number of pueblos reported.

Coronado reports only one pueblo, "Chia" (Zia, LA 28 or possibly LA 384), and does not include it in his "Quirix" (Keres) province, which consisted of the Keres pueblos in the Santo Domingo Basin.[80] The chronicler of the Chamuscado expedition cites four pueblos visited in this subregion, which he called the "Atotonilco Valley."[81] Luxán's report on the Espejo expedition mentions only one pueblo, "Ziaquebos," but according to him it is in "Punames" province, distinct from his "Quires" province, indicating the presence of other pueblos on the lower Jemez.[82] Espejo himself says there were five pueblos in this province.[83] Besides Zia, these pueblos probably consisted of Corn Clan Zia, Old Zia, Chackham, and Santa Ana (site unknown). Two of these pueblos can be recognized on Oñate's lists: Zia ("Tzia"/"Acotziya") and Santa Ana ("Tamaya"/"Tamy"). Because his other names cannot be linked to the remaining sites and only Zia and Santa Ana are shown on the 1602 map, it could, perhaps, be concluded that these were the only pueblos on the lower Jemez still occupied at the end of the contact period.[84] Although it seems certain that Santa Ana people lived in this area during the contact period, the site they occupied then has not been found.[85] According to Santa Ana or Tamayame tradition, they had finally settled beside the Jemez River beneath a broad mesa by the time the first Spaniards arrived.[86] This pueblo, or one near it, might be the one on the west side of the Jemez River shown on the 1602 map, a pueblo that perhaps was subsequently destroyed by floods.[87]

Santo Domingo Basin

Explorers found between four and seven pueblos in the Santo Domingo Basin, which lies above the Rio Grande–Jemez River junction (table 6).

Some of these Keres pueblos were located along a fourteen-mile stretch of the Rio Grande and others on the lower reaches of eastern tributaries: the Santa Fe River, Galisteo Creek, and Tunque Arroyo. The seven "Quirix" (Keres) pueblos that Coronado reports (distinct from those on the lower Jemez) probably included Old San Felipe, Katishtya, "Cochiti" (site unknown), La Bajada, Gipuy, Tunque, and possibly San Marcos in the Galisteo Basin to the east.[88] At that time the Santo Domingo people were probably living at Gipuy on lower Galisteo Creek.[89]

Chamuscado visited seven pueblos: three on the Rio Grande, one on the lower Santa Fe River, and three in what he called "Valle Vicioso," which was probably lower Galisteo Creek.[90] Travelling north along the Rio Grande from the Jemez River junction, his party encountered what was probably Old San Felipe Pueblo and named it "Castilleja." The next, much larger, pueblo, which was most likely Katishtya (LA 922), located on the west side of the Rio Grande near its junction with Galisteo Creek, was named Castildabid and was still occupied by San Felipe

Table 6. Pueblos Reported by Sixteenth-Century Spanish Explorers: Santo Domingo Basin Subregion

Pueblo Name	LA No.[a]	Coronado 1540-1542	Chamuscado 1581-1582	Espejo 1583	Castaño 1591	Oñate 1598	1602 Map
Cochiti	[b]		Suchipila	Cochita	Unnamed	Cochiti	Chicotin
La Bajada	7		Talaván	Tipolti	Unnamed	Tipoti	Tipotin
S. Dom.	[c]			Gigue	S. Dom.	Quigui	S. Dom.
Gipuy	182		Castilblanco				
La Vega	412				Unnamed		
Katishtya	922		Castildabid				
Old S. Felipe	3137[d]		Castilleja	Cachiti	[d]	Cachichi	S. Felipe
Tunque	240		Buena Vista	Sieharan	Unnamed	El Tuerto	
TOTAL		[7][e]	6[f]	5	6	5	4

[a] New Mexico State Laboratory of Anthropology site number.
[b] Sixteenth-century site unknown but probably in the vicinity of the present site LA 126.
[c] The Santo Domingo people occupied the site of Gipuy Pueblo (LA 182) until sometime in the early 1580s by which time they occupied a pueblo they had built on the east side of the Rio Grande in the vicinity of their present site LA 1281.
[d] The San Felipe people might also have been living at Katishtya Pueblo (also called Oldest San Felipe, LA 922) when Coronado was in New Mexico and possibly later into the early 1580s. Although not mentioned by Castaño in 1691, the San Felipe people were undoubtedly at LA 3137 or at LA 2047, a refuge site on the mesa above.
[e] The seven "Quirix" pueblos reported by Coronado probably included San Marcos (LA 98) in the Galisteo Basin but not LA 412, occupation of which is questionable even in Chamuscado's time. .
[f] The seventh pueblo, "La Barranca," is listed in Table 7.
[ ] Total number of pueblos reported.

people while others lived at Old San Felipe.[91] Above this point they visited two other pueblos, "Suchipila" and "Talaván," the first of which was probably Cochiti and the other possibly La Bajada on the lower Santa Fe River.[92] The location of Cochiti Pueblo during the contact period is uncertain, but probably it was in the vicinity of its present site (LA 126). The difficulty of trying to match explorers' descriptions to archeological sites is further seen in locating sites for the three pueblos Chamuscado claims were in his Valle Vicioso. Castilblanco, which he locates opposite Castildabid, was probably Gipuy and was mostly likely still inhabited by the Santo Domingo people. Identification of the other two pueblos, "Buena Vista" and "La Barranca," presents problems because there are no other appropriate sites on lower Galisteo Creek. Because their names suggest a location near mountains, these two pueblos might be Tunque and some other unknown site near the north end of the Sandia Mountains if the definition of Valle Vicioso can be stretched to include other tributaries in the southern part of the Santo Domingo Basin.[93] The unknown site that might have been La Barranca could have been located closer to the north end of the Sandia Mountains than Tunque and is included in the Sandia Periphery subregion.

Luxán of the Espejo expedition, as well as Espejo himself, mention five pueblos in the Santo Domingo Basin.[94] Three of these can be quite definitely identified: San Felipe ("Cachiti," "Catiete," "La Tiete" [also called "Los Confiados"]), Santo Domingo ("Gigue"), and Cochiti ("Cochita"). Gigue also referred to Gipuy Pueblo, but by this time its inhabitants, having been flooded out, had moved to the Santo Domingo Pueblo site on the east side of the Rio Grande near the present pueblo (LA 1281). They had definitely moved eight years later when Castaño de Sosa visited this area. The pueblo Luxán called "Tipolti" was probably La Bajada.[95] The fifth pueblo, "Sieharan," was probably the one he earlier called "La Milpa Llana." On that occasion the Espejo party went to a pueblo a league and a half (4.5 miles) from San Felipe and from there five leagues (fifteen miles) west to the Jemez River and then on to Ziaquebos (Zia Pueblo) in their Punames province.[96] Given this itinerary, it is possible that La Milpa Llana/Sieharan was Tunque, even though the distances do not fit well.[97]

Castaño de Sosa's reconnaissance party first entered the Santo Domingo Basin from the north. Their route would not have been directly south along the Rio Grande through the extremely narrow White Rock Canyon; more likely they cut across the Caja del Rio Plateau or retraced their route along the Tesuque River before descending La Bajada escarpment (which overlooks lower Santa Fe River) into the Santo Domingo Basin. There, according to Castaño de Sosa, they found four pueblos in view of one another.[98] The identity of the four pueblos so situated has been a puzzle to scholars and the source of some disagreement because most of the pueblo sites in this area that are located close together had been abandoned well before 1540.[99] He spent two days visiting the four pueblos and obtaining their oaths of allegiance. Cochiti was likely one of the four as was Santo Domingo Pueblo, which its inhabitants had built about a decade earlier after being forced to abandon Gipuy as previously mentioned.[100] Castaño later camped overnight at the ruins of Gipuy before going on to the new pueblo, which he named "Santo Domingo" and where he made his headquarters.[101] La Bajada, located on the south side of the Santa Fe River below La Bajada Escarpment, is another possible pueblo in the group. The fourth pueblo seems to be a mystery, but it might be the same pueblo where he later stopped on his return from the Southern Tiwa pueblos in the upper Albuquerque-Belen Basin. This pueblo, where he was informed of the arrival of the Morlete expedition sent to arrest him for entering New Mexico without permission, was located a league (2.6 miles) south of Santo Domingo.[102] Old San Felipe Pueblo was about seven miles south and not a likely possibility. If La Vega Pueblo, about three miles south of Santo Domingo on the east side of the Rio Grande, was reoccupied at that time, its location would have made it a candidate for Castaño de Sosa's stopping place as well as one of the four pueblos he initially visited.

Oñate mentions five pueblos in the Santo Domingo Basin, and the 1602 map shows four.[103] Oñate's list of "Cheres" (Keres) pueblos consists of San Felipe ("Castixe," "Cachichi"), Santo Domingo ("Quigui"), Cochiti, "Tipoti/Olipoti," and "El Puerto"/"El Pueblo Quemado." Cochiti is named "Chicotin" on the 1602 map, and Tipoti/Olipoti corresponds to "Tipotin," whose location on the map between Cochiti and Santo Domingo suggests that it was at the La Bajada site. Fifteen years earlier, when the Espejo expedition was in this area, Luxán mentioned a pueblo named Tipolti. This consistency of naming cannot be ignored despite lack of congruence with La Bajada's Tano name, *Tzenatay*.[104] Although ceramics at the site do not clearly support occupation at this time, they give some evidence of a minor late sixteenth-century occupation that is reinforced by the 1602 map.[105] Some scholars have linked La Bajada with Oñate's El Puerto because of its description as a burned pueblo, but others have suggested that the latter might have been the same as the one he passed through en route from his headquarters near San Juan Pueblo to the Estancia Basin, a pueblo he called "El Tuerto."[106] El Puerto/El Tuerto might have been Tunque, a pottery-making and trading center that was probably inhabited by Tano and Tiwa as well as Keres people.[107]

The distances travelled fit well, and Arroyo del Tuerto is part of the upper drainage of Tunque Arroyo. Archeological evidence indicates that Tunque was not abandoned until the end of the sixteenth century or shortly thereafter.[108] The pueblo is not Paa-ko because "Paaco" appears on one of Oñate's lists.[109] The 1602 map does not, however, indicate a place that might be Tunque. According to Oñate and the 1602 map, San Felipe, Santo Domingo, Cochiti/Chicotin, and La Bajada/Tipotin were still inhabited at the end of the contact period, but La Vega, if indeed it had been occupied during Castaño's time, had probably been abandoned before Oñate's arrival.

Sandia Periphery

In a transitional area between the northern Albuquerque-Belen Basin, the southern Santo Domingo Basin, and the Galisteo Basin farther east lie the Sandia Mountains, which rise from about five thousand to over ten thousand feet above sea level. A number of pueblos have been established on their wetter eastern side, two of which were occupied at some time during the contact period according to evidence provided by explorers and archeologists.[110] These pueblos, Paa-ko and San Antonio, were probably two of the seven that Coronado associates with his "snowy mountains," undoubtedly a reference to the Sandia-Manzano chain (table 7).

Pueblo Name	LA No.[a]	Coronado 1540-1542	Chamuscado 1581-1582	Espejo 1583	Castaño 1591	Oñate 1598	1602 Map
			Table 7. Pueblos Reported by Sixteenth-Century Spanish Explorers: Sandia Periphery Subregion				
?		Unnamed	Barranca		Unnamed		
Paa-ko	162	Unnamed	Unnamed		Unnamed	Paaco	
S. Antonio	24	Unnamed	Unnamed		Unnamed		
Silva Site	12924					Portezuelo	
TOTAL		3[b]	3	[5][c]	3	2	n.d.

[a] New Mexico State Laboratory of Anthropology site number.
[b] Three of the seven unnamed pueblos Coronado associates with the "snowy mountains" but did not visit. See Table 3 for the four other pueblos.
[c] Espejo reports five pueblos in his Ubates province.
[] Total number of pueblos reported.

He mentions three pueblos on the slope of the mountain and four on the plain. The latter were farther south, in the Estancia Basin east of the Manzano Mountains. The former included, besides Paa-ko and San Antonio, a third pueblo that may have been the one on the north end of the Sandias alluded to by subsequent explorers but for which no contact-period site has been identified. Las Huertas Canyon, which is located in this area and which had a significant Pueblo population earlier, was apparently not occupied during the contact period.[111] In Coronado's time Paa-ko and San Antonio may have been occupied by refugees from the Tano pueblos of the Galisteo Basin, which, he was told, had been attacked by a people from the eastern plains.[112] Baltasar de Obregón, writing about Coronado's Tiguex province, states that there were two pueblos southeast of the twelve along the Rio Grande, a likely reference to Paa-ko and San Antonio.[113]

Chamuscado also alludes to pueblos that were probably Paa-ko and San Antonio. When he was in his Valle Vicioso at La Barranca Pueblo, he was informed that thirteen pueblos lay three days' journey upriver and to the south.[114] In this case the river was Galisteo Creek and, because there were not that many pueblos in the adjacent Galisteo Basin, it is likely that they were located south of it on the east side of the Sandia-Manzano Mountains and included Paa-ko and San Antonio along with the eleven pueblos of the Estancia Basin. Later, at a Galisteo Basin pueblo, he was told that there were two large pueblos on the slopes of the "Sierra Morena" (his name for the Sandia-Manzano Mountains), most probably another reference to Paa-ko and San Antonio.[115]

Although it is not mentioned by his chronicler Luxán, Espejo reports a province of five pueblos he calls "Ubates" that he encountered after leaving the Keres pueblos in the Santo Domingo Basin but before reaching the Tano pueblos of the Galisteo Basin.[116] Just which pueblos they were is impossible to say with certainty, but presumably they included Paa-ko and San Antonio, possibly the Silva Site at the mouth of Tijeras Canyon to the south, and a pueblo or two at the north end of the Sandias. Chamuscado's pueblo La Barranca was likely located in the latter area, as discussed in the previous section.

That pueblos on the periphery of the Sandia Mountains were occupied in the contact period is reinforced by Castaño de Sosa, who, after leaving Santo Domingo Pueblo to look for mines, took possession of various pueblos near the north end of the Sandias before crossing to their east side, where he found two recently deserted pueblos—probably Paa-ko and San Antonio.[117] Among the pueblos he took possession of might have been some of the five in Espejo's Ubates province, possibly including Coronado's third mountain-slope pueblo and Chamuscado's La Barranca. The only pueblos Oñate identified in this subregion were Paa-ko, which he so named, and another he called "Portezuelo."[118] He arrived at this latter pueblo after moving north among the salinas pueblos of the Estancia Basin, headed for the Tiwa pueblos along the Rio Grande that were most readily reached through Tijeras Canyon. The Silva Site at the mouth of Tijeras Canyon could well have been Oñate's Portezuelo.[119]

All of the explorers mention pueblos located on the fringes of the Sandia Mountains, but none grouped them into a province except Espejo. The reason may have been that they were not perceived to have a common language. That condition may have resulted from their location in a zone of movement among surrounding Keres-, Tano-, and Tiwa-speaking peoples, a situation similar to that of nearby pueblos such as Tunque in the Santo Domingo Basin and San Marcos in the Galisteo Basin, where linguistic affiliation was probably mixed, as different groups came to dominate these pueblos at various times.

Galisteo Basin

Explorers found three to four pueblos in the Galisteo Basin, which is located east of the Santo Domingo Basin and north of the Estancia Basin (table 8).

Table 8. Pueblos Reported by Sixteenth-Century Spanish Explorers: Galisteo Basin Subregion							
Pueblo Name	LA No.[a]	Coronado 1540-1542	Chamuscado 1581-1582	Espejo 1583	Castaño 1591	Oñate 1598	1602 Map
S. Marcos	98	[b]	Malpartida	S. Catalina	S. Marcos	S. Marcos	S. Marcos
S. Lázaro	92	Unnamed	Malagón		Unnamed		
Galisteo	26	Ximena	Galisteo	Jumea	S. Lucas	Sta. Ana	Calisteo
S. Crist.	80	Silos	Piedrahita	Pocos	S. Crist.	S. Crist.	S. Crist.
TOTAL		3	4	3	4	3	3

[a] New Mexico State Laboratory of Anthropology site number.
[b] Coronado probably considered San Marcos to be a "Quirix" (Keres) pueblo.

They were inhabited by Southern Tewa people who spoke a dialect called Tano, although the population of San Marcos pueblo might have been linguistically mixed and is considered by some scholars to have been Keres.[120] When Coronado travelled through this area in 1541, he notes much destruction and was told that it was the result of attacks made sixteen years before by Teyas, a people from the eastern plains.[121] He describes three pueblos: a small one that was occupied ("Ximena"), a large one that was partially so ("Silos"), and a third one, also large, that was destroyed. His captain, Hernando de Alvarado, notes seven pueblos that were possibly in this area that had been abandoned and ruined as a result of attacks by people from the eastern plains.[122] Archeological evidence also supports the existence of seven occupied pueblos prior to Coronado's entrada, four in the northern sector of the basin and three in the south.[123]

The route Coronado took across the Galisteo Basin from Pecos Pueblo to his Tiguex province cannot be known with certainty, but modern reconstructions favor a route through the northern part of the basin—through Glorieta Pass, along Galisteo Creek, and around the north end of the Ortiz Mountains that separate the Galisteo and Santo Domingo Basins.[124] Data from the later explorers seem to support the hypothesis that the pueblos inhabited in the contact period were those in this northern sector. If such were the case, the three sites in the southern part were most likely abandoned when attacked in the 1520s and not reoccupied—some of their inhabitants possibly having sought refuge at Paa-ko and San Antonio pueblos on the Sandia periphery. Coronado does not mention a fourth pueblo in the northern sector. It could have been San Marcos, which conceivably he included in his group of seven "Qurix" pueblos, of which the other six were located in the adjacent Santo Domingo Basin.[125]

Forty years later Chamuscado and his party visited four pueblos in the Galisteo Basin (their "San Mateo Valley"), which they describe as large, an indication that the pueblos of Coronado's time had been rebuilt and enlarged.[126] They named one of them "Galisteo" and another "Malpartida." The latter, located near mines, was most likely San Marcos, the site of which is near the Cerrillos Hills where turquoise and lead deposits were mined.[127] The very large masonry pueblo they named "Pie-drahita" could well have been San Cristóbal, and the fourth pueblo, "Malagón," might have been San Lázaro, although there is disagreement over the latter.[128]

A year or so later the Espejo expedition reports three pueblos in the Galisteo Basin, or "Atamues"/"Tamos" province as they called it.[129] They associated the one they named "Santa Catalina" with mines, an indication that it probably was San Marcos.[130] From Santa Catalina the Espejo group travelled three leagues (eight miles) to "Jumea," probably Galisteo Pueblo, and then to a very large pueblo, "Pocos," which was probably San Cristóbal. Possibly they failed to take a side trip to the fourth pueblo (San Lázaro) as they made their way across the basin to Pecos Pueblo. That four pueblos were occupied seems likely, not only on the basis of the Chamuscado report but also because the Castaño de Sosa report supports it.

Castaño de Sosa's advance party passed through the Galisteo Basin on its way to rejoin the main body of the expedition camped on the Pecos River, which they refer to as the "Río Salado."[131] They then returned en masse to the Rio Grande, again crossing the Galisteo Basin. On the outward journey three pueblos are mentioned, the first located near some mines. On the return trip these pueblos are named "San Cristóbal," "San Lucas" (Galisteo), and "San Marcos," where they had previously discovered mines.[132] Several days later Castaño de Sosa led a party from San Marcos to another pueblo two leagues (five miles) away that he had not previously visited. This pueblo could have been San Lázaro; ceramic evidence indicates that it was oc-cupied during the sixteenth century.[133] The pueblo might have been abandoned for a time following the raids of the 1520s and, as such, might have been the unnamed pueblo Coronado describes as completely destroyed but that was rebuilt sometime before the Chamuscado expedition arrived in the area.[134]

Seven years later, Oñate and his advance party entered the Galisteo Basin, where they visited three pueblos before continuing on to Pecos. The names given were those bestowed by Castaño de Sosa except that to the name Galisteo they added "Santa Ana" instead of San Lucas.[135] This convergence of names is the first of its kind and is probably the result of Oñate's having as interpreters two Mexican natives who had been left behind by Castaño de Sosa. Oñate may also have seen a copy of Castaño de Sosa's report.[136] Oñate does not mention San Lázaro, and there is some evidence that it was abandoned again, if only temporarily, when his party passed through the area.[137] As Castaño de Sosa notes in 1591, attacks by native peoples still caused inhabitants to flee their pueblos in this area.[138] The 1602 map shows only "S. Marcos," "Calisteo," and "San Cristóual."

Upper Pecos River

East of the Galisteo pueblos and forty miles east of the Rio Grande lies Pecos. This easternmost pueblo of the Rio Grande Pueblo Region was built on a small narrow mesa near Glorieta Pass, a major link between the farming communities of the Rio Grande Valley and the nomadic tribes of the Great Plains farther east. It was visited by all of the Spanish explorers, who were, without exception, impressed by its size and position of power. Coronado reports that "Cicuye" (Pecos) was feared throughout the land and that its people were proud that they could not be` conquered but could subjugate any pueblo they wished.[139] Identification of Pecos in the reports of the Chamuscado expedition is not very clear, but the pueblo called "Tlaxcala" or "Nueva Tlaxcala" seems best interpreted as Pecos.[140] In the Espejo documents it is called "Siqui," similar to Coronado's rendering of the name.[141] Al-though Pecos was the first pueblo encountered by Castaño de Sosa, he did not name it. The name "Pecos" (possibly derived from the Keres name) first appears when Oñate made his initial reconnaissance of the Rio Grande Pueblo Region, and it is also on the 1602 map.[142] Pecos was the only pueblo of Towa speakers besides those located in the Upper Jemez River subregion. How and when these people became dominant at Pecos is still a matter of conjecture.[143] Possibly they were survivors of an earlier, more widespread distribution of Towa people—a situation similar to that of the Acomans to the west.

Upper Jemez River

In the deeply dissected plateau country on the southwestern flank of the Jemez massif, the Towa-speaking Jemez people established numerous pueblos. Nine of these probably survived into the contact period, although the Spanish explorers reported from seven to fifteen pueblos (table 9).[144]

Table 9. Pueblos Reported by Sixteenth-Century Spanish Explorers: Upper Jemez River Subregion

Pueblo Name	LA No.[a]	Coronado 1540-1542	Chamuscado 1581-1582	Espejo 1583	Castaño 1591	Oñate 1598	1602 Map
Unshagi	123	Aguas Cal.					
Nanishagi	541	Aguas Cal.	Puerto Frío				
Guisewa	679	Aguas Cal.	Baños			Guiusta	
Kiatsukwa	132-133						
Seshukwa	303						
Amoxiumqua	481						
Kwastiyukwa	482						
Tovakwa	483						
—	484						
TOTAL		[10]	[15]	[7]	n.d.	[11][b]	[6][c]

[a] New Mexico State Laboratory of Anthropology site number.
[b] Eleven Upper Jemez pueblos were reported to Oñate. Of the eight he assigned to a priest, only "Guiusta" (Guisewa) can be identified.
[c] The map shows six pueblo symbols placed without regard to specific sites.
[ ] Total number of pueblos reported.

Coronado mentions three pueblos in the hot springs area ("Aguas Calientes") and seven others in his "Hemes" province.[145] The three hot springs pueblos could well have been Guisewa, Unshagi, and Nanishagi.[146] Chamuscado visited two pueblos in what he called the "Valley of Santiago" (through which the Jemez River flows) and was informed that there were thirteen others. He named one of the two pueblos he visited "Baños," an indication it was located in the hot springs area. It might have been Guisewa, and the second pueblo, called "Puerto Frío," might have been nearby Nanishagi.[147] Espejo reports seven pueblos, but there is some question about whether he actually contacted any of them.[148] Castaño de Sosa did not visit or mention the Jemez pueblos. Oñate visited eight, including the "great pueblo," probably Tovakwa (also called Stable Mesa, LA 483), and the pueblos near the hot springs. He was told there were eleven altogether; however, his list of Jemez pueblo names consists of nine, one of which is Zia, a Keres pueblo. The only recognizable Towa pueblo name is "Guiusta" (Guisewa).[149] The 1602 map shows a group of six pueblos along the upper Jemez River but without regard to specific locations. Walatowa, the pueblo that is the present home of the Jemez people, was not established until the 1620s.[150]

Pajarito Plateau

The dissected plateau structure known as the Pajarito Plateau, which comprises the eastern flank of the Jemez massif, had been largely depopulated by the contact period. None of the explorers reports settlements there. However, archeological evidence indicates that some of the pueblos still might have been at least partially occupied. Their location in very rugged terrain remote from the explorers' routes of travel could have been the reason for failure to report them. Tree-ring data indicate that Puye was probably occupied into the 1570s and Tsirege into the 1580s.[151] Tree-ring dates for Sankawi'i, Potsuwi'i, and Tyuonyi are not as late, but parallel ceramics argue for their inclusion in this group, if only for the early contact period.[152] Kuapa, located at the southern end of the plateau, might also have been occupied into the contact period.[153] These pueblos were probably all of waning importance as their inhabitants, prompted by increasingly severe drought conditions, moved to pueblos on the Rio Grande such as San Ildefonso, Santa Clara, and Cochiti.[154] The only historical evidence to support occupation of the Pajarito Plateau during the contact period is the 1602 map, which shows a pueblo called "Messillas" located west of the Rio Grande between Santa Clara and Cochiti. This information fits the archeological evidence that only one pueblo survived to the end of the contact period. The pueblo was probably Tsirege, which is considered the last pueblo in the area to have been abandoned. It has also been suggested that the four "mountain" pueblos that Coronado's officer Francisco de Barrionuevo mentions when inspecting the pueblos at the Rio Grande–Rio Chama confluence were located on the Pajarito Plateau rather than in the Chama Basin and were possibly Puye, Potsuwi'i, Tsirege, and Sankawi'i.[155]

Española Basin

North of the Santo Domingo Basin, the Española Basin stretches some thirty-five miles to the confluence of the Rio Grande and Rio Chama. The Rio Grande hugs the west side of the basin along the base of the Pajarito Plateau, and its principal tributaries arise in the Sangre de Cristo Mountains to the east. The southernmost tributary is the Santa Fe River, which drains a substantial area but one that was without settlement in the contact period. It is another case, such as those of the Rio Puerco Valley and Las Huertas Canyon already mentioned, where abandonment about 1450 followed an era of substantial Pueblo settlement.[156] Reasons for abandonment of such a favorable location as the Santa Fe River Valley are not clear, although competition among surrounding Tewa, Keres, Tano, and Pecos peoples might have led to its becoming a buffer zone.[157] The smaller Santa Cruz Valley, located farther north in the Española Basin, experienced a similar settlement history, but its abandonment was not likely caused by hostilities among neighboring peoples because it is well within Tewa territory.[158]

Contact-period settlement in the Española Basin, home of Tewa-speaking people, was concentrated in the Pojoaque Creek drainage area and in the northern part of the basin in the vicinity of the Rio Grande–Rio Chama confluence (table 10).

Table 10. Pueblos Reported by Sixteenth-Century Spanish Explorers: Española Basin Subregion

Pueblo Name	LA No.[a]	Coronado 1540-1542	Chamuscado 1581-1582	Espejo 1583	Castaño 1591	Oñate 1591	1602 Map
Rio Grande-Rio Chama							
Pioge	144				Unnamed		
San Juan	874	Unnamed			Unnamed	S. Juan	S. Juan
Yunque	59	Unnamed			Unnamed	S. Gabriel	S. Gabriel
Santa Clara	925				Unnamed	Caypa	Sta. Clara
Tsama	908					Tzooma	Sama
Te'ewi	252				Unnamed		
?							
?							
SUBTOTAL		[6][b]	n.d.	n.d.	5	4[b]	4
Pojoaque Creek							
S. Ildefonso	6188				Unnamed	Bove	S. Ildef.
Jacona	1065				Unnamed		
Pojoaque	61				Unnamed		Unnamed
Nambe	17				Unnamed		Unnamed
Cuyamunge	38				Unnamed		Unnamed
Tesuque	1064				Unnamed		Unnamed
SUBTOTAL		n.d.	n.d.	n.d.	6	incomplete[c]	5

[a] New Mexico State Laboratory of Anthropology site number.
[b] Besides two pueblos visited by Coronado's men, four others were reported to them.
[c] Oñate's list of "Teguas" (Tewa) pueblos includes some in both the Chama and Pojoaque areas but only five can be linked to sites.
[ ] Total number of pueblos reported.

Pueblos in the Pojoaque drainage area were not reported until the entrada of Castaño de Sosa in 1591.[159] Although two of Coronado's captains, Alvarado and Barrionuevo, visited Taos Pueblo farther north, neither mentions pueblos on the Pojoaque or its tributaries, making their routes to and from Taos the subject of continuing speculation. The Chamuscado and Espejo expeditions did not reach as far north as the Española Basin. Castaño de Sosa approached it from Pecos Pueblo, probably moving through Glorieta Pass, around the southern end of the Sangre de Cristo Mountains, across the unoccupied valley of the Santa Fe River, and into the upper Rio Tesuque Valley. On this tributary of the Pojoaque he and his advance party visited two pueblos one league (2.6 miles) apart that were probably Tesuque and Cuyamungue. They then went on to three others, also a league from each other, which were likely Nambe, Pojoaque, and Jacona.[160] Travelling west another two leagues (five miles) along Pojoaque Creek, they reached its junction with the Rio Grande and San Ildefonso Pueblo. From there they marched north and later, returning to this area, stopped at a pueblo located on the Rio Grande about five miles north of San Ildefonso that is best interpreted as Santa Clara.[161]

Oñate visited San Ildefonso (his "Bove") and Santa Clara (his "Caypa") during the initial reconnaissance he made of the region and mentions them again when he assigned priests to the various groups of pueblos.[162] The Pojoaque Creek pueblos cannot be identified on Oñate's lists, but the 1602 map shows four sites located along an eastern tributary of the Rio Grande. They could be Pojoaque, Nambe, Cuyamungue, and Tesuque, with Jacona abandoned by Oñate's time. San Ildefonso and Santa Clara are specifically named on the map.

The other area of settlement in the Española Basin centered on the confluence of the Rio Grande and the Rio Chama. There, two important pueblos were located: Yunque west of the Rio Grande above the confluence and San Juan opposite it on the east side. Pioge, a small pueblo ancestral to San Juan and located about six miles above it, was probably still occupied in the contact period.[163] Francisco de Barrionuevo, on a mission to round up provisions for the Coronado expedition, visited San Juan and Yunque before going farther north to Taos.[164] Castaño de Sosa, the next explorer to penetrate this far north, passed through a pueblo that was very probably San Juan and stopped overnight at a second that was likely Pioge before going on five leagues (thirteen miles) to Picuris. Upon their return from Picuris to the pueblos they had previously visited—Pioge and San Juan—Castaño de Sosa and his party crossed the Rio Grande to a pueblo on the west side that was probably

Yunque.[165] Seven years later Oñate made his initial headquarters in the vicinity of San Juan.[166] At some point—just when is the subject of controversy—his colonists took over Yunque, renaming it "San Gabriel" and making it their capital.[167] San Juan and Yunque were among those pueblos to which Oñate assigned a priest, but Pioge was not, possibly because it had been abandoned sometime before his arrival.[168] Only San Juan and San Gabriel are shown on the 1602 map.

At the time Barrionuevo and his party visited San Juan and Yunque in 1541, he mentions that the inhabitants had fled to four very substantial pueblos in the mountains, but they did not visit them, claiming that the terrain was too rugged for their horses.[169] The identity of these pueblos has been the subject of scholarly inquiry for many years but without any conclusive results.[170] It has generally been assumed that the four pueblos were in the adjacent Chama Basin, but an alternate suggestion places them on the Pajarito Plateau, an area of much more rugged terrain but farther from the location of San Juan and Yunque. As previously discussed, no explorer mentions any settlement on the Pajarito Plateau, but there is tree-ring and ceramic evidence that as many as six pueblos there might have been occupied, at least in the early contact period.

It is thought that pueblos in the Chama Basin were abandoned by 1500 or shortly thereafter.[171] However, the ceramic evidence on which this opinion is based is equivocal and there is historical evidence, besides Barrionuevo's comment about four pueblos in the mountains, that points specifically to occupation in the Chama Basin in the contact period. After Castaño de Sosa visited Yunque he spent the night at another pueblo a league (four miles) away before continuing his journey southward on the west side of the river. The closest pueblo site, Te'ewi, located five miles up the Rio Chama, might be the one he referred to. Whether it was Te'ewi or some other closer pueblo that subsequently eroded away, it does seem that there was an occupied pueblo on the Rio Chama besides Yunque.[172] Another pueblo in the Chama Basin, one that possibly was occupied in Oñate's time, was Tsama. "Tzooma," as he called it, was one of the Tewa pueblos to which he assigned a priest.[173] Tsama ("Sama") also appears on the 1602 map.

This information from the Castaño de Sosa and Oñate expeditions indicates there was probably some late contact-period settlement in the Chama Basin of a limited or intermittent sort. Whether it was related to possible earlier settlement in Coronado's time cannot be known. Because Barrionuevo did not visit the four "mountain" pueblos, it is not known if they were in the Chama Basin or on the

Pajarito Plateau; or whether they were still occupied or abandoned, or just used from time to time for purposes such as defense, ceremonials, a base for resource exploitation or, as on that occasion, a refuge. If these pueblos were in the Chama Basin, perhaps they were in the process of being abandoned for ones on the Rio Grande, as seems to have been happening to the Pajarito Plateau pueblos.

The Far North

Farther north two pueblos were still occupied in the contact period: Picuris and Taos, in both of which the Northern Tiwa language was spoken. Both also were located on Rio Grande tributaries that drained the west side of the Sangre de Cristo Mountains, with Taos about twenty miles north of Picuris. Two of Coronado's captains visited Taos.[174] Hernando de Alvarado is reported to have reached it after he visited Pecos Pueblo.[175] Francisco de Barrionuevo travelled twenty leagues (fifty-two miles) north of Yunque to the northern limits of settlement, where he found a pueblo known as "Braba" ("Uraba") that he named "Valladolid," a pueblo that was most certainly Taos. There is no record that Picuris was visited until the arrival of Castaño de Sosa fifty years later.[176] He did not go on to Taos, which was only visited again by Spaniards in 1598 when Oñate and his advance party made it and Picuris the northernmost stops on their reconnaissance of the Rio Grande Pueblo Region.[177] Both Picuris and Taos appear on the 1602 map.[178]

Part One Summary

In combination, the reports of the sixteenth-century Spanish expeditions to New Mexico constitute a rich source of information about the geography of the Rio Grande pueblos. The information they provide about the number and spatial distribution of these pueblos has been integrated with archeological identification of pueblo sites to establish the overall pattern of settlement. In the course of combining both sources of information, it became apparent that about one hundred pueblos were occupied at some time during the fifty-eight years of the contact period. In addition to the separate pueblos of Acoma and Pecos, they formed ten loose groupings that occupied distinct hydrographic subregions and consisted of as few as two and as many as twenty-one pueblos. Most of these groupings were linguistically distinct.

Almost half of the pueblos were located along the Rio Grande, mainly in the middle and southern parts of the region. Most of the others were established on tributary streams. Few occupied elevated sites chosen for defense purposes, as had been common at an earlier time. But Acoma and Pecos, isolated pueblos located respectively on the western and eastern frontiers of the region, fit this pattern, as did some pueblos in the Upper Jemez subregion that were still typically located on high narrow mesas. The pueblos in the Chama Basin and on the Pajarito Plateau were apparently in the process of being abandoned as inhabitants sought lower-elevation sites along the Rio Grande. In the Chama Basin some limited residual occupation is indicated in the Coronado, Castaño de Sosa, and Oñate reports as well as on the 1602 map. Although the explorers do not mention pueblos on the Pajarito Plateau, which for them was rather inaccessible and remote from their main routes of travel, good archeological evidence supports occupation of a few pueblos there, at least in the early contact period. The reports of the explorers confirm the existence of pueblos in the southern part of the Albuquerque-Belen Basin where sites have been difficult to locate, thus establishing that there was no substantial no-man's-land separating the Piro and Southern Tiwa territories despite reported hostility between the two groups.

The explorers' reports reveal that some parts of the Rio Grande Pueblo Region were uninhabited even though archeological evidence establishes the existence of substantial settlement in these areas not many decades earlier. The Rio Puerco Valley, Las Huertas Canyon, Santa Fe River Valley, Santa Cruz River Valley, and possibly Chupadera Basin were all devoid of settlement during the contact period. Reasons for the abandonment of such attractive areas can only be speculative, although in the case of the Santa Fe River Valley, competition among surrounding Tewa, Tano, Keres, and Southern Tiwa peoples might have created a buffer zone. Reports from the Coronado and Castaño de Sosa expeditions mention pueblos in the Galisteo Basin and on the eastern periphery of the Sandia Mountains abandoned as a result of attacks by nomadic tribesmen from the eastern plains. Espejo reports a number of ruined pueblos in the central and southern parts of the Southern Rio Grande subregion. Such unsettled conditions just prior to and during the contact period indicate that the processes of settlement change at work within Pueblo societies were continuing. However, it should be noted that ceramics found at about half of the contact-period pueblos indicate occupation from early in the Classic Period. Although this occupation may have been intermittent in some cases, there was a tradition of settlement continuity as well as the one of change that the explorers encountered.

The explorers themselves contributed to disturbed conditions. Their need to requisition food and clothing from the pueblos, in addition to other matters, caused considerable friction that led in some cases to Spanish attacks on pueblos, especially by members of the Coronado expedition, who destroyed a number of pueblos in the northern Albuquerque-Belen Basin. In the same area the people of Puaray Pueblo may have destroyed their pueblo and moved to another because they were linked to the killing of the two Spanish priests from the Chamuscado expedition. It has been suggested that the ruined pueblos reported in the Southern Rio Grande sub-region might have been abandoned as the result of epidemics of European diseases that preceded the arrival of the Spaniards, but so far definite supporting evidence is lacking. Reports from later explorers seem to indicate that pueblos damaged or destroyed by Spaniards were rebuilt. The number of pueblos and their overall location pattern within the Rio Grande Pueblo Region did not change significantly as a result of Spanish intrusions during the 1540–98 contact period. Thus, the reports of the Coronado, Chamuscado, Espejo, Castaño, and Oñate expeditions provide a geography of Pueblo settlement influenced by the needs of those societies, one that only changed drastically once Spanish settlement replaced exploration.

PART
TWO

Colonization and Its

Consequences

1598–1680

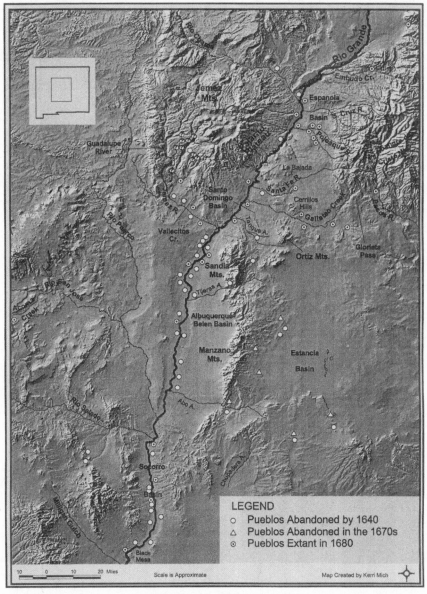

Map 3. Rio Grande Pueblos, 1600–1680.

At the end of the sixteenth century, after nearly sixty years during which seven Spanish expeditions explored the Rio Grande Pueblo Region of New Mexico, the number of Pueblo settlements and their overall pattern of location remained essentially the same as they had been prior to contact despite the depredations and demands of the Spaniards, which often led Pueblo peoples to flee their settlements when the former approached. These dislocations were, for the most part, temporary, and few pueblos were permanently abandoned as a result of Spanish actions. However, changes did begin with the arrival of Spanish colonists in New Mexico in 1598 under the command of Juan de Oñate. During the next eighty years several factors contributed to a reduction in the number of pueblos by 62 percent and to the abandonment of a major part of their territory. These factors will be taken up following a discussion of the changes in the number of pueblos that were occupied at various times between 1600 and 1680. The number of pueblos is, of course, related to the size of the population and its changes; for this reason the available population data will be presented. It is the fate of the Pueblo settlements, rather than population per se, that will be of central concern.

CHAPTER THREE
Periods of Change

A t the time Oñate's expedition arrived in the Rio Grande Valley in 1598, there were as many as eighty-one occupied pueblos (table 11). They comprised nine loose geographical groupings of linguistically related pueblos and four individual pueblos, all located along 215 miles of the Rio Grande and in tributary areas, a distribution that had been approximately the same during the previous fifty-eight years since the beginning of Spanish exploration (map 3). During the subsequent eighty-two years—up to the Pueblo revolt of 1680—the number of pueblos was reduced to thirty-one, and the Estancia Basin was abandoned along with large parts of the Socorro and Albuquerque-Belen Basins. Table 11 is a summary of seven reports that give information about which pueblos were extant at various times from Oñate's initial reconnaissance until Governor Otermín's retreat in the face of the revolt by the northern pueblos.

Identification of the pueblos occupied at the time of Oñate's entrada is provided mainly from an interpretation of the 1602 map that was based on information obtained from one of Oñate's men who had returned to New Spain (map 2). Oñate's lists of pueblos to which he assigned priests and from which he extracted pledges of obedience contain many duplications and errors and are used only to supplement information provided on the 1602 map.[1] The pueblos in the Estancia Basin were omitted from that map but were mentioned by Oñate when he led a party to inspect the salt flats in the area.[2] Between Oñate's first and last salinas pueblos—Chilili and Quarai—are three sites that were probably occupied: Tajique, LA 371, and LA 372. Pueblo Pardo, located near Las Humanas Pueblo farther south in the Estancia Basin, was also probably inhabited. All have late ceramics.[3] The 1602 map shows only two pueblos on the lower Jemez River, Santa Ana and Zia, but Oñate mentions a total of five.[4] Based on ceramic evidence, there were three other pueblos in the area that could have been occupied at that time: Old Zia (Kohasaiya), Chackham, and Corn Clan Zia.[5] The number of inhabited pueblos in the Upper Jemez River subregion is uncertain. Oñate claims to have visited eight and was told there were eleven.[6] Six are shown on the 1602 map without regard to their individual locations. Archeological evidence best supports the

Table 11. Rio Grande Pueblos: 1598-1680

Pueblo	LA No.	Oñate 1598 1602 Map	Benavides 1626-1629	"Marquez" 1641	Vetancurt 1660	Cardoso 1663-1666	Villagutierre ca. 1680	Otermín 1680 Retreat
Southern Rio Grande								
?		Unnamed						
Sevilleta	774	Nueva Sevilla	Sevilleta	Sevilleta	Sevilleta	Unnamed	Sevilleta	Sevilleta
P. de Arena	31717		Unnamed					
Alamillo	—	Unnamed	Unnamed	Alamillo	Alamillo	Unnamed	Alamillo	Alamillo
El Barro	283		Unnamed					
Pueblito Pt.	31751		Unnamed					
Pilabo/Socorro	791	Teypama/Socor.	Pilabo	Socorro	Socorro	Socorro	El Socorro	Socorro
Teypama	282		Unnamed					
Plaza Montoya	31744		Unnamed					
Qualacu	757	Qualacu	Unnamed					
Nra. Señora	19266	Unnamed	Unnamed					Ruin
San Pascual	487	Unnamed	Unnamed				San Pascual	Ruin
Tiffany	244	Unnamed						
Senecu	—	Tzenequel	Senecu		Senecu	Senecu	Senecu	Senecu
Magdalena	284	Possible	Unnamed					
Bear Mountain	285	Possible	Unnamed					
Total		11	15/11†	3	4	4	5	4
Estancia Basin								
Pueblo Blanco	51	Xenopuy	Unnamed	Tabira	Tabira	Unnamed		
Pueblo Colorado	476	Patasci	Unnamed					
Pueblo Pardo	83	Unnamed	Unnamed					
Las Humanas	120	Cueloze	Xumanas	Jumanos		Jumanos		
Tenabo	200	Second Abbo	Unnamed		Tenabo			
Abo	97	Abbo	Unnamed	Abo	Abbo	Abo		
Quarai	95	Last salinas P.	Unnamed	Cuarac	Cuarac	Cuarac		
Tajique	381	Possible	Unnamed	Tajique	Taxique	Tajique		
—	372	Possible	Unnamed					
—	371		Unnamed					
Chilili	874	1st salinas P.	Unnamed	Chilili	Chilili	Chilili		
Total		11		6	6	6		

Table 11. Continued

Pueblo	LA No.	Oñate 1598 1602 map	Benavides 1626-1629	"Marquez" 1641	Vetancurt 1660	Cardoso 1663-1666	Villagutierre ca. 1680	Otermin 1680 retreat
Middle Rio Grande								
Abo Confluence	50241	Unnamed	Unnamed					
Casa Colorado	50261	S. Juan Bautista	Unnamed					
Ladera del Sur	50257	Unnamed	Unnamed					
Valencia	953	Unnamed	Unnamed					
Bei-jui Tu-ay	81	Unnamed	Unnamed					
Isleta	724	Unnamed	Isleta	Isleta	Isleta	Isleta	Isleta	Isleta
Pur-e Tu-ay	489	Mesilla	Unnamed					
P. Marcadas	290	Unnamed						
Calabacillas	289	Unnamed						
Chamisal	22765	Unnamed	Unnamed					
Alameda	421	Unnamed	Unnamed	Alameda	Alameda	Unnamed	Alameda	Alameda
?	—	Unnamed						
Maigua	716	Unnamed	Unnamed					
Puaray	717	Puarai	Unnamed	los P....	Puray	Unnamed	Puaray	*
Corrales	288	Unnamed	Unnamed					
Sandia	294	Unnamed	Sandia	Sandia	Zandia	Sandia	Sandia	Sandia
Watche	677	Unnamed	Unnamed					
Santiago	326	Santiago	Unnamed					
	325	Unnamed	Unnamed					
Kuaua	187	Unnamed	Unnamed					
Silva Site	12924	Portezuela	Unnamed					
Paa-ko	162	Paaco	Unnamed	San P...o				
Total		21	16/18†	5	4	4	4	4
Rio Puerco-Rio San Jose								
Acoma	112	Acoma	Acoma	Acoma	Acoma	Acoma	Acoma	Acoma
Lower Jemez River								
Corn Clan Zia	241	Possible	Unnamed					
Old Zia	384	Possible	Unnamed					
Zia	28	Tzia/Sia	Unnamed	Sia	*	Sia	Zia	Zia
Santa Ana	?/2049	Tamaya/S.Ana	Unnamed	Santa Ana	Santa Ana	Unnamed	*	Santa Ana
Chackham	374	Possible	Unnamed					
Total		5	4	2	2	2	2	2

Table 11. Continued

Pueblo	LA No.	Oñate 1598 1602 map	Benavides 1626-1629	"Marquez" 1641	Vetancurt 1660	Cardoso 1663-1666	Villagutierre ca. 1680	Otermín 1680 retreat
Santo Domingo Basin								
Old San Felipe	3137	Cachiti/S.Fel.	San Felipe	San Felipe	San Felipe	Unnamed	San Felipe	San Felipe
Santo Domingo	1281	Quigui/S.Dom.	Unnamed	Sto. Domingo	Sto. Domingo	Sto. Domingo	Sto. Domingo	Sto. Domingo
Cochiti	126	Coch./Chicotin	Unnamed	Cochiti	Cochiti	Cochiti	Cochiti	Cochiti
La Bajada	7	Tipoti/Tipotin						
Tunque	240	El Tuerto						
La Cienega			Unnamed	La Cienega	La Cienega	Unnamed	Cieneguilla	La Cienega
Total		5	4	4	4	4	4	4
Galisteo Basin								
San Marcos	98	San Marcos	San Marcos	San Marcos	San Marcos	San Marcos	San Marcos	San Marcos
San Lázaro	91		Unnamed	San Lázaro	San Lázaro	Unnamed	San Lázaro	San Lázaro
Galisteo	26	S.Ana/Calisteo	Galisteo	Galisteo	Galisteo	Galisteo	Galisteo	Galisteo
San Cristóbal	80	San Cristóbal	Unnamed	San Cristóbal	San Cristbal	Unnamed	San Cristóbal	San Cristóbal
Total		3	4	4	4	4	4	4
Upper Pecos River								
Pecos	625	Pecos	Pecos	Pecos	Pecos	Pecos	Pecos	Pecos
Upper Jemez River								
Tovakwa	483	Unnamed	Possible					
—	484	Unnamed						
Kwastiyukwa	482	Unnamed	Possible					
Seshukwa	303	Unnamed	Possible					
Kiatsukwa	132-133	Unnamed	Possible					
Nanishagi	541	Unnamed						
Unshagi	123	Unnamed						
Guisewa	679	Guiusta	San José					
Amoxiumqua	481	Unnamed	Possible					
Patokwa	96	Unnamed						
Boletsakwa	136	Unnamed	Possible					
Walatowa	8860	Unnamed	S.Diego.Cong.	Jemez Pueblo	Hemes	Jemez	Xemes	San Diego...
Total		11	Incomplete/8†	Incomplete	Incomplete	Incomplete	Incomplete	Incomplete
Pajarito Plateau								
Tsirege	170	Messillos						

Table 11. Continued

Pueblo	LA No.	Oñate 1598 1602 map	Benavides 1626-1629	"Marquez" 1641	Vetancurt 1660	Cardoso 1663-1666	Villagutierre ca. 1680	Otermin 1680 retreat
Española Basin								
Tesuque	1064	Unnamed	Unnamed	Tesuque	Tezuque	Unnamed	Tezuque	Tesuque
Cuyamungue	38	Unnamed	Unnamed	Cuyamungue	Cuya Mangue	Unnamed	Cuyamungue	Cuyamungue
Nambe	17	Unnamed	Unnamed	Nambe	Nambe	Nambe	Mambe	Nambe
Pojoaque	61	Unnamed	Unnamed	Unnamed	*	Unnamed	Pujuaque	Soxuaque
Jacona	1065		Unnamed	Unnamed	Jacona	Unnamed	Jacona	*
San Ildefonso	6188	Bove/S.Ildef.	San Ildefonso	San Ildefonso	San Ildefonso	San Ildefonso	San Ildefonso	San Ildefonso
Santa Clara	925	Caypa/S.Clara	Santa Clara	Santa Clara	Santa Clara	Santa Clara	Santa Clara	Santa Clara
San Juan	874	San Juan	Unnamed	San Juan	San Juan	San Juan	San Juan	San Juan
Yunque	59	San Gabriel						
Total		8	8	8	8	8	8	8
Chama Basin								
Tsama	980	Tzooma/Sama						
Far North								
Picuris	127	Picuries	Picuries	Picuris	Pecuries	Picuris	Pecuries	Pecuries
Taos	3932	Taos	Taos	Taos	Taos	Taos	Taos	Taos
Total		2	2	2	2	2	2	2
Total		81	71/75†	37	37	38	32	31

? Pueblo mentioned but not identified.
* Pueblo possibly overlooked or temporarily abandoned but included in the total.
† Adjusted figure.
LA New Mexico State Laboratory of Anthropology site number.

presence of nine pueblos, although two others, Patokwa and Boletsakwa, might have been occupied at that time if the Jemez people resided in eleven pueblos.[7] In other areas there were three pueblos, never mentioned by Spanish explorers, for which ceramics indicate occupation as late as Oñate's time. They were Magdalena and Bear Mountain in the Rio Salado drainage some twenty miles due west of the Rio Grande and Tsirege on the Pajarito Plateau.[8] Altogether, Pueblo peoples probably occupied eighty-one pueblos in the Rio Grande region at the end of the sixteenth century.

Changes: 1620s

After Oñate, the next information about settled pueblos in the Rio Grande Pueblo Region comes from Fray Gerónimo de Zárate Salmerón, who served as missionary in New Mexico from 1621 to 1626. He worked among the people of the upper Jemez pueblos as well as at the Keres pueblo of Zia on the lower Jemez and the Southern Tiwa pueblo of Sandia in the Middle Rio Grande subregion (Albuquerque-Belen Basin).[9] However, the information he provides is limited.[10] The only places he mentions as pueblos are Acoma, Santa Ana, Zia, Tsama, Amoxiumqua, and "Quiumziqua," the latter possibly Guisewa.[11] His other place names are associated with mines, although they were also the names of pueblos: Socorro, Puaray, Tunque, San Marcos, Galisteo, Jemez, and Picuris.[12] While working among the Jemez people, he established a mission dedicated to San José at Guisewa Pueblo and, to serve a numerous scattered population in the area of the Vallecitos drainage, he founded a new pueblo-mission, San Diego de la Congregación, located near the site of the present Jemez pueblo, Walatowa.[13] Studies of the early mission establishment in the Rio Grande Pueblo Region indicate there were other inhabited pueblos during Zárate Salmerón's tenure and before, but they do not purport to give a full enumeration of Rio Grande Pueblo settlements.[14] Zárate Salmerón states that he had been told by Conchos people, who lived well south of Pueblo country, that there were more than forty pueblos, but the general nature of this statement is not helpful.[15]

A more complete picture of the Rio Grande pueblos during the first three decades of Spanish settlement is seen in the data provided by Zárate Salmerón's successor, Fray Alonso de Benavides. Benavides served into 1629 and, after returning to Spain the following year, wrote a lengthy report about his work. In 1634 he completed a revised version, and both memorials have been used to determine which pueblos were extant during his tenure in New Mexico.[16] Benavides's population data are based on estimates rather than actual accounts, but the number and names of pueblos he mentions accord well with those of Oñate's time and with the ceramic evidence.[17] Between 1600 and 1630 some pueblos were abandoned, reoccupied, or newly built, but on the whole, there were no major changes in the number of pueblos or pattern of their distribution. This stability is particularly true in the area north of the junction of the Santa Fe River with the Rio Grande, where the loss of three pueblos—Tsirege on the Pajarito Plateau, Yunque at the junction of the Rio Grande and the Rio Chama, and Tsama in the Chama Basin—was balanced by the gain of one that was reoccupied: Jacona in the Pojoaque drainage.[18] Yunque was taken over by Oñate and his colonists soon after their arrival in 1598, and the inhabitants of Tsirege and Tsama, the last pueblos in their respective areas to be abandoned, were probably in the process of moving to pueblos on the Rio Grande at the time of Oñate's arrival.[19]

Reasons for the abandonment of Keres pueblos are less clear. If Benavides's estimate of seven Keres pueblos is correct—he counts San Marcos as a Tano pueblo—La Bajada and Tunque in the Santo Domingo Basin were probably abandoned before his time. Tunque, an important ceramic-making center, was subject to inter-pueblo strife and might have been abandoned not long after Oñate's arrival.[20] Perhaps La Bajada suffered the same fate. Chackham, on the lower Jemez River, also might have been abandoned, leaving four Keres pueblos in that area and three—Cochiti, Santo Domingo, and San Felipe—on the Rio Grande. La Cieneguilla Pueblo (LA 16), located on the Santa Fe River at the head of Las Bocas Canyon, and San Lázaro in the Galisteo Basin might have been reoccupied by Benavides's time and included as two of his five Tano pueblos, although the former was later considered to be a Keres pueblo by Diego de Vargas when he was governor of New Mexico in the 1690s.

For the Upper Jemez subregion, Benavides mentions only Zárate Salmerón's two mission-pueblos: San José (Guisewa) and San Diego de la Congregación (Walatowa). Was Benavides reporting only mission-pueblos or all pueblos? He states: "We have congregated the Jemez nation into two pueblos."[21] He further reports that the Jemez people were unsettled when he arrived in New Mexico and almost depopulated by famine and wars, with more than half of the people dead. He gives a figure of 3,000 tributaries, which is about half of the 6,566 souls whom Zárate Salmerón claims to have baptized only a few years earlier. Even though these figures are not comparable and their accuracy suspect, it would appear that there was a substantial population loss among the Jemez in the 1620s. But even with this reduced population, it is not likely that they lived in just two pueblos. Unlike the other Rio Grande Pueblo groups, where missions were established at the larger pueblos and the smaller ones—designated "visitas"—were served by the clergy who resided in the mission convents, no visitas were reported among the Jemez. Given the reputation of the Jemez as great idolaters and the most indomitable and belligerent of the Pueblo peoples, as noted by Benavides, it is possible that they might have resided in additional pueblos that were beyond mission control. Although it is unclear how many settlements they occupied or which ones, there is historical and archeological evidence for their occupation of more than the two mission-pueblos.[22]

In the Middle Rio Grande subregion there were fifteen or sixteen pueblos according to Benavides, whereas in Oñate's time there had been twenty-one.[23] The changes occurred among the pueblos clustered at the northern end of the area where four pueblos were abandoned (Watche, Calabacillas, Piedras Marcadas, and an unidentified site), and one, possibly LA 325, was added.[24] With the possibility that the two Tiwa pueblos on the periphery of the nearby Sandia Mountains, Paa-ko and Silva Site, were still occupied, the total could have been as high as eighteen. Given the problems with dating sites based on their ceramics, it is difficult to be certain which Southern Tiwa pueblos were occupied in Benavides's time, but there were at least sixteen sites with late ceramics that could have been inhabited.

In the Southern Rio Grande subregion (Socorro Basin) there were also more sites with late ceramics than the number—fourteen—that Benavides gives as the total.[25] Compared with the nine Piro pueblos on the 1602 map, fourteen represents a significant increase, one that mainly affected the northern part of the area. Pueblo de Arena, El Barro, Pueblito Point, Pilabo, and Plaza Montoya were the pueblo sites with late ceramics that were most likely reoccupied.[26] In addition, Piro people probably still inhabited the two outlier pueblos, Magdalena and Bear Mountain, making a total of fourteen when the loss of Nuestra Señora and a small pueblo near Sevilleta is factored in. The only area where the number of pueblos claimed by Benavides exceeds the number of sites with late ceramics is the Estancia Basin. His total of fourteen or fifteen is more than the eleven accounted for earlier and more than the number of appropriate sites available.[27]

The total number of Rio Grande pueblos claimed by Benavides is seventy-one. If this figure is modified to account for his overestimations in some areas, notably the Estancia Basin, and underestimations in others, notably the upper

Jemez, the adjusted total would be seventy-five, a number close to the total of eighty-one at the time of Oñate's arrival.

Changes: 1630s

The next comprehensive report on the Rio Grande pueblos was made some ten years later, possibly about 1641, thus reflecting changes that took place during the 1630s.[28] It indicates a drastic reduction in the number of pueblos. The greatest losses took place in the Southern Rio Grande subregion, where only three of the fourteen Piro pueblos survived, and in the Middle Rio Grande subregion, where only five of the eighteen Tiwa pueblos remained occupied. Losses were also significant in the Estancia Basin, where five of the eleven pueblos were abandoned, and on the lower Jemez, where two of four Keres pueblos were also abandoned. There might have been further losses among the upper Jemez pueblos, but it is unlikely they were reduced to the single pueblo reported. This pueblo was the mission San Diego de la Congregación. San José, the other mission-pueblo, was abandoned by the Jemez sometime during this decade. Abandonments reduced the number of pueblos by about half, from seventy-one (using Benavides's figure) to thirty-seven (including only one upper Jemez pueblo) and resulted in a changed pattern of distribution. None of the nine geographical groupings was entirely abandoned, but the reduction left the greater number of pueblos north of the Rio Grande–Jemez River junction, whereas previously the greater number had been in the areas to the south, especially the Middle and Southern Rio Grande subregions where the greatest losses occurred. In 1643 Governor Alonso Pacheco de Herédia reports the number of Rio Grande pueblos as thirty-eight, giving support to the number in the 1641 document.[29]

Changes: 1660s

The Franciscan historian Fray Agustín de Vetancurt provides the next set of data. Although he was writing in the 1690s, he includes information that appears to be taken from a 1660 census in his attempt to compare the Pueblo situation before and after the 1680 revolt.[30] He lists thirty-four pueblos but does not mention three others that are reported in the previous and subsequent documents and that he possibly overlooked: Zia on the lower Jemez, San Cristóbal in the Galisteo Basin, and Pojoaque in the Española Basin. With the three additions, the total number of pueblos, thirty-seven, is the same as that reported in 1641, with the difference that Senecu was again occupied and Paa-ko was finally abandoned. The thirty-eight Rio

Grande pueblos enumerated by Fray Domingo Cardoso, who was reporting on the places served by Franciscan missionaries in New Mexico in the years 1663 to 1666, include the addition of a visita of San Marcos that might have been La Cienega, a small new pueblo.[31] Cardoso also mentions that Santa Fe had three visitas, one of which might have been La Cienega.

The only other changes in the 1660s are the gain of Tabira (Pueblo Blanco, LA 51) and the loss of Tenabo, a reversal of their status in the 1660 census, leaving one to wonder whether these changes in the Estancia Basin were real or mistakes in reporting. The pueblo called Tabira in the 1660 census might have referred to Las Humanas Pueblo (LA 120), a name by which the latter was known in the colonial period even though it was also applied to Pueblo Blanco. In his 1665 residencia, former governor of New Mexico Diego de Peñalosa claims that he visited all of the forty-two pueblos, omitting only two small ones.[32] Assuming that this number included the five Hopi and six Zuni pueblos, the total would have been thirty-three in the Rio Grande Pueblo Region, a number somewhat lower than others reported in the 1660s.[33] On the whole, the number of Rio Grande pueblos remained stable from about 1641 through the 1660s.

Changes: 1670s

The 1670s was the second period in which loss of pueblos was notable. By the end of the decade the Estancia Basin pueblos were abandoned, leaving a total of thirty-one in the Rio Grande Pueblo Region. Fray Francisco de Ayeta, custodian of the Franciscan province of New Mexico from 1673 to 1679, reports the depopulation of Chilili, "Cuarac" (Quarai), "Las Salinas" (probably Tajique), Abo, and Las Humanas, in addition to Senecu, the southernmost pueblo of the Rio Grande Pueblo Region.[34] The sixth Estancia Basin pueblo, Tabira or Pueblo Blanco, had been abandoned by 1672.[35] Ayeta attempted to resettle Senecu and Tajique in late 1677, but only Senecu was mentioned when the Spaniards retreated south in 1680.[36] It was among the thirty-two pueblos listed by Juan de Villagutierre y Sotomayor as extant in 1680 before the revolt.[37] Besides Senecu, his list also includes the old Piro site called San Pascual, both of which might have been resettled by refugees from the Estancia Basin. According to Ayeta there were forty-six pueblos in all. If the eleven Hopi and Zuni pueblos are deducted as well as the four Estancia Basin pueblos that remained depopulated (Chilili, Quarai, Las Humanas, and Abo), Ayeta's total is thirty-one. Thirty-one pueblos are also mentioned in the reports that document the Spanish

Table 12. Seventeenth-Century Rio Grande Pueblos:
Number of Pueblos and Population by Subregion

Subregion	1626-29[1] No. of Pueblos	1626-29[1] Popu-lation	1641[2] No. of Pueblos	1641[2] Popu-lation	1629-41 % Pop. Loss	1660[3] No. of Pueblos	1660[3] Popu-lation
Southern Rio Grande	14	6,000	3[a]	400	93.3	4	900
Estancia Basin	15/11[b]	10,000	6	2,972	70.3	6	2,200
Middle Rio Grande	16/18[b]	7,000	5	990	85.9	4[c]	5,500
Acoma	1	1,500	1	600	60.0	1	1,500
Lower Jemez River	4	{4,000	2[d]	800	{50.0	2	{1,050
Sto. Domingo Basin	3			1.200		3	
Galisteo Basin	5[e]	[e]4,000	5[e]	1,777[e]	55.6	5[e]	1,400[e]
Pecos	1	2,000	1	1,189	40.6	1	2,000
Upper Jemez River	2[f]/6[b]	3,000	1[f]	1,860	38.0	1[f]	5,000
Española Basin	8	6,000	8	1,423	76.3	8	2,100
Far North	2	4,500	2	1,164	74.1	2	5,000
Total	71/73[b]	48,700	37	15,575	68.0	37	26,650[g]

Sources:
[1] Benavides, *The Memorial of...1630*, 17-27; Benavides, *...Memorial of 1634*, 63-72.
[2] Scholes, "Documents for the History," 47-50; Scholes, "Correction," 245-46.
[3] Ventancurt, *Teatro Mexicano*, 4:309-25; Bandelier, *Final Report*, 1:122-23n.

[a] Senecu, n.d.
[b] Adjusted figure.
[c] Paa-ko abandoned.
[d] Chackham and Corn Clan Zia abandoned.
[e] Figures include La Cieneguilla Pueblo (LA 16), located on the Santa Fe River.
[f] Mission pueblos only.
[g] Sum of thirty-seven Rio Grande pueblos. In this same source a total of 24,000 is given for all of New Mexico. After Spanish, Zuni, and Hopi populations are subtracted, the total population of the thirty-seven Rio Grande pueblos is 18,000.

retreat from Pueblo country in August and September 1680.[38]

On the eve of the 1680 revolt, the settlement pattern of the Rio Grande pueblos had changed significantly from what it had been when Spanish colonists arrived in 1598. In number, pueblo settlements were reduced by 62 percent, from eighty-one to thirty-one (not taking into account the possibility of more than one Jemez pueblo). The greatest reduction took place in the 1630s, when the number of pueblos declined by about half, reflecting a population loss of 68 percent between 1626–29 and 1641 (table 12).[39] Although the 1626–29 population figures have been criticized as being inflated, there is less room for error in the number of pueblos reported, and together they give support to the occurrence of drastic decline.[40] In 1638 Fray Juan de Prada, the Franciscan commissary-general in Mexico, reports that information supplied to him by missionaries in New Mexico indicates that the population there had declined from more than sixty thousand baptized persons to less than forty thousand (table 13), a lesser decline than the data in table 12 indicate, but still a substantial loss.[41] A further population loss of 10 percent is reported for 1640.[42]

Table 13. Reported Population Totals, Rio Grande Pueblo Region: 1598-1678

Date	Source	Population	Unit	Comment
1598	Oñate	60,000*	Indians	1601-1609 estimates: 60,000 to 20,000 native people
1621-1626	Zárate S.	34,650*	Baptized	Excluding many not yet converted
1626-1629	Benevides	48,700	Baptized	Sum of 71 Rio Grande pueblos
		60,000	Baptized	Total of 80,000 minus Zuni and Hopi populations of 10,000 each
1638	Prada	>40,000*	Baptized	Reduced from 60,000+. 30 missions + many *visitas*
1641	"Marquez"	15,575	Souls	Sum of 37 Rio Grande pueblos
1643	Pacheco	16,904	Indians	Sum of 38 Rio Grande pueblos
1660	Vetancurt	26,650	Persons	Sum of 37 Rio Grande pueblos
		18,000	Persons	Total of 24,000 minus Spanish, Zuni, and Hopi
1678	Ayeta	17,000*	Baptized	Total of 46 pueblos of which 25 are missions

Sources:
1598: Hammond and Rey, *Don Juan*, 483, 619, 629, 639, 652, 695, 702, 838, 851, 863, 1012, 1030, 1067, 1095.
1621-1626: Zárate Salmerón, *Relaciones*, 35.
1626-1629: Benavides, *The Memorial of...1630*, 17-27, 30; Benavides, *...Revised Memorial of 1634*, 63-72.
1638: Hackett, *Historical Documents*, 3:108.
1641: Scholes, "Documents for the History," 47-50; Scholes, "Correction," 245-46.
1643: Scholes, ibid., 246; Baldwin, "A Reconsideration," 413.
1660: Vetancurt, *Teatro Mexicano*, 4:309-25; Bandelier, *Final Report*, 1:122-23n.
1678: Hackett *Historical Documents*, 3:299.

* Includes population of Zuni and Hopi pueblos.

Table 12 also shows that the greatest reduction in the number of pueblos and among the greatest population losses took place in the Southern and Middle Rio Grande subregions and in the Estancia Basin. So many pueblos in these areas were abandoned that the majority of pueblos was thereafter located north of the Rio Grande–Jemez River confluence, where no pueblos were abandoned despite large population losses (although the situation in the Upper Jemez River subregion remains unclear). From about 1641 the settlement pattern and population remained fairly stable for several decades, but the settlement pattern in the south was further weakened during the decade of the 1670s, by the end of which all of the pueblos in the large area of the Estancia Basin had been abandoned.

It should also be noted that the practice of using field houses was greatly diminished, if not abandoned, in many parts of the Rio Grande Pueblo Region in the early decades of the seventeenth century. After Apacheans adopted the use of the horse, their attacks became a menace not only to pueblos but also to isolated family groups in field houses. In addition, greatly reduced population and abandonment of pueblos made unnecessary the maintenance of distant fields.[43]

The settlement changes between 1598 and 1680 were the most drastic to affect the Rio Grande pueblos in historic times, whether compared with the previous period of Spanish exploration (1540–98) or any time subsequent to 1680, despite the great hardships and losses suffered during the reconquest of the 1690s. Reasons for these changes in the pattern of Rio Grande pueblo settlements are not always well documented, but there is some evidence that the factors discussed in chapter 4 contributed to them in varying degrees and combinations at different times.

CHAPTER FOUR
Reasons for Pueblo Abandonments

The Spanish presence in New Mexico disrupted the Pueblo people's way of life in many ways and, in so doing, led to large-scale population loss and forced abandonment of pueblos. Factors contributing to losses include the disruption of native subsistence activities in conjunction with legal and extralegal exactions of labor and goods, expansion of Spanish settlements and land grants, attacks by Apachean tribes, environmental factors such as droughts, epidemics of diseases introduced by Spaniards, and possibly the Spanish policy of congregating Pueblo populations in order to facilitate civil and religious administration. Pueblo response to these factors took several forms. Uprisings in various parts of the Rio Grande Pueblo Region have been reported, but until 1680 they were always put down.[1] In some cases the people fled, often joining Apachean peoples or other Pueblo people such as the Zuni or Hopi to the west.[2] An early recorded case of flight involved the people of Taos Pueblo, who in 1639, joined Apaches living along the Arkansas River in the vicinity of the present Colorado-Kansas border.[3] There they established a settlement called El Cuartelejo. By 1642 many had been brought back, but others remained until the Spaniards forced them to return in 1662.

Congregation

The Spanish colonial practice of congregating the populations of two or more settlements into one to facilitate administration would have reduced the number of pueblos in the Rio Grande region but not necessarily the size of the population.[4] There is no evidence that Spanish authorities in New Mexico systematically carried out congregación or reducción for this purpose, although the 1610 instructions to the new governor gave him the authority to carry out such consolidation.[5] The fact that the number of pueblos did not differ greatly between 1598 and 1626–29 indicates as much. The only reference to congregation in New Mexico in this period involves the Towa communities of the Upper Jemez River subregion, where the pueblos were located for the most part on high mesa tops separated by very broken terrain. Fray Zárate Salmerón established a mission at the centrally located pueblo of Guisewa, and, to serve the more distant pueblos in the Vallecitos drainage, he established (also in the early 1620s) the mission-pueblo he called "San Diego de la Congregación," located lower down the valley of the Jemez River near the present Jemez Pueblo (Walatowa).[6] Fray Alonso de Benavides reports that he had these missions reestablished later in the decade and that the Jemez nation was then congregated in these two mission settlements.[7] He implies that all of the Jemez people were so congregated, but, as previously discussed, some may have continued to live in additional pueblos.

Population loss, rather than administrative efficiency, seems to have been the reason for the drastic reduction in the number of pueblos among Rio Grande Pueblo peoples in the 1630s. Although there are no records of formal congregation proceedings, the greatly diminished number of pueblos in the 1641 census indicates that some form of amalgamation of surviving people took place. The need for consolidation would have been especially critical in the Southern and Middle Rio Grande subregions and in the Estancia Basin, where population losses were among the greatest and where the pueblos, in general, were smaller.[8] A specific case of population aggregation is that of Chilili in the Estancia Basin, mentioned in the 1641 census as a pueblo where ". . . there have been assembled many people from the other pueblos . . ."[9] In other areas of great population loss—the Española Basin and the Far North—congregation did not take place, possibly because the pueblos were larger and more geographically proximate. It appears that the practice of congregation was not a cause of the decline in the number of pueblos, but a consequence of other factors that caused population loss and subsequent pueblo abandonment.[10]

Tribute

Spanish policies and practices that led to the disruption of subsistence activities substantially reduced the ability of Pueblo peoples to maintain themselves and their settlements. Legal and extralegal exactions of goods and labor by civil and religious officials as well as by settlers placed great burdens on Pueblo peoples, the negative effects of which accumulated and worsened over time. Goods were extracted legally by means of the encomienda system, under which a designated amount of tribute goods was paid periodically either to the Crown or to individual settlers who had been awarded an encomienda grant by a royal official who had been given the right to make such grants. In New Mexico this right was held by the governor, and the grants persisted throughout the prerevolt period.[11] The governors themselves held encomiendas granted by the viceroy in Mexico. Under this system each Pueblo household was assessed each year one fanega of maize (2.6 bushels) and a piece of cotton cloth (about

5.5 square feet) for which a buffalo hide or deer skin could be substituted.[12] Although this does not seem like a great burden, it still represented a diversion of resources from people living in a marginal environment and, in the case of maize, a smaller surplus to set aside for the inevitable drought years. Furthermore, encomenderos abused the system by assessing tribute on individuals instead of households and by demanding payment for abandoned houses, claiming that several families moved into a single house to reduce their tribute payments.[13] As early as 1609 the viceroy noted in his instructions to the new governor that ". . . the tribute levied on the natives is excessive and that it is collected with much vexation and trouble to them. . . ."[14]

Labor

Tribute labor had been outlawed in the Spanish colonies as early as 1549, but forced paid labor was not, although attempts to do away with it were made in the seventeenth century.[15] Crown officials could require villages to supply workers for public and private enterprises. The law specified the pay and conditions of work, but abuses were widespread.[16] Studies based on documents from this period indicate that governors, in particular, commonly forced Pueblo people to work in their various enterprises, paying them little or nothing, even though governors were prohibited from engaging in such ventures in the first place.[17] Local officials such as alcaldes mayores also made use of Pueblo labor, as did settlers and clergy who needed it to work their fields and tend their livestock.[18]

Land

Generally, the fields and pasture lands on which Pueblo workers were forced to labor for Spaniards were lands that were once their own. Although Crown law forbade Spaniards from living in or adjacent to pueblos or encroaching on their lands, the scarcity of good agricultural land, especially cropland with access to water for irrigation, meant that as the Spanish settlers, as well as encomenderos and the clergy, sought to secure a better income and food supply, they found ways to utilize Pueblo lands.[19] Pueblo lands were also desired because the source of labor was near at hand and lands farther away were vulnerable to Apachean raids.[20] To safeguard native lands, the amount of land to which natives had a right and the distances of surrounding buffer zones were set forth in law, but these were often violated.[21] An example of such violation is reported in 1633 by Fray Estevan de Perea, the missionary at Cuarac (Quarai), who complains that the governor gave settlers permission to establish stock farms for raising cattle and sheep on the cultivated fields of the Indians.[22]

At each pueblo, plots of land were set aside to be cultivated for the missionaries. The latter's herds of livestock, some of the largest in the colony, were pastured on Pueblo land, where Pueblo herdsmen were obliged to tend them without pay.[23] Although support of the clergy was in accordance with Crown law, Pueblo food production suffered, as it did when livestock owned by the clergy or by settlers invaded Pueblo fields and destroyed crops.[24] Crown prohibition against such invasions did little to prevent their happening.[25] Even though there were never more than twenty-five hundred Spanish/mestizo people in New Mexico in the prerevolt period and fewer than one thousand during the first three to four decades of the colony, their demands for Pueblo land did deprive many Pueblo peoples of land they needed for their own sustenance.[26]

An idea of the expansion of Spanish landholdings (estancias) can be gained from the 1641 and 1663–66 reports, which show that the total number of landholdings increased from some twenty-five to more than fifty-five.[27] Because these are essentially ecclesiastic censuses, the estancias enumerated may have belonged to the missions.[28] A 1639 report mentions ten or twelve farms between Senecu Pueblo and Santa Fe (a distance of about 130 miles) that belonged to Spaniards, a number that may have been in addition to those mentioned in the 1641 census, if the latter includes only mission estancias.[29] Although Spaniards established themselves early in the Santa Fe River Valley, where their capital was officially founded in 1610 and where there were no occupied pueblos at that time, and in parts of the Española Basin such as the Santa Cruz River Valley that were also bereft of occupied pueblos, they began to move south into areas such as the Santo Domingo Basin and the Albuquerque-Belen Basin where there was more irrigable land, land that was occupied by Keres and Southern Tiwa peoples.[30] In 1641 about 64 percent of the estancias were located in the Albuquerque-Belen Basin, and by 1663–66 this figure was 80 percent. By 1680 there was in this basin a concentration of seventeen estancias on both sides of the Rio Grande along the eight-mile stretch between Atrisco and Alameda Pueblo.[31]

This expansion took place after the severe decline in both population and number of pueblos of the 1630s, which was especially notable in these latter areas and which must have forced much Pueblo cropland to be abandoned. The governor could declare such land vacant (tierras baldías) and then make grants (mercedes) of it to others, including Spaniards, as long as the former inhabitants were not deprived of land they needed to support themselves.[32] It is likely in these circumstances that the surviving population was congregated into the thirty-seven pueblos listed in the 1641 census. The absence of records of formal congregation proceedings or other pertinent documents makes it impossible to know how the aggregation was carried out and to what degree Pueblo land rights were protected. When deaths occurred in the pueblos they held in encomienda, encomenderos were forbidden to take over these lands.[33] If people were removed to a settlement not far from their old one, their original fields were to be retained, but, if they had to move farther away, they were to be assigned new lands.[34] Such laws provided little protection to subject people in a remote frontier area.

Trade

Besides interfering with Pueblo peoples' ability to raise their own food, Spaniards in New Mexico also disrupted the arrangements by which food and other items were redistributed among Pueblo peoples themselves and traded with their Apachean neighbors. Within the Rio Grande Pueblo Region, tribute payments and diversion of labor away from their own subsistence activities reduced the surplus of items such as corn and cotton that they could use to trade with each other. Acquisition of cotton cloth by people in the northern pueblos where cotton could not be grown was not only important for their personal use but to meet tribute payments. When maize crops failed in one part of the region, the ability to remedy food shortages by trading with pueblos in surplus areas was largely eliminated because Spanish demands reduced surpluses in all pueblos.[35] In time of famine Pueblo peoples had to rely on the missions, and to some extent the governor, for relief.[36]

The exchange of maize for bison meat and fat was an important part of the trade between Pueblo peoples and Apache tribes to the east. This trade was especially important because large game was no longer abundant within the Rio Grande region.[37] The allied trade in bison hides was also important to Pueblo peoples, in part because the hides could be used instead of cotton cloth to meet that part of their tribute requirement. As Spaniards, particularly governors, arranged direct trade with Plains Apache tribes and exported hides and other goods to the mining districts of northern New Spain, Pueblo peoples were deprived of their traditional sources of meat, fat, and hides, while their trade with Plains tribes also diminished because they had little surplus to exchange as a result of continued Spanish exploitation of their economy.[38] This trade was further disrupted beginning in 1664 when Governor Diego de Peñalosa issued a decree forbidding "enemy Indians," from entering pueblos to trade, one result of which was to cut off both Pueblo and Apache peoples from sources of food they had traditionally exchanged.[39]

Apachean Raids

Some scholars believe that the decline in the number of pueblos prior to the mid-seventeenth century was chiefly caused by the kinds of Spanish exploitation described above.[40] But other factors, such as raiding by Apachean tribes, also contributed to the weakening and abandonment of pueblos. Although hostile relations with their Apachean neighbors were not unknown prior to the arrival of the Spanish colonists, the establishment of a Spanish presence brought on an increase in the number and intensity of attacks, which escalated during the period up to the 1680 revolt. The brunt of Apachean attacks was mainly suffered by pueblos because their inhabitants were seen as acquiescing to and therefore supporting the Spanish presence and because Pueblo men were used as auxiliaries in Spanish attacks on them. The Apacheans rightly saw Spanish domination as a threat to their own way of life. In addition, Spanish slaving practices, illegal though they were, provoked retaliation.[41]

Some of the earliest Apachean attacks were made by Navajo Apaches who lived in the area west of the Rio Grande Pueblo Region. It is reported that in 1606 and 1607 Juan Martínez de Montoya, encomendero of a Jemez pueblo, led attacks against Apaches, presumably against those who had been raiding in the area of his encomienda and who would likely have been Navajo Apaches.[42] He also took part in an expedition led by Oñate against Apaches who had attacked San Gabriel, the Spanish capital until 1610.[43] Given the proximity of the Navajos to the Tewa pueblos in the Española Basin, it was probably they who made this attack. In 1608 Fray Lázaro Ximénez, who had recently returned from New Mexico, reports to the viceroy in Mexico that ". . . Christian and peaceful natives in New Mexico are frequently harassed by attacks of the Apache Indians, who destroy and burn their pueblos, waylay and kill their people by treachery, steal their horses and cause other damages . . ."[44] The effectiveness of Apache raids was undoubtedly enhanced by their use of the horse, which was brought to the Americas by the Spaniards. Early acquisition of the horse and knowledge about its use may have diffused from native peoples to the south, aided and abetted by Pueblo peoples on the frontiers of the Rio Grande Pueblo Region.[45]

Benavides describes the Jemez people as dispersed, unsettled, and depopulated by famine and wars.[46] It was not only the Jemez people who suffered from raids in this early period. Benavides mentions that the Tewa pueblo of Santa Clara was frequently attacked by Navajo Apaches.[47] He also describes the plight of Sevilleta and several other Piro pueblos that had been burned by enemy Indians and where many of their people were killed. He found survivors wandering about in neighboring hills.[48] Fray Juan de Prada, writing in 1638, states that people in the frontier pueblos lived in constant danger from the continuous attacks of the warlike Apaches who lived in the vicinity.[49] In 1640 burning and pillaging took place in such widely separate pueblos as Sandia in the Middle Rio Grande subregion, Quarai east of the Manzano Mountains, and Socorro in the Southern Rio Grande subregion.[50]

Despite such Apachean depredations, some Pueblo peoples were willing to enter into alliances with them and help them acquire horses because they too wished to be rid of the Spaniards and saw that Apache raiding might help accomplish that goal. As early as 1609, the viceroy, in his instructions to the new governor, notes that frontier Pueblo peoples sheltered Apaches and colluded with them to make war against the Spaniards.[51] Governor Fernando de Arguello (1644–47) had twenty-nine Jemez men who had plotted rebellion with Apaches hanged as traitors.[52] In 1650 a number of Pueblo peoples (Southern Tiwans, Keres, Jemez) joined Apaches in another rebel plot in which the former were to turn over to the latter herds of horses belonging to the Spaniards.[53]

Relations with the various Apachean tribes worsened in the 1650s as the Spaniards, including the governors, sold large numbers of captives as slaves, sending many to New Spain.[54] In retaliation Apacheans raided frequently and widely, from the Jemez pueblos to the Tompiro pueblos in the Estancia Basin.[55] As a result, in 1659 the governor reversed the removal of the people of Sevilleta to Alamillo Pueblo, a removal that had been requested by the clergy, because this abandonment of Sevilleta, located on the Rio Grande west of Abo Pass, aided Apache penetration of that area.[56]

The 1660s saw an intensification of Apache raiding. At this time the subdivision of New Mexico into the Rio Arriba and Rio Abajo (the latter beginning with the Keres pueblos in the Santo Domingo Basin) was created, partly to better counter the more numerous Apache raids in the latter, especially on pueblos in the Estancia Basin.[57] The 1664 edict issued by the governor forbidding enemy Indians from entering pueblos to trade was another attempt to control contacts that could lead to further warfare, but only resulted in increased Apache hostility, which took the form of not only raiding pueblos but destroying them.[58] By 1669 Fray Juan de Bernal, commissary for New Mexico, could write from the custodial seat at Santo Domingo Pueblo that ". . . the whole land is at war with . . . the Apache Indians . . ."[59]

The relentless Apache warfare continued into the 1670s and by the end of that decade had helped bring about the abandonment of the Estancia Basin pueblos. Fray Francisco de Ayeta reports that between 1672 and 1677 the Estancia Basin pueblos and Senecu, the southernmost Piro pueblo, were abandoned and that he attempted to resettle them when reinforcements arrived from New Spain in the latter year.[60] Resettlement of Senecu was successful to the extent that it was inhabited at the time of the Spanish retreat in 1680.[61] But the fate of the Estancia Basin pueblos in the late 1670s is less clear.[62] Tajique was apparently the only Estancia Basin pueblo to be resettled, although Ayeta, in 1678, indicates there were others, claiming they were maintaining themselves despite being under attack.[63] But this was probably a false hope because Governor Otermín does not mention any Estancia Basin pueblos on his retreat to the El Paso area.

Pueblos elsewhere in the Rio Grande Pueblo Region were also under attack, notably those in the northwestern part of the region where Navajos were active, but none were abandoned as a result of these attacks.[64]

Drought and Famine

From time to time drought and famine exacerbated the weakened condition of pueblos that had been brought on by Spanish exploitation and Apachean raids. Famine (severe food shortage) can be caused by a number of factors, but drought (deficient moisture for plant growth sufficient to cause crop failure) is usually the basic reason. Although the severe drought conditions of the sixteenth century were not repeated, New Mexico in the seventeenth century suffered a number of shorter-term droughts. Average precipitation in New Mexico for the years 1602–80 (reconstructed from tree-ring data) was similar to present conditions, but these are not conditions favorable for agriculture, and the potential for drought caused by a shortfall in the already low level of precipitation was considerable. Precipitation data for the Albuquerque area show an annual average of 8.37 inches for 1602–80 and 8.53 inches for 1950–95 (table 14). Summer, not winter, was consistently the season of maximum precipitation but that amount was low. See appendix table E for 1602–99 seasonal and annual precipitation data for the Albuquerque area.

The temperature regime was also similar to that of the present. The average summer temperature in Santa Fe for 1602–80 was 68.48 degrees Fahrenheit, compared with 68.50 for 1950–95.[65] Average winter temperatures were 32.80 and 31.80, respectively, while average annual temperatures were 49.60 and 50.50. See appendix

Table 14. Average Annual Precipitation,* Albuquerque, NM, 1602-1680 and 1950-1995

	Winter	Spring	Summer	Fall	Annual Total
1602-80	0.82	2.33	3.08	2.39	8.37
1950-95	1.36	1.47	3.43	2.28	8.53

Source: For 1602-80 data see Appendix Table E. 1950-95 data are from the Midwestern Climatic Center, a cooperative project of the National Climate Data Center and the Illinois State Water Survey, Champaign, Illinois.

* In inches.

table F for 1602–99 seasonal and annual temperature data for the Santa Fe area. Temperature reconstructions for western North America in the seventeenth century indicate that this region did not share with eastern North America and Europe the lower temperatures associated with the Little Ice Age.[66]

Although it should be emphasized that seventeenth-century climatic data are reconstructions, not direct measurements, there are a number of drier than normal episodes in the tree-ring data that coincide with historical reports of famines.[67] Drier than normal years occurred in the first few years of the century, in the mid-1620s, and in many of the years from 1657 through 1676, especially from the mid-1660s into the early 1670s. In the Albuquerque area precipitation averaged 8.27 inches in the years 1602–8, and in southern New Mexico the annual average for the years 1602–08 was 10.35 inches. A drier period occurred in the 1620s, when the 1622–26 average in the Albuquerque area was 6.73 inches and in southern New Mexico 7.88 inches. Drier yet was the 1660–70 period, when 6.69 inches was the 1664–72 average in the Albuquerque area and 6.95 inches the 1666–74 average in southern New Mexico, with precipitation ranging from 4 to 5 inches in both regions in 1667 and 1668. Some relief came from the mid-1630s into the early 1640s, when nearly every year was wetter than normal. Annual precipitation averaged 9.01 inches in the Albuquerque area (1634–44) and 11.03 inches in southern New Mexico (1634–41). Wetter than normal conditions also prevailed in the years 1677–80, when the Albuquerque area averaged 8.95 inches and southern New Mexico 11.27 (appendix tables D and E).

The Pueblo peoples used irrigation to supplement such low rainfall, but water for irrigation is diminished as stream flow is reduced during drought periods. Most pueblos were located on tributaries of the Rio Grande where water for irrigation depends on precipitation within the region, in contrast to the Rio Grande itself, which is also fed by outside sources. On the whole, climate in the Rio Grande region was marginal for subsistence agriculture even with the practice of irrigation. In pre-Spanish times Pueblo peoples relied on their reserved crop surpluses for short-term droughts and on mobility and greater dependence on wild plant and animal food resources to see themselves through prolonged drought periods. Under Spanish rule these options were restricted and famine became more severe.

The earliest report of failed rains coincided with the drought conditions of the initial years of the seventeenth century. Fray Juan de Escalona, writing to his superior from New Mexico in 1601 about the difficulty of maintaining the colony, mentions the severe shortage of food caused by the Spaniards' consumption of the Pueblo peoples' reserves and by a shortfall of rain that caused many maizefields also to dry up (appendix tables A, C, D, and E).[68] Famine conditions at that time were also described by Fray Francisco de San Miguel, who might have exaggerated the suffering because he was trying to convince authorities to abandon the colony but he nevertheless supplies evidence that there was a famine.[69]

In the latter 1620s Benavides describes the Jemez people as ". . . depopulated by famine and war. . . ."[70] In this case the cause of the famine might have been dispersal of people away from their pueblos and fields because of their resistance to the imposition of Spanish rule combined with attacks by the Navajo, but drought during the three years from 1623 to 1625 was probably a factor too. Famine was reported in 1640 at a time when precipitation was somewhat higher than normal and drought was not involved. Rather, famine conditions at that time were mainly caused by Apache destruction of Pueblo food supplies, which involved burning an estimated twenty thousand fanegas or fifty thousand bushels of maize.[71] Apache raids often involved theft or destruction of Pueblo food supplies, partly to harm the Pueblo-Spanish subsistence base and partly to obtain the food they would have bartered for with Pueblo peoples in precolonial times.

In 1659 the Franciscan custodian Fray Juan Ramírez reports that New Mexico had just been through a serious famine and that the upcoming harvest was in jeopardy because the governor had requisitioned eight hundred Pueblo men to accompany Spaniards on a slaving expedition. According to him 840 fields of maize were subject to ruin. During the famine Pueblo people and Spanish colonists alike were reduced to eating wild plants. Even seed maize for the next planting had been consumed in the pueblos most affected by the governor's levy. Ramírez further reports that Apache tribespeople also were suffering food deprivation to the extent that they came to the convents to exchange captives they held and even their own children for a little meat and flour and that the friars at the missions in Senecu, Socorro, La Isleta, Tajique, Quarai, and others gave their parishioners a week's rations every Sunday during the time of the famine.[72]

Ramírez's prediction of ongoing calamity was correct. The 1660s were characterized by continuing famine during which nearly every year was drier than normal, many significantly so. The 1664 edict forbidding Apaches from entering pueblos worsened food shortages by cutting off the limited Pueblo-Apache exchange of food items that still took place.[73] At the end of the decade Fray Juan de Bernal describes a situation of extreme hunger in which the dead could be found lying along the roads and in the ravines as well as in their huts.[74] In Las Humanas Pueblo in the Estancia Basin 450 people died of hunger. He states that for two years people, including Spaniards, had been eating toasted cattle hides and that even the herds were dying for lack of forage. This latter fact indicates that drought conditions prevailed that would also account for the crop failures of the previous three years as reported by Bernal.[75] A plague of locusts reported by custodian Juan de Talabán in 1667 also contributed to food shortages in the Rio Grande Pueblo Region.[76]

But drought alone might not have produced such extreme famine conditions without the cumulative effects of Spanish exploitation and Apachean raiding.[77] It is not surprising that Apache attacks intensified significantly during this decade and that the combination of all three factors—Spanish exploitation, Apache raids, and drought—resulted in a famine severe enough to cause the abandonment in the 1670s of some of the most vulnerable pueblos, namely those in the Estancia Basin, as these conditions continued to prevail into that decade. Although wetter conditions returned late in the 1670s, they were insufficient in themselves to save the pueblos from abandonment.

Epidemics

Epidemic disease was yet another scourge that contributed to the decline of the Rio Grande pueblos in the seventeenth century. According to Fray Francisco de Ayeta, a great pestilence carried off many people in 1671.[78] He does not, however, identify the disease or give any information about its duration or distribution within the region.[79] In combination with the ongoing famine and Apachean raids previously described, the epidemic must have been devastating, with the worst consequences suffered in the Estancia Basin where all of the pueblos had to be abandoned in the following years.

The time of greatest pueblo abandonment, however, was not the 1670s but the late 1630s and early 1640s. In 1638 Fray Juan de Prada writes to the Council of the Indies that the population of New Mexico had been reduced by about one third, a decline he relates to the ". . . very active prevalence during these last years of smallpox and the sickness which the Mexicans called cocolitzli."[80] In this case the disease is known, it was of at least several years duration, and it was probably widespread. The term "cocolitzli" can be interpreted either as a particularly virulent form of smallpox—the fulminating type—or as a great or major disease event with generally more than one disease involved.[81] Another report, referring to the year 1640, states that a peste had spread among the Indians, taking a toll of three thousand persons or more than 10 percent of the total population.[82] Whether this epidemic was distinct from the one reported by Prada or a continuation, the late 1630s and 1640 were times when epidemic disease caused major population loss. The period from 1629 to 1641 is the time during which the greatest loss of population (68 percent) and abandonment of pueblos (some 50 percent) took place (table 12).

Was epidemic disease the principal cause of this great loss? In 1640 there was not only an epidemic but an increase in Apache raids, including the burning of fifty thousand bushels of maize, which must have caused severe food shortages in many pueblos. After four decades of Spanish rule, the various forms of Spanish exploitation and Apachean raiding had caused Pueblo peoples great hardship, leading many to leave their pueblos—note the flight of Taos people to El Cuartelejo at this time—but the cumulative effects of these factors became much worse in later decades without causing the scale of population loss and pueblo abandonment that took place between 1629 and 1641. Furthermore, drought was not a problem during this period. Something more catastrophic must have happened, and it is likely that the epidemic(s) that occurred then played a major role in such a drastic decline.

As previously discussed, the greatest losses took place in the Southern and Middle Rio Grande subregions. Losses were also significant in the Estancia Basin and in the lower Jemez. Because no pueblos in the area farther north had to be abandoned, it is possible that the strength of the epidemic might have abated by then, but, because the northern pueblos were generally larger, they also had a better

chance to survive.[83] Neither did the epidemic cause Acoma and Pecos, large outlying pueblos, to be abandoned, although the population of Pecos declined about 40
percent between 1622 and 1641.[84] The pattern of abandonment suggests that the
disease was introduced from New Spain and spread northward up the Rio Grande,
perhaps with one of the triennial supply trains from Mexico.[85] The smallpox epidemic noted in the years 1636–38 in Zacatecas, Monterrey, and the Parral district
could have been the source of this epidemic in New Mexico.[86]

The resulting 68 percent Pueblo population loss is of the order of magnitude of
losses suffered by a virgin soil population.[87] It is difficult to believe, however, that
the Pueblo population had not been previously affected by epidemics of European
diseases, particularly smallpox, during the one hundred years that had elapsed since
Spaniards first entered the region, especially during the three decades after missionization was initiated. The absence of documents that mention early disease
events in New Mexico has given the impression that the Pueblo population escaped
the epidemics that afflicted other American peoples shortly after, or sometimes in
advance of, contact with Europeans. The silence of records from the sixteenth-
century Spanish exploring expeditions to New Mexico on the subject of disease and
the apparent absence of large-scale reduction in the number of settlements during
that time combine to reinforce the idea that the Pueblo population did not suffer
epidemics of European diseases until the 1636–41 period.

It has been suggested that diseases such as smallpox and measles reached New
Mexico before Europeans were in the area, perhaps as early as the Mexican pandemic of 1520–24 that diffused widely and apparently devastated native populations
from Peru to the present United States.[88] If so, the surviving population would
have gained a certain immunity that later generations would have lost, leaving the
possibility that other epidemics could have occurred but were unrecorded or the
records lost.[89] Many disease episodes in northwestern New Spain in the sixteenth
century have been recorded, making it possible that this region could have served
as a disease reservoir for New Mexico.[90]

If there were such earlier epidemics among the Rio Grande pueblos, they did
not cause the large-scale abandonment of settlements during the contact years that
took place in the 1636–41 period, but they could have so diminished Pueblo populations that by the latter time, when they had lost any previously acquired immunity,
this epidemic was the one that finally caused wholesale abandonment of pueblos.
Whether the 1636–41 pestilence was the first epidemic of a European disease to

afflict the Rio Grande Pueblo population or had been preceded by others, this particular one played an important role in causing the single greatest loss of Pueblo settlements in historic times.[91]

Part Two Summary

Rio Grande Puebloans suffered the most devastating period of their history during the decades between 1600 and 1680. It is indeed remarkable that they managed to throw off the yoke of Spanish rule for a time, given their reduced condition. An investigation of the changing settlement pattern of Rio Grande pueblos during this period reveals a loss of some fifty pueblos (62 percent) and abandonment of large areas of territory, namely the Estancia Basin and much of the Socorro and Albuquerque-Belen Basins. In these areas 81 percent of the settlements were lost prior to the revolt. By far the greatest part of the total loss occurred early in the period—from the late 1630s into the early 1640s. The many stresses to which Pueblo peoples were subjected undoubtedly contributed to their weakened condition, but the epidemic of smallpox that occurred from about 1636 to 1641 was likely a key factor in the catastrophic decline in the number of pueblos, one from which they never recovered. Eighty-eight percent of the total settlement loss occurred during those years, to which was added the abandonment of the six Estancia Basin pueblos in the 1670s. Although the region suffered further loss of people, settlements, and territory during the later years of revolt and reconquest, the greatest abandonment of pueblos took place earlier in the seventeenth century.

PART THREE

Revolt, Reconquest,
and Resettlement

Introduction

The accumulated effects of the various forms of deprivation visited upon the Rio Grande Pueblo peoples during the first eighty years of Spanish rule led to a revolt in 1680 that forced the retreat of the Spanish population to the El Paso area. The revolt was carried out mainly through the coordinated efforts of the pueblos north of the Rio Grande–Jemez River junction. The southern half of the Rio Grande Pueblo Region was lost because the retreating Spaniards destroyed the Southern Tiwa pueblos in the Albuquerque-Belen Basin, and because the inhabitants of the Piro pueblos in the Socorro Basin, who had been excluded from knowledge of the revolt, either fled south with the Spaniards or sought refuge with other Pueblo or non-Pueblo peoples.

The campaigns of reconquest led by Governor Diego de Vargas during the years 1692–96 brought about the desertion of most of the remaining pueblos, some of which were never reoccupied. Inhabitants moved to refuge sites in their bitter but ultimately unsuccessful resistance to the reimposition of Spanish rule. The discord that prevailed among various Pueblo groups during the twelve years following the departure of the Spaniards contributed to their inability to achieve the unity needed to defeat the Spaniards again.[1] Factions within some pueblos saw the return of the Spaniards to be in their interest, especially after Vargas's initial reconnaissance in 1692.[2] Where these factions had the upper hand, the pueblos became the allies of the Spaniards. These pueblos were Pecos; the Keres pueblos of San Felipe, Santa Ana, and Zia; and later, the Tewa pueblo of Tesuque.[3]

During the years of resistance, inhabitants of pueblos were forced to move about in response to Spanish attacks, often splitting up. They were subject to exposure during the cold winters as well as to drought that contributed to famine. They were also under duress because they could not properly tend their fields and because their food stores were confiscated by the Spaniards, who not only used this deprivation to subdue them but to obtain food for their own people, who were also starving. After more than three years of such conditions and an unsuccessful revolt in 1696, many Pueblo peoples returned to their villages, but their populations were much reduced in number as exposure, starvation, military action, and flight took their toll. The process of resettlement of such shattered populations took many years, in some cases extending well into the first half of the eighteenth century. And not all pueblos were reoccupied. Twelve out of thirty-one were lost, and only one, La Laguna, was added.

The basic source of information about settlement patterns during the reconquest period has been the journals of Governor Diego de Vargas, and the recent edition produced under the direction of John L. Kessell has been heavily relied upon. Vargas's reporting of activities aimed at bringing the Rio Grande pueblos back under Spanish rule reveals much about the movements of Pueblo peoples in their attempts to avoid such subjugation. Other published collections of primary documents edited and translated by J. Manuel Espinosa, Charles Wilson Hackett, Hackett and Charmion Clair Shelby, Alfred Barnaby Thomas, Eleanor B. Adams, and Adams and Fray Angelico Chávez have also been important sources of information, as have many published secondary works.

CHAPTER FIVE
Environmental Context

T he turmoil of the reconquest and resettlement years was not only a matter of the repeated dislocations of Pueblo peoples as they sought refuge at sites where Spanish forces could not reach them. Their suffering was intensified by exposure during the long cold winters and, more importantly, by conditions of near starvation related to disruption of their agricultural activities, Spanish confiscation of their food stores, destruction of their fields, and drought.

Frequent comments in Vargas's journals emphasize the harsh winter conditions endured by both Spaniards and Puebloans. Climate-wise, what Vargas considered extreme conditions were probably only relative to what he knew in central New Spain and were not seen as extraordinary by local people; nevertheless, conditions were not mild. Vargas, as Benavides had in the 1620s and Coronado as far back as the 1540s, particularly notes the severity of the winters, with snow as early as October and as late as April, the former at times preventing people from harvesting their maize and the latter postponing planting until May.[1] Such conditions are not unusual in New Mexico at present, where winters are considered cold but not extremely so. An examination of tree-ring reconstructions for the 1690s shows that the average winter temperature at Santa Fe was 32.84 degrees Fahrenheit compared with 31.80 degrees Fahrenheit for 1950–95 and 32.76 degrees Fahrenheit for the seventeenth century as a whole (appendix table G).[2] Data in appendix table E also indicate that the 1690s was not a decade of extreme cold. Nevertheless, for people under siege who had left their pueblos to seek refuge in the mountains, the abundant snow, heavy frosts, and icy winds exacerbated already difficult conditions, particularly in the latter phase of the reconquest when many Pueblo peoples were split up trying to hide from Vargas's forces and living in caves and rancherías. Vargas hoped that these conditions and the catarrh that was common among Puebloans in winter, and from which many died, would force them back to their pueblos.[3] The food shortages and consequent malnutrition prevalent during the reconquest made the Pueblo population especially vulnerable to sickness and death during the long cold winters.

A basic if not overriding concern throughout the reconquest was the inadequacy of food supplies. When Vargas returned with colonists in October 1693, he planned to barter beef for grains to feed his people, who numbered about one thousand.[4] To these were added about 240 colonists from Mexico City who arrived in June 1694 and 176 from Zacatecas who arrived in May 1695.[5] Taking into account deaths and desertions that occurred, the Spanish population probably remained between one thousand and fourteen hundred during the reconquest period.[6] The Rio Grande Pueblo population was probably about twelve to thirteen thousand in 1680, declining to some seven to eight thousand by 1706, the reduction partly caused by deaths but mainly by flight from the region.[7]

During the early phase of the reconquest Vargas pursued a barter approach, rather than outright requisition, in order to avoid antagonizing the Puebloans, but their response was to give as little as possible—sequestering as much as they could and in some instances claiming that a plague of locusts or worms had left them little to harvest.[8] Even the Spaniards' Keres allies pleaded the latter case, which Vargas later learned was made up.[9] During November and December 1693, prior to laying siege to Santa Fe at the end of December, Vargas attempted to bargain for food with the rebels at their refuge pueblos—the Jemez on the peñol of San Diego (Guadalupe) Mesa, the rebel Keres on Horn Mesa, and the Tewans and Tanos on San Ildefonso Mesa—as well as with the Tanos and Tewans who occupied Santa Fe. Token amounts of maize were offered in exchange for slaughtered beef.[10] Some seventy sacks were sent to Horn Mesa to be filled, but nearly all were returned only half full.[11] Horn Mesa, referred to then as either the sierra or mesa of La Cieneguilla, is located at the southern end of the Pajarito Plateau about five miles northwest of Cochiti Pueblo. Vargas's allies at Pecos did somewhat better, sending some seventy–three bushels of maize in the ear and five bushels of maize flour in December.[12] The rebels in Santa Fe were particularly reluctant to give up foodstuffs even when paid for them, and according to an informant were removing their provisions to the mountains at night, hoping the Spaniards, who were camped nearby, would not see them.[13] However, when Vargas and his men finally forced their way into the villa, they found the houses well supplied with maize, beans, peas, lentils, and other dried vegetables.[14]

The foodstuffs available during the fall and winter of 1693 were mainly those harvested from the fields near their home pueblos, although Vargas notes milpas in the vicinity of the San Diego Mesa and Horn Mesa refuges and points out to the rebels that such fields were small and poor and that they would be better off to return home.[15] (San Diego Mesa is situated at the confluence of the Guadalupe and Jemez Rivers.) Although the rebels refused to do so, they did attempt to cultivate their home fields when the Spaniards were not in the vicinity. The following spring Vargas notes that the Tanos had planted milpas near their pueblos in the Santa Cruz Valley even though they lived at the refuge on San Ildefonso Mesa, and some Tewans from the mesa were later seen in a milpa near Jacona Pueblo.[16] Others went farther afield to plant. Some Tewans on San Ildefonso Mesa as well as those at Embudo went to Picuris and Taos to plant, while people from Nambe and Tesuque planted at San Juan Pueblo and the Embudo refuge.[17] Still others established fields near their refuges. Some of the San Ildefonso Mesa rebels planted below their mesa refuge, which is also known as Black Mesa and is located immediately north of San Ildefonso Pueblo on the east side of the Rio Grande at its junction with Pojoaque Creek.[18] Keres rebels on Horn Mesa planted in a barranca near a spring.[19] A Jemez prisoner caught by Zians confessed that he was scouting the area below San Diego Mesa to see if it was safe to come down to plant, and Vargas notes later, after he had defeated the Jemez in July, that they had many milpas in the area.[20]

Maintaining their milpas was not easy because Vargas, having failed by peaceful means to persuade the Puebloans to return to their pueblos, spent most of 1694 trying to subdue them by force. It was at this time that food came to be a weapon of war as Vargas turned to looting food stores in deserted pueblos and taking food as booty when he defeated the Puebloans at their refuge pueblos. Large amounts of foodstuffs were taken from the refuges on Horn and San Diego Mesas after the rebels were defeated there in April and July respectively.[21] Prior to the defeat of the Jemez in July, Vargas, noting the shortage of provisions in Santa Fe, decided to again search for supplies in abandoned pueblos.[22] In June he ranged as far north as Taos, which he found deserted and its inhabitants in a nearby canyon refuge that they refused to leave even while for two days Vargas's men plundered their food stores, shelled the ears of maize, sacked it, and loaded as much as they could on the pack train they brought with them.[23] To avoid being attacked by rebels, the Spaniards returned via a circuitous route through Ute country carrying some 780 bushels (300 fanegas), which Vargas estimates was about one fourth of the maize stored in the Taos pueblo.[24] The success of this trip relieved the crisis in Santa Fe, where provisions were nearly exhausted.[25] They were further replenished by the 624 bushels of shelled maize taken from the defeated Jemez.[26]

While confiscated food fed Vargas's people, its loss to the rebels, along with military defeats, forced most of them to return to their pueblos by the end of 1694. After repeated campaigns and patrols to prevent the rebels on San Ildefonso Mesa from obtaining food from their milpas and water from the Rio Grande, the rebels agreed to Vargas's demands in September when their milpas were about ready to be harvested.[27] The capitulation of these Tewa and Tano rebels signaled the end of major resistance and the beginning of the return to their pueblos by the various Pueblo peoples in time for the October harvest of those milpas they had been able to plant.

During 1694 Vargas also attempted to get the colonists to raise some of their own food. In April he ordered the settlers in Santa Fe to plant the fields near the villa that the occupying rebels had previously cultivated, even requiring the soldiers to work them.[28] He assigned the latter to outlying fields so they could act as guards to prevent the settlers working in the fields from being ambushed by Pueblo rebels who lurked about the villa looking for opportunities to steal crops and livestock and otherwise harass the Spaniards.[29] At their request, Vargas also sent some soldiers to his San Felipe allies to protect them while they planted their milpas, but later in June, with the soldiers gone, they were ambushed in their fields by some Jemez.[30]

By September 1694, realizing that the colonists would not raise enough foodstuffs to feed themselves and that he had confiscated nearly all of the Puebloans' food stores, and noting that the Tewans and Tanos were already reduced to consuming immature maize from their milpas, Vargas attempted to ensure adequate provisions for his people through purchases in New Spain and by getting the colonists to produce more. To accomplish the first goal he requested 3,000 fanegas (7,800 bushels) of maize and 1,070 head of cattle, sheep, and goats, but despite the viceroy's approval and numerous attempts to negotiate purchases in the towns of northern New Spain, supplies were not forthcoming until the spring of 1697.[31] He also failed in his second goal. In April 1695 he installed the Mexico City colonists in the Tanos' San Lázaro Pueblo in the Santa Cruz Valley, evicting the latter so the colonists would have ready-made houses, cleared fields, and an established network of irrigation ditches. Knowing that the colonists were urban artisans, he thought they needed this help if they were to succeed in raising their own food. But even with these advantages and paying some Tanos to work for them, they were unable to harvest much; nor were the settlers in Santa Fe.[32] Thus by the end of 1695, despite peaceful conditions, the colonists were as dependent as ever and the shortage of food was greater.

Vargas was loath to press the Puebloans to sell him foodstuffs because he knew they had no surplus from their harvest of 1695 and he wanted to retain their hard-won acquiescence. The Pueblo rebel leaders were aware of the dire situation of the Spaniards and strengthened their position by seizing the livestock of the missions that had been reestablished at the beginning of 1695.[33] By June of the following year they felt they could again try to force the Spaniards out of New Mexico. During this uprising Vargas was no longer reluctant to use food as a weapon of war and did so with a vengeance. Previously he had taken pains not to destroy planted fields. Hoping to gain the cooperation of the inhabitants of a pueblo, he would set up camp at a distance from their milpas so his horses would not trample them.[34] He had also recognized the need for the Pueblo peoples to produce food so that he might barter for it, but, seeing that they were still determined to drive him out, he set aside these considerations and proceeded to destroy or threaten to destroy milpas as a means of subduing the rebels.[35] At this time many of the rebels were not concentrated in refuge-pueblos but were split up into smaller groups hiding in the mountains, with their provisions sequestered in many sealed clay caches (coscomates), also hidden in numerous places.

Vargas mounted many campaigns to hunt down these rebel groups and their food stores, often causing them to flee farther into the mountains, with many migrating out of the Rio Grande region or ending up at the pueblos farthest from Santa Fe— Taos in the north or Acoma to the southwest.[36] Half of the Jemez and the Keres of Cochiti were reported to have gone to the Hopi.[37] The Picuris and others headed for the eastern plains, taking their sheep and goats with them.[38] In August, unable to defeat the rebels on the peñol of Acoma, Vargas had his men destroy many of the milpas planted at its base.[39] He also sent a Zuni prisoner to Zuni Pueblo with the message to submit or suffer the same fate. At Taos in September Vargas promised the people not to harm their milpas if they would surrender, but when they refused, his troops not only went after their provisions in their canyon refuge but began to take maize from the fields, although the Taos governor begged them not to.[40] Only when the Taos people returned to their pueblo in early October did Vargas end the plundering of their fields.[41] Adverse climatic conditions were a major consideration in their decision to return. The region had been struck by a severe drought in 1696 that undoubtedly diminished the harvest, which was further threatened by early heavy snowfalls (appendix tables A, C, D, and E).[42]

Both Puebloans and Spaniards were greatly affected by the drought, the first significant shortfall in a decade. Appendix table E shows 6.78 inches as total precipitation for the year in the Albuquerque area, whereas the average for the decade

1687–96 was 8.36 and for the entire seventeenth century, 8.29. Drought Severity Index values in appendix table A for other areas in the Rio Grande Pueblo Region also indicate a precipitous drop in available moisture. Vargas reports to the viceroy in a letter dated July 30, 1696, that there was a severe drought caused by light snowfall the previous winter and lack of seasonal rains.[43] In August he mentions that delivery of 250 head of cattle from El Paso was delayed because of the drought.[44] Earlier, in June, the municipal council (cabildo) in Santa Fe complained that the crops they planted had been lost because of the great drought and that people were reduced to eating toasted cowhides. They also had to dig wells in a marsh (ciénega) to obtain drinking water, an indication that the Santa Fe River was dry; most likely that was also true of all the other Rio Grande tributaries on which everyone depended for irrigation.[45] The cabildo further reports that, although the "Indians" had sown fields, they were not cultivating them because they had dried up for lack of seasonal rains, and that neither they nor their own people expected to harvest anything.[46] A Keres prisoner caught near Acoma in July stated that little land was planted because the ground was dry.[47] He also mentioned that because of the drought there was no water in the catchments (tinajas) on the peñol. In August and September both Puebloans and Vargas's forces continued to scavenge in old milpas or anywhere some food might be hidden, desperate to garner every last bit.[48] These conditions, in addition to Vargas's assaults, especially on Acoma and Taos, finally brought an unwilling end to active resistance in October. As late as February 1704 Vargas was informed that an uprising was being planned that involved Taos, the Tewans of San Juan and San Ildefonso, the Navajos of Piedra Alumbre Valley, and some Hopis—but nothing came of it.[49]

The year 1696 was the most difficult time of the reconquest period because both Puebloans and Spaniards were experiencing severe food deprivation and because the former were without adequate shelter and subject to attack. The situation was further complicated by the marked drought that struck that year, diminishing the prospects of a harvest that could bring some relief. Vargas's tactics of destroying food in the fields and confiscating hidden stores to send back to Santa Fe, along with the dismal outlook for the 1696 harvest, must have been major factors in the rebels' decision to return to their pueblos.

CHAPTER SIX
Regional Analysis

E ach Pueblo group within the Rio Grande Pueblo Region had its own experience of the revolt, reconquest, and resettlement, as related in the following discussions centered on the geographic subregions.

Southern Rio Grande

Only four pueblos in the Socorro Basin were still occupied in 1680 before the re-volt—Sevilleta, Alamillo, Socorro, and Senecu. Their Piro inhabitants, undoubtedly including Tompiros who had been forced to abandon their pueblos in the Estancia Basin during the previous decade, were not included in the planning of the revolt, the leadership of which was centered on the northern pueblos.[1] The first group of retreating Spaniards, led by Lieutenant Governor Alonso García, found some of the Piros willing to join them in the retreat to the El Paso area, possibly out of fear of retaliation for not joining the rebellion.[2] But not all Piros followed the Spaniards, as Governor Antonio de Otermín found when he led an expedition back into Pueblo country the following year. The Piro pueblos were deserted, but when he reached the Tiwa pueblo of Isleta he found people from Socorro, Alamillo, and Sevilleta there.[3] On the way he had the Piro pueblos burned, and after forcing the people at Isleta to surrender he burned their pueblo and took the inhabitants, including Piro and Tompiro refugees, back to El Paso when he departed the area in January 1682.[4] In this case, also, many escaped—westward to Acoma or the Hopi pueblos or to Rio Grande pueblos farther north.[5] Those who were forced south joined the 317 Piros, Tompiros, and Isletans who had been taken there the previous year.[6]

It was only after Otermín's return to the El Paso area in February 1682 that mission settlements were established there for the Puebloan refugees. Spanish refugees arriving in October 1680 had been settled in three camps in the ford area of the Rio Grande in the vicinity of the Nuestra Señora de Guadalupe del Paso mission previously established for the local Manso tribe, but there is no record of how the Puebloan people who accompanied them were settled at that time.[7] After Otermín's unsuccessful foray into New Mexico during the winter of 1681–82, it became clear that the Spaniards were not going to reestablish their authority in Pueblo country quickly, and so it was necessary to found regularized settlements for both groups of Puebloan refugees.

The Piros and Tompiros were gathered into two mission-pueblos. The first, called "San Antonio Senecu," was located two leagues (about five miles) below the Manso mission, and the other, "Nuestra Señora del Socorro," which also included some Jemez and Tanos, was ten leagues (twenty-six miles) farther south along the Rio Grande.[8] The following year, 1683, Socorro was moved closer to the other settlements because some of its inhabitants had tried to kill their priest and a couple of Spanish families.[9] Apache attacks brought about further consolidation of settlements in 1684 under Governor Domingo Jironza Pétriz de Cruzate, who moved Socorro to within two leagues (about five miles) of Senecu, with the Southern Tiwa pueblo of Isleta halfway between the two.[10] Despite unrest among the Puebloan refugees, their settlements in the El Paso area persisted. In 1754 their priest describes their diligent work in their fields and gardens but notes they were never without the poor.[11] Over time the inhabitants of Socorro and Senecu became "mexicanized" both culturally and genetically, although they maintained some contact with the pueblos farther north. Senecu continued to exist as a small but organized community into the first decade of the twentieth century, although Socorro ceased to function thus a little earlier.[12]

When Governor Diego de Vargas passed through the Socorro Basin in the fall of 1692, he found the Piro pueblos destroyed.[13] After he succeeded in reimposing Spanish authority in the region, he considered resettling these pueblos, but no actual attempt was made to do so.[14] Perhaps officials thought it too difficult to administer them in view of continued Apache raiding or perhaps the absence of a native population in the area would leave it open to further Spanish settlement. Puebloan occupation of the Socorro Basin effectively ended with the 1680 revolt, and the territory of the Rio Grande Pueblo Region was thus reduced.

Middle Rio Grande

Sandia, Alameda, Puaray, and Isleta were the only Southern Tiwa pueblos that remained occupied in the Albuquerque-Belen Basin on the eve of the 1680 revolt. All joined in the revolt except Isleta, which did not receive notice of its premature outbreak and which was used as a gathering place by Spanish officials and residents of the Rio Abajo while they decided what to do.[15] The Isletans, who were showing signs of joining the revolt, were taken south with the group of retreating Spaniards led by Alonso García, although some did escape.[16] When Governor Otermín reached

Isleta twenty days later, on September 3, 1680, it was deserted.[17] He had previously found Sandia deserted and its church and convent largely destroyed.[18] Before continuing south he ordered Isleta burned. Presumably Puaray and Alameda suffered the same fate, although he does not mention them.

When Otermín returned in the winter of 1681–82, he found the four Southern Tiwa pueblos repopulated. Reaching Isleta, by then the southernmost Rio Grande pueblo, he staged a surprise attack and forced its surrender.[19] The inhabitants of the other Tiwa pueblos—Alameda, Puaray, and Sandia—then fled and were said to have gone to the "sierra." Apparently they joined the Keres of Santa Ana and Zia in the Sierra de los Jemez (Cerro Colorado or Red Mesa), and at least some of the men joined other Keres on the Sierra de la Cieneguilla (Horn Mesa).[20] When they visited the three deserted Tiwa pueblos, Otermín and his men found them well supplied with maize, which they looted before burning the pueblos, a fate also suffered by Isleta when Otermín ordered the retreat to El Paso on January 1, 1682.[21] The population of Isleta was forced to go along, although many managed to escape. Of the 511 persons in the pueblo when Otermín captured it, only 385 were left to be marched south to El Paso.[22] Defections continued, and by the time they reached Estero Largo twenty-eight leagues (seventy-three miles) above El Paso, only 305 remained.[23]

Otermín's return to El Paso in February 1682 with additional refugees occasioned the founding of mission-pueblos for all Puebloan refugees. Besides the two missions for Piros and Tompiros already mentioned, a third was established for the Isletans. It was located between the other two, about a league (2.6 miles) south of Senecu mission.[24] Initially it was named "Sacramento de la Isleta" or "El Santísimo Sacramento" and later called "Corpus Christi de la Ysleta."[25] Eighteenth-century reports give its name as "San Antonio de la Isleta."[26] Isleta was the largest of the three El Paso area pueblos and has managed to persist as an organized community up to the present, although much "mexicanized." Commonly referred to as Isleta del Sur, it is located on the east bank of the Rio Grande fourteen miles below the city of El Paso.[27] Sometime during the second half of the nineteenth century a daughter colony, Tortugas, was established in Las Cruces, New Mexico.[28]

The Southern Tiwa pueblos do not appear to have been reoccupied during the nearly eleven years that elapsed until Vargas made his appearance in the fall of 1692, when he found them abandoned and in ruins.[29] Many of the Tiwans seem to have sought refuge among the Hopi during that period.[30] There is a tradition that they occupied a separate pueblo, Payupki, although this is not certain and it was not mentioned during Vargas's visit to the Hopi in 1692.[31] The Tiwa pueblos apparently remained abandoned until well into the eighteenth century, although Alameda was reoccupied for a short time early in the century. It was reestablished in 1702 by Fray Juan de Sabalita and Governor Pedro Rodríguez Cubero and listed by Fray Juan Álvarez in his 1706 census.[32] The latter notes that it was a small mission of only fifty people but that others were still coming in. In 1708 they were apparently moved by Fray Juan de la Peña to Isleta, perhaps marking the beginning of resettlement of that ruined pueblo, to which were added Isletans returning from Hopi country in 1716–18.[33] That Isleta had been reconstituted as a pueblo and mission by 1730 is confirmed in a report by the Bishop of Durango, Benito Crespo, who visited the New Mexico missions that year.[34] It was not until the 1740s that larger numbers of Southern Tiwans returned to the Rio Grande Pueblo Region. In 1742 two missionaries, Carlos Delgado and Ygnacio de Pino, went to the Hopi pueblos and brought back 441 people, most of whom were from Sandia, Alameda, and Puaray.[35] They were initially crowded into various pueblos, mainly Jemez, with others going to Isleta, because Governor Gaspar Domínguez de Mendoza refused to grant permission to open new settlements.[36] Only in 1748 after Fray Miguel Menchero arrived with an order from the viceroy were these refugees, who included a number of Hopis, able to settle at Sandia, building a new pueblo near the site of the old ruined one.[37] As late as 1759 visiting Bishop Pedro Tamarón y Romeral found Tiwans and Hopis living in Sandia pueblo, each in separate roomblocks.[38] An anonymous report dated possibly 1765 also lists Sandia as a pueblo of Tiguas (Tiwas) and Moquinos (Hopis); over time, however, the Hopis ceased to be an identifiable element in the Sandia population.[39] Sandia and Isleta are the only Southern Tiwa pueblos that continued to be occupied up to the present.

Lower Jemez River

The people of the two lower Jemez River pueblos, Zia and Santa Ana, allied themselves with the Spaniards after Governor Diego de Vargas returned to recolonize New Mexico in 1693, although they had earlier demonstrated their opposition to continued Spanish rule by joining the revolt in 1680. They had further reason to oppose submission after they were brutally attacked in 1687 and 1689 by the forces of previous governors. In 1687 a party led by Governor Pedro Reneros de Posada attacked and burned Santa Ana.[40] They attempted to do the same to Zia but strong resistance forced them to retreat. In 1689 Governor Domingo Jironza Pétriz de Cruzate and his men sacked Zia in a bloody battle that destroyed the pueblo and caused the deaths of more than six hundred Zians. In addition, some seventy or more were taken to El Paso, where they were condemned to ten years of servitude among the Spanish soldiers and settlers, thus adding Keres to the mix of Puebloan peoples forced into exile in El Paso.[41]

These assaults undoubtedly emphasized to the people of Zia and Santa Ana just how vulnerable their position was to further Spanish attacks. They also had to contend with harassment by Puebloan enemies, particularly the Tewans, Tanos, and Jemez.[42] Although their pledge of allegiance made to Vargas during his initial reconnaissance of the pueblos in 1692 may have been insincere, as it was for almost all of the Pueblo peoples, they may have decided the following year when they saw him return with Spanish settlers that the reestablishment of Spanish rule was likely and that they could benefit more from Vargas's protection than they could gain by opposing him.[43] The influence of Bartolomé de Ojeda also may have been crucial to their decision. He was a Keres from either Zia or Santa Ana whom Jironza took to El Paso as a captive and who, after returning with Vargas, became an important leader of his people.[44]

Where did the Zians and Santa Anans live during the years between the revolt and Vargas's return in 1692? At the time of the revolt Zians were most probably living in their traditional pueblo on the east side of the lower Jemez River where they still live today (LA 28). It is less clear where the Santa Anans lived, whether in a pueblo on the banks of the river, perhaps in an as yet unidentified pueblo in the vicinity of their present one (LA 8975) or above on Santa Ana or Black Mesa—possibly in Canjillon Pueblo (LA 2049), located on the mesa overlooking the confluence of the Jemez River with the Rio Grande.[45] When Governor Otermín returned in the winter of 1681–82 the Zians and Santa Anans fled to Cerro Colorado three leagues (eight miles) west of Zia Pueblo. It is variously referred to as a "high mesa near the pueblo of the Jemez," Sierra de los Jemez, or Cerro Colorado.[46] The site (LA 2048) is located on a small mesa in the mountains west of the Jemez River and about two miles due west of present Jemez Pueblo. After Otermín left for El Paso, it is possible that the Santa Anans went to live at Canjillon Pueblo on Santa Ana Mesa.[47] After Reneros attacked Santa Ana in 1687, he then went on to Zia, an indication that the two peoples were no longer together on Cerro Colorado. The Zians were in their traditional pueblo when Jironza attacked them in 1689.

After these disasters the people of Zia and Santa Ana again retreated to Cerro Colorado, where they built a new pueblo, the one where Vargas found them in 1692.[48] He urged them both to return to their separate pueblos but apparently only the Santa Anans did so. It might have been at this time that they established their pueblo at its present site on the east bank of the Jemez River about eight miles above the Jemez–Rio Grande junction, and it was possibly there they received him in November 1693.[49] The Zians remained in the pueblo on Cerro Colorado, where Vargas and his men had to struggle up the steep slopes to reach them, but they received the Spaniards cordially and promised to return to their ruined pueblo and rebuild their church.[50] A month later, in December 1693, a missionary was assigned to them, and by the following spring a mission was established.[51]

As allies of the Spaniards, the Keres of the lower Jemez River aided Vargas in many of his battles to subdue the other Pueblo peoples, and this support continued after the second uprising in 1696.[52] Zia Pueblo was especially important as a staging point for campaigns against the Jemez and the rebels who retreated to Acoma.[53] As a result of this alliance their populations did not suffer the dispersal, exile, and losses experienced by most of the other Rio Grande Pueblo peoples.

Upper Jemez River

At the time of the 1680 revolt the Jemez people were probably living in a number of settlements, although there was only one mission-pueblo—San Diego de la Congregación—located at Walatowa, the present Jemez pueblo. (This site will henceforth be referred to as Walatowa.) It is unclear which other pueblos were occupied then, but they might have included sites such as Tovakwa (the main ceremonial center), Kwastiyukwa, and Boletsakwa.[54] Unlike most Jemez pueblos, which were built on high mesa tops, Walatowa is located on a terrace on the eastern margin of the Jemez River floodplain about four to five miles below the river's exit from its canyon (San Diego Canyon). The Jemez people seem to have been divided between those living in the more inaccessible pueblos and those residing at the mission.

When Governor Antonio de Otermín led an expedition into Pueblo country from the El Paso area in the winter of 1681–82, he was informed, upon reaching Isleta Pueblo, that word of his entrada had spread quickly and that many Pueblo peoples had fled to refuge sites. The Jemez were reported to be on a high mesa near their pueblo, where they were joined by people from Zia and Santa Ana.[55]

The refuge-pueblo referred to was most probably Cerro Colorado, located about two miles due west of the mission-pueblo. Following Otermín's intrusion, which did not reach the Jemez, they possibly returned to Walatowa, but when Governor Diego de Vargas arrived a decade later to reinstate Spanish authority he found them at the refuge-pueblo Astialakwa.[56] Located about eight miles north of Walatowa at 6,660 feet on a peñol at the summit of San Diego (Guadalupe) Mesa, some 900 feet above the canyon floor, it was a formidable site.

Before Vargas returned the following year, the Jemez apparently moved down from the peñol and established themselves, not at the old site of Walatowa as he had urged, but on a low outlier at the foot of San Diego Mesa where they built a pueblo on the old Patokwa site.[57] That they had not done so earlier can be assumed from Vargas's failure to mention such a settlement during his October 1692 visit. When Vargas approached the Jemez in November 1693, they again retreated to the peñol. The meeting was outwardly cordial, but they offered only a meager amount of maize in exchange for the beef that Vargas tried to barter, explaining that worms had attacked their crop and they had harvested little; however, he had already been informed that they had moved their provisions into the forest (monte).[58] Although Vargas wanted them to return to the more accessible site of Walatowa, he agreed when they insisted on staying at their new pueblo (Patokwa) where their fields were by then established.[59] The Jemez's resistance to the reimposition of Spanish rule was soon more forcefully revealed when they sent warriors to aid the Pueblo defense of Santa Fe at the end of December.[60] Later, some Jemez joined Keres and Tewa peoples who were resisting the Spaniards at refuge sites on Horn Mesa (Mesa de la Cieneguilla) and San Ildefonso Mesa (Black Mesa).[61]

In retaliation for their continued actions against him and his allies from Zia, Santa Ana, and San Felipe, Vargas, in July 1694, launched a large-scale attack on the Jemez, who had by then again retreated to Astialakwa.[62] The success of this attack dealt the Jemez a severe blow. Besides confiscating all of their provisions and burning their refuge-pueblo, the Spaniards killed sixty-seven people and took as prisoners 361 women and children.[63] Others escaped and scattered—some to join the Cochiti on Horn Mesa and some to Taos and even to the Navajos in the Largo Canyon area.[64] The remainder promised to return to Patokwa and, in September 1694 when Vargas arrived there on an inspection tour, he named the pueblo and the mission he established "San Diego del Monte" to distinguish it from the old San Diego mission-pueblo at Walatowa that they had abandoned.[65]

On the day before Vargas's visit to Patokwa he received at Santa Ana Pueblo representatives of the Jemez faction that had separated from the other Jemez in years past and that was living with Santo Domingo rebels on the next mesa three leagues (some eight miles) from the peñol of San Diego Mesa.[66] Given that distance, their refuge might have been Kwastiyukwa on Holiday Mesa, the "next" mesa, or Tovakwa on Stable Mesa, which fits the distance better.[67] These pueblos, in the Guadalupe drainage west of the Jemez River, were among the more remote settlements likely occupied by some of the Jemez during the seventeenth century; after the defeat at Astialakwa or earlier, one of them might have become the refuge for those Jemez who had not fled the Jemez homeland but who had not gone with the Jemez who returned to Patokwa. In his report on the meeting with representatives of this faction, Vargas states that they lived on San Juan Mesa.[68] It is the opinion of some scholars that Vargas's San Juan Mesa was not in the Guadalupe drainage but was the mesa known today by that name in the Vallecitos drainage east of the Jemez River.[69] Vargas continues to refer to this group as the San Juan Jemez to distinguish them from the San Diego Jemez who lived at the Patokwa site (San Diego del Monte). Although the San Juan Jemez came to the meeting with Vargas at Patokwa, they apparently continued to live on San Juan Mesa for many months, because the following January (1695) Vargas reports that the Jemez were still there with the Santo Domingo rebels while the priest and alcalde for the Jemez people were at Patokwa.[70] As late as September of that year the San Juan Jemez are described as "of the cordillera," but sometime before March 1696 they apparently moved to the old San Diego mission-pueblo (Walatowa), where they were assigned their own priest. Vargas also transferred to them the priest, alcalde, and armed guard from Patokwa as a safety measure in view of Walatowa's strategic location only two leagues (five miles—actually about eight miles) from Zia Pueblo.[71] At this time the priests at the Rio Grande pueblos were increasingly concerned about signs of another uprising.[72]

An uprising did occur beginning June 4, 1696, in which the Jemez people took part.[73] After killing a priest and three Spaniards they moved to their refuge site on the peñol of San Diego Mesa where, with allies who joined them from Acoma, Zuni, Hopi, and Cochiti in addition to some Navajo Apaches, they made plans to attack Zia and Santa Ana.[74] Before they could carry out their attack, Vargas, who had been informed of their plans, sent a force against them on June 29 and defeated them after battles in the vicinity of Patokwa and Walatowa.[75] The result of this defeat was another dispersal of the Jemez people, who abandoned both of their pueblos. A reconnaissance of the area in August, led by one of Vargas's captains, revealed it to be deserted. Reports indicate that some Jemez people sought refuge at Acoma while others went west to the Zuni and Hopi pueblos and still others moved north to their ancestral homeland in the Largo Canyon area—some joining the Navajos who lived in that area.[76] Although a large number remained in exile for many years, and some permanently, the Walatowa site began to be repopulated by the early years of the eighteenth century. Fray Juan Álvarez reports in 1706 that the Jemez were still in a state of rebellion but that three hundred were to be counted at Walatowa with more coming in, and the building of a new church was underway.[77] Although it is unclear how many pueblos the Jemez people occupied at the time of the revolt, only Walatowa was reoccupied after the reconquest was completed, and it has remained their only pueblo up to the present.

Rio Puerco–Rio San Jose

Two pueblos, both occupied by Keres people, are located in the Rio Puerco–Rio San Jose area: Acoma, whose origin dates back to about the twelfth century, and Laguna, which was established in the late seventeenth century.[78] The people of Acoma continued to occupy their pueblo throughout the revolt and reconquest period. Their location atop a small 357-foot butte made it unnecessary to seek refuge elsewhere, and their great distance from Santa Fe (about 110 miles) meant that the Acomans were not subject to successful attack even though they consistently opposed efforts to reinstate Spanish rule. The priest at Acoma was one of the twenty-one killed on the opening day of the revolt, August 9, 1680.[79] Their remote location protected them from the depredations of Otermín, Reneros, and Cruzate when their respective forces made forays up the Rio Grande during the 1680s. Vargas did visit Acoma in 1692 during the course of his initial reconnaissance, but he was too preoccupied with rebellious pueblos closer to Santa Fe, after returning to New Mexico in 1693, to lead an expedition against it until several months after the second revolt, begun in June 1696, was well underway.[80] In the meantime the Acomans formed alliances with Zunis, Hopis, Jemez, and several Apache tribes with the intention of gathering at Acoma to launch an attack that would drive the Spaniards out of New Mexico.[81] This campaign was never carried out, but attacks were made during June and July 1696 in the vicinity of Zia and Santa Ana.[82]

In this last phase of the reconquest Acoma was an important refuge for the many different Pueblo peoples fleeing Vargas's forces. It was to subdue this concentration of rebels that Vargas led his first expedition against Acoma. By the time Vargas reached the peñol of Acoma on August 15, 1696, he had obtained information about which Pueblo peoples had retreated there. They comprised groups of Jemez; Keres from Santo Domingo, Cochiti, La Cienega, and San Marcos; Tanos; and Tewans from Santa Clara.[83] A certain amount of discord must have existed in this situation, which led some of them to move on to Zuni, and in November it was reported to Vargas that the Acomans had expelled the Jemez and Santo Domingo refugees who remained in their midst.[84] These latter refugees, who included Keres people from the pueblos listed above accompanied by some disgruntled Acomans, fled first to nearby mountains, but by the end of 1697 they had established a settlement fourteen miles north of the peñol near a small lake fed by the Rio San Jose.[85] The next year the people of this settlement, called La Laguna, and the Acomans of the peñol sued for peace, and on June 30, 1699, Governor Rodríguez Cubero gave them formal recognition.[86] Both Laguna and Acoma are listed in Fray Juan Álvarez's census of 1706 and both have persisted to the present.[87] A number of Rio Grande pueblos were abandoned and never resettled during the revolt and reconquest period, but La Laguna, founded by Keres people from a number of their different pueblos, was the only new pueblo to be established in the Rio Grande Pueblo Region then or at any time later.

Santo Domingo Basin

Keres people also occupied pueblos along the Rio Grande north of its confluence with the Jemez River. These Santo Domingo Basin pueblos were San Felipe, Santo Domingo, and Cochiti. About twenty miles east of the Rio Grande, on the western edge of the Galisteo Basin, Keres people also occupied San Marcos Pueblo. A fifth pueblo was La Cienega.[88] All of these pueblos were major players in the revolt and all except San Felipe staunchly opposed the return of the Spaniards.

San Felipe joined its neighbors Santa Ana and Zia in siding with the Spaniards when the latter returned under the leadership of Governor Diego de Vargas. During the colonial period up to the revolt, the people of San Felipe had occupied a pueblo (Katishtya or Tamita—LA 3137) located near the base of La Mesita just east of the Rio Grande and about six miles north of its junction with the Jemez River. When Governor Otermín returned in the winter of 1681–82, they fled, along with the people of Santo Domingo and Cochiti, to Horn Mesa northwest of Cochiti Pueblo.[89]

It is unclear whether they returned to their riverside pueblo after Otermín retreated to El Paso or whether they then stayed on Horn Mesa with Keres from Cochiti and San Marcos at the refuge-pueblo Potrero Viejo (LA 84).[90] When Vargas found them there during his reconnaissance in the fall of 1692, they told him they were seeking refuge from the Tewans, Tanos, and Picuris, who were making war against them.[91] He urged them to return to their pueblo on the Rio Grande, promising to protect them from their enemies. When he again encountered them upon his return to the region the following year, they were living in a pueblo they built on Santa Ana or Black Mesa (LA 2047) above their old pueblo on the river.[92] Because they cooperated with Vargas, they were then threatened by other Keres who remained on Horn Mesa in defiance of the Spaniards.[93]

The people of San Felipe opted to cast their lot with the Spaniards not only to receive protection from their Puebloan enemies but because they, like their neighbors in Santa Ana and Zia, felt very exposed to Spanish attack if they chose to oppose them. Although they were not attacked by Reneros in 1687 or Cruzate in 1689, nor earlier in the decade by Otermín, they knew of the devastation that those forces visited upon nearby pueblos and realized that their geographical position left them also readily accessible to attack.[94] The people of San Felipe not only cooperated with Vargas in his efforts to subdue Jemez and pueblos to the north, they continued to support him when the second uprising began in June 1696 and participated in the campaign against Acoma in August.[95] Its geographical position above a much-used ford of the Rio Grande and its potential as a refuge for the Spanish colonists living in the Bernalillo area made San Felipe very useful to Vargas.[96] In August 1696 the San Felipe people were still living in their mesa-top pueblo, but by the end of the year, when the rebellion was largely put down, they began to build a new pueblo below on the west side of the Rio Grande (LA 2232), where they were reported living by Fray Juan Álvarez in 1706 and where their descendants still live today.[97]

The remaining Keres pueblos—Santo Domingo, Cochiti, La Cienega, and San Marcos—also participated in the revolt, but unlike San Felipe, Santa Ana, and Zia they continued to oppose the Spaniards throughout the reconquest period.[98] Otermín's forces reached as far north as Cochiti in the winter of 1681–82, only to find that the people of these pueblos had retreated to Horn Mesa and defied the Spaniards, who were too few in number to defeat them.[99] On that occasion, when his men passed through Santo Domingo and Cochiti, they took provisions but did not destroy the pueblos.[100] Their next encounter with the Spaniards was with the 1692 reconnaissance expedition led by Governor Diego de Vargas, who found these four pueblos deserted and their inhabitants scattered to various refuge sites.[101] The people of Santo Domingo were on Cerro Colorado with the Zians and Santa Anans.[102] The Cochitis were on Horn Mesa with the San Felipe and San Marcos people.[103] It is not clear where the inhabitants of La Cienega Pueblo were, but it is likely they were with their fellow Keres on Horn Mesa.[104] The situation was much the same when Vargas returned the next year. The Santo Domingans remained in Jemez territory, living with some of the Jemez people on a remote mesa to avoid the attacks they claimed the Tewans, Tanos, and Apaches made on their pueblo.[105] The people of Cochiti, San Marcos, and presumably La Cienega were still on Horn Mesa.[106] Only the San Felipe people had returned to their home area. When Vargas approached the three Keres groups on Horn Mesa in November 1693, they again promised to come down to their former pueblos but failed to do so.[107] Because they continued to defy him, Vargas attacked the stronghold the following April—killing some of the men and taking many prisoners.[108] After the pueblo was emptied of its food stores, it was burned.[109]

Despite this defeat, some of the rebel Keres refused to surrender. They retreated to adjoining areas and continued to attack Vargas's men and his Pueblo allies.[110] However, Vargas's defeat of the Jemez on San Diego Mesa in July and his successful siege of the Tewa on San Ildefonso Mesa in early September made it more difficult for the Keres rebels to hold out. When Vargas made an inspection tour of the pueblos that fall, the leaders of the Cochitis, representing the Keres in the Horn Mesa area, met him at the still deserted Santo Domingo Pueblo and pledged to accept Spanish authority, which implied a return to their home pueblos.[111] The Cochitis seem to have complied. By January 1695 they had been assigned a priest, who was resident at the pueblo in the spring of 1696.[112] The pueblo of La Cienega is mentioned and might have been briefly repopulated—possibly by Vargas, who might have resettled there a mixed group of Puebloans who had been displaced during the many battles fought during the reconquest.[113] San Marcos Pueblo is not mentioned, and possibly its people remained with the Cochitis. A San Marcos man later reported that both groups were together as refugees on the peñol of Acoma.[114]

The people of Santo Domingo also sought refuge with fellow Keres on Horn Mesa at the time of Otermín's return, but on the occasion of Vargas's first entrada in the fall of 1692 they joined the Keres of Santa Ana and Zia on Cerro Colorado.[115] Although the latter pueblos became allies of the Spaniards, Santo Domingo did not and sometime later, at the latest by March 1694, joined the faction of the Jemez that had been living apart from the main group in a remote area on what Vargas called "San Juan Mesa."[116] After the Jemez were defeated on San Diego Mesa, leaders of the Santo Domingans approached Vargas in the fall of 1694 to make peace.[117] By January 1695 a priest had been installed at Santo Domingo Pueblo and an alcalde appointed, indications that they were repopulating their pueblo on the Rio Grande, but the situation seemed unsettled.[118] As late as September 1695 some of them were still in the mountains with the San Juan Jemez, where they probably remained until they retreated to Acoma the following year. By the spring of 1696 Santo Domingo no longer had a resident missionary.[119]

With the beginning of the uprising in June 1696 the people who had remained in Santo Domingo Pueblo, like their neighbors the Cochitis (who probably included the people of La Cienega and San Marcos pueblos), again abandoned their pueblos and scattered to the mountains in the vicinity of Horn Mesa, where they were living in primitive shelters called "rancherías."[120] Vargas led several forays against them and, although he failed to obtain their surrender, he confiscated some of their food caches.[121] The precarious nature of their existence must have led some of them to seek shelter at the isolated pueblo of Acoma. Some Cochitis and Santo Domingans were reported there in August.[122] But as this uprising failed to gain momentum and overcome Vargas's countermeasures, various Pueblo groups began to sue for peace. The Keres refugees at Acoma initiated the new settlement La Laguna in the vicinity of Acoma in 1697, but those who had remained in the mountains in the Horn Mesa area returned to reestablish Cochiti and Santo Domingo pueblos on the Rio Grande.[123] The pueblos of La Cienega and San Marcos seem to have been permanently abandoned.

Galisteo Basin

The people of the three Tano pueblos in the Galisteo Basin were among the first to attack Santa Fe during the initial days of the 1680 revolt. Men from San Cristóbal, San Lázaro, and Galisteo were reported marching on Santa Fe on August 13, having already killed their priest in Galisteo.[124] It is uncertain how soon the rebels made the abandoned capital their residence after Governor Otermín withdrew following a nine-day siege.[125] In October of the next year when Otermín returned, the Tanos were reported to be gathering at Galisteo Pueblo, possibly indicating that they had not yet abandoned their Galisteo Basin pueblos.[126] However, when Vargas arrived in the fall of 1692, he found these pueblos deserted. The people of Galisteo were ensconced in Santa Fe, where they had converted the governor's palace into a pueblo-style building; the people of San Lázaro and San Cristóbal had established pueblos in the Santa Cruz Valley on lands held by Spanish colonists prior to the revolt.[127] These moves seem to have been prompted partly by the opportunity to obtain lands near better water supplies and partly by vulnerability in the Galisteo Basin to hostilities from neighboring Keres and Pecos peoples as well as from Plains Apaches.[128]

Vargas succeeded in retaking Santa Fe at the end of December 1693.[129] The Galisteans, who were the majority of its defenders within the walls, suffered the loss of many men, although some escaped to join the Tewans, while the prisoners, some four hundred, mainly women and children, were distributed among the Spaniards as servants.[130] The Tanos who had been living in the Santa Cruz Valley did not return to their pueblos after the siege but retreated to a refuge site with some of the Tewans. Whether this site was atop San Ildefonso Mesa or on a summit in the vicinity of San Juan Pueblo cannot be known with certainty because witnesses give conflicting testimony.[131] The Tano people were distantly related to the Tewans, from whom they were separated as early as the late thirteenth century;[132] their language is regarded as a dialect of Tewa.[133] In 1692 Vargas describes San Cristóbal Pueblo as three leagues (eight miles) from San Juan Pueblo and San Lázaro as one league (2.6 miles) beyond San Cristóbal.[134] However, his later discussion infers that it was San Lázaro Pueblo that was closer to San Juan and that San Cristóbal was farther up the Santa Cruz Valley. The San Lázaro people built their pueblo near an old site (LA 269) where Vargas later founded the Spanish settlement of La Villa Nueva de Santa Cruz, and the San Cristóbal Pueblo in the Santa Cruz Valley was established on the site of Tswari (LA 36) some 3.5 miles upstream.[135]

The San Lázaro and San Cristóbal people finally returned to their pueblos in the Santa Cruz Valley some nine months later, in September 1694, but apparently some of them had temporarily returned from their refuge earlier in order to plant and tend their fields, as Vargas notes when travelling through this area in July.[136] In October a priest was installed in San Lázaro to serve both pueblos.[137] This seemingly peaceful state of affairs did not last long because Vargas was under pressure to find lands on which to settle Spanish colonists, especially lands that had been cleared and prepared for crops. Because the Tanos were occupying lands that had been worked by Spaniards until they had been forced out in 1680, Vargas felt justified in displacing them.[138] He announced his plans in March 1695, offering to the people of San Lázaro the lands of the abandoned Tewa pueblo of Yunque, called San Gabriel by the Spaniards, with the proviso that they live in one of the roomblocks of San Juan Pueblo, an arrangement that he saw as equable because the former were few in number and the latter had much land.[139] When they objected to this removal, he agreed that they might join their fellow Tanos at San Cristóbal Pueblo.[140] To the people of San Cristóbal he offered lands in the vicinity of Chimayó at the head of the Santa Cruz Valley, stating that they had one month to establish a new settlement there and prepare the land for cultivation.[141]

A major objection the Tanos had to this latter arrangement was the lack of time to carry it out. Because it was already mid-March, they claimed it would be too late to plant by the time they cleared the land and dug the irrigation ditches. Consequently, they requested permission to remain at San Cristóbal Pueblo until they harvested their crops in October.[142] Although Vargas was anxious to settle the new colonists, who apparently were not experienced farmers, he recognized the need for successful harvests to ease the chronic food shortage that affected all and in the end agreed to this arrangement, specifying that during the summer they must build a new pueblo on their Chimayó lands.[143] The San Lázaro people were evicted from their pueblo in April, following which Vargas installed the sixty Spanish families who had arrived the previous June and declared it to be La Villa Nueva de Santa Cruz.[144] He wanted San Cristóbal Pueblo for the forty-four colonist families who subsequently arrived in May.[145]

It does not appear that the Tanos ever moved to Chimayó or even attempted to build a pueblo there.[146] When Vargas visited San Cristóbal Pueblo the following March (1696) they were still there, and he ordered them to go to Galisteo Pueblo, presumably because they had not built a pueblo at Chimayó and he still needed their pueblo for his colonists.[147] The Tanos complained to their priest that Vargas was doing them harm first by evicting them from their pueblos and sending them to open land at Chimayó and then by ordering them to return to the Galisteo Basin where conditions were also hostile.[148] According to this priest the Tanos had moved their food stores and weapons to a refuge in the nearby mountains. Toward the end of March the custodian of the missionaries reported to Vargas that the priest had taken refuge in La Villa Nueva and refused to carry out his duties at San Cristóbal Pueblo without an armed guard, and that most of the inhabitants had retreated to the sierra.[149] When the alcalde of the villa confirmed this situation, Vargas again went to the Tanos to try to convince them to return.[150] They appeared to acquiesce but in fact continued in a state of rebellion and were among the instigators of the uprising that took place in June.[151] By the end of that month they were still in the Sierra de Chimayó.[152] During July some were reported at Embudo, located near the junction of Embudo Creek and the Rio Grande where the latter flows through a narrow steep-sided canyon.[153] Others were seen crossing the Rio Grande, headed into the mountains west of Santa Clara Pueblo.[154] This latter group was probably the one reported to be with the Navajos.[155]

As the uprising continued, the Tanos became even more dispersed. While some remained in the mountains north of Santa Cruz Valley, collaborating with those Tewans and Northern Tiwans of Taos and Picuris pueblos who were attempting to force Pecos to join them, others made their way west to Acoma and the Zuni and Hopi pueblos.[156] The Tanos were among the last holdouts. Those east of the Rio Grande preferred to live among Plains Apaches rather than endure life under Spanish rule. In late October they joined some Tewans and the people of Picuris Pueblo in a march to the eastern plains.[157] Vargas caught up with them in the Mora Valley and broke up the flight, capturing many while numerous others got away.[158] In November when most groups were beginning to return to their pueblos, the Tanos were still absent, but apparently they were expected because a request for clergy to man the New Mexico missions mentions need for a priest at La Villa Nueva and its Tano visita of San Cristóbal.[159] It is not likely, however, that the Tanos returned to the Santa Cruz Valley.[160] Early the next year Vargas moved the remnant population of San Cristóbal and San Lázaro Tanos still in the area to the old Galisteo Pueblo.[161] This settlement did not persist, and by 1700–01 the residents had migrated to First Mesa in Hopi country, where they established a pueblo known at present as Hano or Tewa Village.[162] Another attempt was made in 1706 to repopulate Galisteo Pueblo with the Tanos who were still dispersed among various settlements in the Rio Grande Valley. According to the Álvarez report of that year these Tanos were about to go to settle Galisteo.[163] Among them were eighteen families that had been living with the Tewa of Tesuque Pueblo.[164]

Occupation of Galisteo Pueblo continued for most of the rest of the eighteenth century. It is listed in all of the ecclesiastic censuses up to 1790, some of which mention the Comanche menace that the pueblo was subject to because of its frontier location. Bishop Pedro Tamarón y Romeral describes Galisteo in 1760 as a walled and gated pueblo and mentions that war with the Comanches kept it in a bad way.[165] Fray Francisco Atanasio Domínguez mentions its fortified tower in 1776.[166] He also writes that the Galisteans' wretched condition was related to drought conditions as well as to Comanche raids.[167] The 1780–81 smallpox epidemic undoubtedly took its toll and added to their inability to maintain themselves.[168] Galisteo Pueblo is last listed in the 1782 document of Fray Juan Agustín de Morfi and missing from the Revilla Gigedo census of 1790.[169] In February 1792 it is mentioned as extinct, its people then living with the Keres in Santo Domingo Pueblo.[170] That move put an end to the Tanos as a distinct people with their own lands and pueblo and left the Galisteo Basin without Pueblo settlements.

Upper Pecos River

Pecos had long been considered one of the largest and most powerful pueblos in the Rio Grande Pueblo Region, occupying a strategic position on the eastern frontier not far from a major pass leading to the Rio Grande. Pecos participated in the 1680 revolt, but even then there was a pro-Spanish faction that had given early, but unheeded, warning of impending rebellion.[171] When the Spaniards returned in 1692 under Governor Vargas, factionalism among the Pecos showed itself again. The people demonstrated their hostility by deserting their pueblo and refusing to meet with him, unlike most of the other pueblos, which gave nominal, if feigned, allegiance.[172] Vargas learned during the five days he stayed at Pecos Pueblo that its governor and elders would have come down to the pueblo but were prevented by the younger men, who were adamant in their opposition to the Spaniards. By the time Vargas returned to Pecos three weeks later on October 17, the governor and his supporters had apparently gained the upper hand and Vargas received a friendly reception, partly owing to his not having harmed the pueblo in retaliation for the hostile reception of his previous visit.[173] When he returned in the fall of 1693, the Pecos leaders were not only friendly but offered him their support, despite efforts by the Jemez to persuade them otherwise.[174] They were invaluable in supplying information, provisions, and military support.[175] One hundred forty Pecos warriors helped the Spaniards retake Santa Fe, and others participated in the defeat of the Tewans' stronghold on San Ildefonso Mesa.[176]

The decision to ally themselves with the Spaniards probably rested with the judgment of the Pecos governor and elders that the Spaniards would prevail and that they could use protection from their Tewa, Tano, and Apache enemies as well as obtain better conditions for trade with their Apache friends.[177] Although it was still a relatively large pueblo, Pecos, like all of the Rio Grande pueblos, had lost population during the eighty years of Spanish colonial rule. It was reduced by more than half by 1694, making defense more difficult in such an isolated location.[178] Vargas estimates their number at 1,500 in 1692, compared with 736 reported by the head missionary in 1694, but gives a figure of 800 to 900 in mid-1696.[179] Nevertheless, Pecos was considered by the rebel pueblos to be an important force that could help defeat the Spaniards. When the second uprising began in June 1696, the Jemez again sent an emissary to Pecos, hoping to take advantage of the factionalism there to bring it over to their side.[180] They were no more successful than the force of Taos, Picuris, and Tano warriors that later marched against Pecos in an attempt to help the rebel faction there take over.[181] The governor of Pecos remained a staunch ally of Vargas, and when he heard of the uprising he brought one hundred warriors to Santa Fe to help.[182] In the following months they participated in battles against Cochitis, Tanos, various Tewa groups, and the Picuris and Taos peoples, helping Vargas defeat the rebels.[183]

Given its prominent position and alliance with the Spaniards, it is surprising that Pecos was not one of the pueblos that have survived up to the present. A number of factors conspired against it. Factionalism continued to plague Pecos, its members further embittered by incidents that took place during the reconquest period.[184] One group was so alienated that it requested permission in 1700 to relocate to the then deserted Tewa pueblo of Pojoaque, a request denied by Governor Pedro Rodríguez Cubero, who had succeeded Vargas.[185] Their once favorable location on a major route connecting the Rio Grande with the eastern plains became a disadvantage during much of the eighteenth century with the displacement of the Apaches by the more warlike Comanches, who made Pecos one of their prime targets.[186] This situation adversely affected Pecos's position as a trade center and, by the end of the century, as more commerce was handled by Spaniards through their settlement on the Pecos River at San Miguel del Vado, the importance of Pecos Pueblo declined even further.[187]

The Comanches' frequent attacks not only disrupted the trade on which the pueblo depended but cost lives. The population, which had been declining during the seventeenth century, continued to drop during the eighteenth century, with some dozen epidemics, especially the smallpox epidemic of 1780–81, contributing to the decline.[188] Pecos was not only diminished in numbers and commerce but also in land. The peace treaty with the Comanches was still holding at the beginning of the nineteenth century, making it feasible to settle land in the vicinity of Pecos. Settlers began petitioning for this land, and at the same time Pecos land was for the first time confined to the "pueblo league," the amount of land encompassed within the boundaries set by measuring one league (2.6 miles) in each of the four cardinal directions (17,350 acres).[189] In 1825 under the Mexican regime even these lands were opened to settlement. With conditions worsening, some Pecos families moved away from the pueblo, finding employment mainly in the new Hispanic settlements nearby.[190] In 1838 the remaining seventeen residents moved to Jemez Pueblo, home of the only other Towa speakers.[191] The loss of Pecos in 1838 reduced the territory of the Rio Grande Pueblo Region and the number of Pueblo settlements to what it is today—eighteen.

Española Basin

In 1680 the eight Tewa pueblos were the largest grouping in the Rio Grande Pueblo Region and one of the strongest forces that defeated the Spaniards. These pueblos were Tesuque, Cuyamungue, Nambe, Pojoaque, Jacona, San Ildefonso, Santa Clara, and San Juan. Tewans were among the four hundred warriors entrenched at the refuge-pueblo on Horn Mesa that Governor Otermín encountered when he returned the following year and that contributed to his decision to retreat to El Paso without further attempting to retake the region.[192] Despite their opposition to Spanish rule, the Tewans met Vargas's attempt to gain their allegiance in 1692 with a façade of compliance. He visited each pueblo in late September and early October and elicited pledges of loyalty.[193] That these pledges were false is seen in their joining in the fight to prevent Vargas from retaking Santa Fe in 1693. Among those involved in this battle were some Tewans who were living with the Tanos in the walled section of the villa.[194] After Vargas's success in Santa Fe at the end of December, it was reported to him that the closest Tewa pueblos—Tesuque, Nambe, Jacona, and Pojoaque—were deserted, their residents having taken shelter near Nambe Falls where they were trying to decide whether to return to their pueblos or go elsewhere.[195] Vargas found the other Tewa pueblos also deserted during his reconnaissance of the area early in January 1694. At that time all of the Tewans except those of San Juan Pueblo had taken refuge on San Ildefonso Mesa.[196] The latter were reported on a summit near their pueblo, where they were joined by at least some of the people from Tesuque and Nambe pueblos as well as by the San Lázaro and San Cristóbal Tanos.[197] When they learned that their location had been reported to Vargas, they moved north to Embudo.[198]

After a number of unsuccessful attempts to persuade the Tewans on San Ildefonso

Mesa to return to their pueblos, Vargas attacked them in early March. With the aid of Pueblo allies he reached the top of the mesa but was unable to secure a peace.[199] Another attack in May also failed.[200] He kept up the pressure on them by removing stored provisions from their pueblos and trying to prevent their descent to the Rio Grande to obtain water.[201] It was not until September that a siege of the mesa was successful, following which the Tewans at Embudo also sued for peace.[202] By mid-September they were returning to their pueblos, and in early October Vargas toured the area installing priests and Pueblo officials.[203]

The Tewans, like the other Pueblo groups, made peace only reluctantly. After nearly a year of disruption, they needed to tend their fields and obtain proper shelter for the coming winter (1694–95). They remained in their pueblos through the following winter as well, but by the spring of 1696 their priests, like those elsewhere in the Rio Grande Pueblo Region, were reporting unrest.[204] However, at Tesuque, the Tewa pueblo closest to Santa Fe, a decision was made to join the Spaniards. The governor, Domingo Tuguaque, sent a letter to Vargas on June 4 warning him that an uprising had begun.[205] Three days later Vargas visited the pueblo, acknowledged the people's loyalty, and invited them to be his allies.[206] From then on they actively aided Vargas in his campaigns against the Keres of Cochiti, fellow Tewans, and the Northern Tiwans (Picuris and Taos).[207] On June 17 Vargas was informed by Domingo that leaders at Santa Clara and San Ildefonso planned to attack Tesuque, but they were foiled by Vargas.[208]

The people of the other seven Tewa pueblos again fled after killing eleven Spaniards and two priests at Nambe and San Ildefonso.[209] During this phase of the reconquest, the Tewans became even more scattered. The four pueblos in the Tesuque-Nambe drainage—Nambe, Cuyamungue, Pojoaque, and Jacona—joined the Tanos in the mountains north of Chimayó.[210] Vargas went after them, but because they were widely scattered over rough terrain, it was difficult to find them.[211] Many of them fled again. A prisoner from Cuyamungue testified that the people of Jacona left to join the Navajos; those from Nambe remained in the Sierra de Chimayó, except a few who went to Taos, which was where the Cuyamungue people also went.[212] He said most of the Pojoaque residents left but did not give their destination. Possibly they, too, sought refuge at Taos.

Meanwhile the San Ildefonso people were reported in the mountains west of their pueblo, but some were also listed with other Tewans and the Tanos in the Sierra de Chimayó.[213] The Santa Clarans were also in the mountains west of their pueblo, where

Vargas hunted down their campsites, causing the survivors to flee farther west.[214] A month later, in August, some of them were reported with the Navajos and others with the Hopis.[215] The Navajos mentioned could have been the band living in the area called Los Pedernales, possibly the one to which the people of Jacona had also retreated.[216] Los Pedernales is described as above or west of the Chama River beyond Abiquiu, probably in the vicinity of Cerro Pedernal.[217] Because Vargas continued to attack the rebels, the Santa Clarans and possibly the Jacona people decided to leave this area and in October were reported moving with their livestock eastward past Embudo on their way to join the Tanos and Picuris in their flight to the eastern plains.[218] The San Juan Tewans retreated to their refuge at Embudo with their governor, although some of them followed a rebel leader farther north to Taos.[219]

By November Vargas's relentless attacks on the rebels and the prospect of another winter without adequate food or shelter must have convinced most Tewa groups to return to their pueblos. At the end of the month Vargas announced that only the people of Santa Clara, Cuyamungue, and Pojoaque still had not been "reduced."[220] After he finally prevailed in his campaign against Taos in early October, the Tewans who had taken refuge there were again dispersed, including the people of Cuyamungue, possibly those of Pojoaque, and the San Juan rebel faction. Many or all of these people joined the Tanos, the Picuris, and the Santa Clara refugees from Los Pedernales (who might have included the people of Jacona) in their march to the eastern plains—to El Cuartelejo, established by Taos people when they fled to join the Apaches along the Arkansas River on the Colorado-Kansas border earlier in the century.[221] Vargas's disruption of this expedition caused further dispersal, from which it became more difficult to recover. The Santa Clarans were said to be scattered among the Navajos in the Sierra de los Pedernales and the Apaches of Embudo, as well as farther away at Acoma and the Zuni and Hopi pueblos.[222] But gradually they, as well as the other Tewans, reestablished their pueblos. Some Santa Clarans were among the refugees brought back from El Cuartelejo in 1706.[223]

The Álvarez report of 1706 accounts for all the Tewa pueblos except Jacona, Cuyamungue, and Pojoaque.[224] The Jacona people are reported returning to their pueblo in November 1696, but when Vargas visited the pueblo he found only twenty-nine individuals, and it might have been the small size of the population that led them to move or be moved to nearby pueblos.[225] The same situation might have prevailed among the people of Cuyamungue, many of whom are reported by Vargas to be living in Tesuque Pueblo.[226] These two pueblos were never reestablished and their lands were subsequently taken up by Spanish settlers. As early as 1699 Cuyamungue became the property of Alonso Aguilar, and in 1702 Jacona was granted to Ignacio de Roybal.[227] Pojoaque was resettled in 1707 with Tewa families that had been dispersed, probably including not only its old residents who survived but others from neighboring Jacona and Cuyamungue.[228] The remaining six Tewa pueblos have survived to the present and form the largest grouping of the eighteen extant Rio Grande pueblos. Pojoaque was considered abandoned from about 1912 to 1934 as its population dwindled and intermarriage with non-Puebloans increased. It has since been revived, although its still small population no longer occupies a typical pueblo and is considered to be the least culturally intact of the present Pueblo peoples.[229]

The Far North

The people of the two Northern Tiwa pueblos, Taos and Picuris, were among the most active in planning the 1680 revolt, and when it began killed their priests and the Spaniards in the area.[230] They also joined in the attack that drove the Spaniards from Santa Fe.[231] The return of Governor Otermín the following year did not affect them because his forces only reached as far north as the Keres pueblos in the Santo Domingo Basin. Vargas, however, did reach the Northern Tiwa pueblos.[232] In October 1692 the residents of Picuris greeted him peaceably and asked him to subdue the people of Taos, who, they said, repeatedly attacked them.[233] He and his men approached Taos the next day prepared for hostilities but found the pueblo deserted.[234] The people had retreated to a canyon in the nearby mountains, and it took Vargas the better part of two days to persuade them to return to their pueblo.[235] When Vargas next met the Northern Tiwa, he encountered much greater hostility. After he retook Santa Fe at the end of 1693, he visited the various pueblos to enlist their allegiance. When he arrived in Northern Tiwa country the following July, he found both pueblos deserted.[236] The people of Taos had retreated to their refuge in the mountains, and this time Vargas could not persuade them to return. When that became evident, he ordered his troops to remove the stores of maize from the pueblo.[237] During this activity, which went on for two days, the Taos people did not relent. Only after Vargas left the area did they and the Picuris, who had not been looted, move back to their pueblos, where they remained until the June 1696 rebellion in which they played an active role.[238] They did not kill their priests because the latter, observing growing hostility, had sought safety in Santa Fe several months earlier.[239] Taos and Picuris rebels, along with some Tano warriors, marched on Pecos to prevail upon its people to turn against the Spaniards but were unsuccessful.[240] Taos, about seventy miles north of Santa Fe, became an important refuge for many Tano and Tewa people.[241]

In late September Vargas launched a campaign against the Northern Tiwa. He found Picuris vacated, its people dispersed in the mountains; and he went on to Taos.[242] When Vargas reached Taos its inhabitants were at their canyon refuge, where the main body of people occupied a ranchería and the men were stationed above on the ramparts of the steep-sided canyon.[243] He laid siege to them for almost two weeks before they began returning to their pueblo.[244] Vargas mainly succeeded by looting maize, clothing, and hides from the ranchería and from other hidden caches in the area. He was also helped by a split between those people who wanted peace, including the governor, and those who wanted to continue fighting.[245] The Picuris were also divided, but most followed their governor, who was a determined rebel.[246] After Vargas's victory at Taos in early October, the Picuris, some of whom fought the Spaniards there, did not return to their pueblo, although their governor promised to do so.[247] Instead, they travelled east with the Tanos and some Tewans to join Apaches on the plains.[248] Although Vargas caught up with them, many were able to escape because they were warned by some Apaches that he was about to attack their camp.[249] These escapees, including most of the Picuris, made their way to the Apaches in the El Cuartelejo area. According to Vargas's report of late November, only eight families had returned to Picuris Pueblo.[250] It was not until 1706 that the remainder was brought back from El Cuartelejo.[251] Since then both Taos and Picuris have remained occupied.

Part Three Summary

The 1680 revolt provided the Pueblo peoples a twelve-year respite from Spanish rule but in the end caused a further setback in terms of the number of people, settlements, and territory lost. The population declined by about 40 percent between 1680 and 1706. It took about a decade after the 1696 uprising was put down for the majority of surviving Puebloans to reoccupy their pueblos, although some refugees were still returning in succeeding decades and others never returned. Twelve of thirty-one pueblos were never repopulated. The abandonment of twelve pueblos does not take into account the situation of the Jemez people, who probably inhabited more than one pueblo in 1680 and who had apparently formed two separate communities—San Diego Jemez and San Juan Jemez—by the time Governor Vargas arrived in 1692. They consolidated into one pueblo, Walatowa, at the end of the reconquest. Tewa pueblos were reduced from eight to six although two—Cuyamungue and Jacona—might have been resettled if Spaniards had not taken over their lands in 1699 and 1702 respectively. Keres pueblos were reduced from seven to five with the loss of San Marcos and La Cieneguilla, but a new pueblo was gained with the establishment of La Laguna about 1697. With the abandonment of San Cristóbal and San Lázaro, the Tanos lost their claim to the Santa Cruz Valley but repopulated their old pueblo, Galisteo, in the Galisteo Basin. Two Southern Tiwa pueblos—Sandia and Isleta—were eventually reestablished in the Albuquerque-Belen Basin, but Alameda and Puaray were not. In the Socorro Basin all four Piro pueblos, Sevilleta, Alamillo, Socorro, and Senecu, were abandoned earlier, in 1680–81. Some of their occupants as well as some Southern Tiwans were taken by the retreating Spaniards to the El Paso area, where they established three pueblos that eventually became substantially "mexicanized." Except for the reestablishment of Isleta about 1720 and Sandia in 1748, the extensive lands along some 125 miles of the Rio Grande between San Marcial and the Jemez River junction were lost. The Galisteo Basin was also lost after 1782, when Galisteo Pueblo was abandoned. Pecos, formerly the eastern stronghold of the Pueblo domain, was not abandoned until 1838, but long before, the territory of the Rio Grande Pueblo Region had shrunk to less than half of its pre-Spanish extent. Today, Pueblo peoples occupy eighteen settlements in this diminished territory.

The Puebloans' opposition to Spanish rule and their determination to maintain their own way of life can be seen in the extraordinary feat of their successful 1680 revolt, their continued opposition over more than three years (including a second but unsuccessful uprising in 1696) to Vargas's many military campaigns, the prolonged period of resettlement, and the decision of many to remain in exile.

CONCLUSION

The settlement geography of the Rio Grande Pueblos had undergone a long history of change prior to the coming of the Spaniards in the sixteenth century, changes that grew out of the dynamics of the various Pueblo societies and their relation to each other and to their natural environment. The sixteenth century saw the appearance of an alien people whose exploratory expeditions led, in the seventeenth century, to colonization of this region, so remote from Spain's main arena of conquest in central Mexico but attractive because of its settled agricultural population. Colonization initiated an era of subjugation and diminishment of a Pueblo society that up to then had still been undergoing growth and development. This decline might have begun earlier during the prolonged period of exploration if European diseases had been introduced then, but as yet there is no direct evidence of such disease events that would have caused substantial reduction in a population with no immunity to them. Whether or not such events occurred, analysis of historical documents and reports of archeological investigations supply evidence that the number of pueblos and their distribution did not undergo any marked change during the contact period. With colonization, however, a series of drastic changes did occur.

Colonization brought exploitation of the Pueblo economy in terms of diversion of goods, appropriation of labor, alienation of land, and disruption of trade—all of which led to increasing impoverishment that was exacerbated by periods of drought and famine and by attacks from surrounding Apache tribes that were intensified by their early acquisition of the Spaniards' horse. Epidemics of European diseases also played a role. Although it is uncertain when the first epidemics took place in the Rio Grande Pueblo Region, a major event that involved smallpox and possibly other contagious diseases was reported to have occurred during the years from 1636 to 1640. It was probably a key factor in the greatest loss of population and settlements suffered by Pueblo peoples in historic times. Fifty of some eighty-one pueblos were abandoned between 1600 and 1680 (62 percent), and forty-four of these were lost between 1600 and 1640 (88 percent of the total loss). The remaining six pueblos in the Estancia Basin were abandoned in the 1670s, leaving that subregion, in addition to most of the Socorro and Albuquerque-Belen Basins, without Pueblo settlement. The majority of settlements in the Rio Grande Pueblo Region shifted to that part north of the Rio Grande–Jemez River confluence where the center of Pueblo settlement has remained ever since. Population declined 75 percent, from about sixty thousand in 1600 to an estimated fifteen thousand in 1680.

It was perhaps the realization of the extent of their losses as much as the ongoing religious and economic persecution that finally galvanized the various Pueblo peoples into achieving a unity of purpose and action they had not previously known, one that was sufficient to expel the Spaniards from the region. The successful revolt in 1680, a rare occurrence in the Americas, is all the more remarkable in view of the Puebloans' greatly diminished state. However, they paid a heavy price for their dozen or so years of freedom before they were again subjugated with further losses of people, settlements, and territory. In the aftermath of reconquest only twenty pueblos were resettled. By the early nineteenth century two of these were abandoned, leaving the Galisteo Basin and upper Pecos River subregions also bereft of Pueblo settlement and the eighteen remaining pueblos with a population of some seven thousand. Compared with a population of perhaps eighty to one hundred thousand living in some one hundred settlements when the first Spaniards arrived in 1540, the extent of the catastrophe that befell the Pueblo peoples is manifest.

NOTES

PART ONE

Introduction 1.   The pueblos mentioned by the explorers are shown on map 1, where they are correlated with known archeological sites. These correlations have been made with varying degrees of certainty because neither the information provided by the explorers nor the dating of the sites is precise enough to make unqualified identifications in all cases. Although there is information about Pueblo settlements in all of the sixteenth-century Spanish chronicles of New Mexico, these accounts cannot be coordinated to give an entirely clear idea of pueblo numbers and location for a number of reasons: The expeditions did not cover exactly the same parts of the region; they probably did not encounter the same occupied pueblos in all cases because some were abandoned and others reoccupied during the period; chroniclers did not report settlement location in an unambiguous manner and gave different names or no names to the pueblos; and they undoubtedly varied in their understanding of what they were told by local people.

Archeological identification of pueblo sites that were occupied during the 1540–98 contact period is also burdened with many problems (Linda S. Cordell and George J Gumerman, eds, "Northern and Central Rio Grande," in *Dynamics of Southwest Prehistory* [Washington, D.C.: Smithsonian Institution Press, 1989], 295). In nearly all cases the dating of sites is based on the presence of certain ceramic types, the chronology of which is derived from such measures as tree-ring analysis from a few sites (David A. Breternitz, *An Appraisal of Tree-Ring Dated Pottery, in the Southwest*, vol. 10 of Anthropological Papers of the University of Arizona [Tucson: University of Arizona, 1966], 105–7). Although there are questions about the region-wide applicability of these dates and the adequacy of surface collections (few sites have actually been excavated), it is the long duration of ceramic-type periods that creates the greatest problem for part I of this study, which has a timeframe of only fifty-eight years (Linda S. Cordell, *Prehistory of the Southwest* [Orlando, Fla.: Academic Press, Inc., 1984], 90–91). The diagnostic ceramic type for this period should be Glaze E—one of a series of glazed ceramic types that began with the introduction of Glaze A (1300–1475) and ended with Glaze F (1650–1700). See A. Helene Warren, "Glaze Paint Wares of the Upper Middle Rio Grande," in vol. 4 of *Archeological Investigations in Cochiti Reservoir, New Mexico*, ed. by Jan V. Biella and Richard C. Chapman (Albuquerque: Office of Contract Archeology, University of New Mexico, 1979), 193. Glaze E has been assigned dates between 1515 and 1650, making it possible that a site with this pottery could have been abandoned before 1540 or built after 1598. Evidence from some sites indicates that one type of Glaze F pottery might have been made as early as 1550, making it a possible indicator of pueblo occupation in the contact period (Amy C. Earls, *The Organization of Piro Pueblo Subsistence, A.D. 1300–1680*, PhD. dissertation [Albuquerque: University of New Mexico, 1985], 30; William M. Sundt, "Pottery of Central New Mexico and Its Role as a Key to Both Time and Space," in *Secrets of a City: Papers on Albuquerque Area Archeology in Honor of Richard A. Bice*, ed. by Anne V. Poore and John L. Montgomery, Papers of the Archaeological Society of New Mexico 13 [Santa Fe, N.Mex.: Ancient City Press, 1987], table 2). In the same way Glaze D may be an indicator because in some areas it continued to be made after 1515, possibly even into the seventeenth century (Sundt, ibid., table 2). Another indicator ceramic type for northern pueblos is Sankawi Black on Cream (1550–1650) (Sundt, "Pottery of Central New Mexico," table 2).

There is a further problem that bears on the identification of pueblo sites. Over time they have been subject to forces of destruction, natural and/or human. The Middle and Southern Rio Grande subregions, in particular, have been affected by intense, long-term agricultural and urban development as well as periodic flooding and river channel shifting. Any of these factors could have obliterated a site or so modified an existing one that accurate dating is not possible.

2. For discussion of this map see Carl I. Wheat, *Mapping the Transmississippi West, 1540–1861* vol. 1 (San Francisco: Institute of Historical Cartography, 1957), 29–33 and George P. Hammond and Agapito Rey, eds. and trans., *The Rediscovery of New Mexico, 1580–1594* Coronado Cuarto Centennial Publications III (Albuquerque: University of New Mexico Press, 1966), 63. Map 2 is a redrawn version of Enrico Martínez's map, commissioned by the University of New Mexico Press and published in the endpapers of *The Rediscovery.* The University has granted the author permission to use this map. Names on this map have been corrected according to the errata published in *The Rediscovery.*

3. Fred Wendorf and Erik K. Reed, "An Alternative Reconstruction of Northern Rio Grande Prehistory," *El Palacio* 62 (1955): 149, 153; Cordell, "Northern and Central Rio Grande," 319–24.

4. Glaze-type ceramics are diagnostic of pueblos occupied during the Classic Period and mainly Glaze-type E was produced during the contact period. Ceramic data for each pueblo are available in the ARMS data base.

Chapter One

1. All distances are based on straight-line measurements taken from 1:250,000 maps prepared by the U.S. Defense Mapping Agency Topographic Center. These measurements are rounded and should be considered approximate, as were the distances mentioned by the Spanish explorers, who gave them in leagues. The standard league measured 2.6 miles and the long league about 4.0 miles. The league used by Luxán of the Espejo expedition quite consistently measured about 3.0 miles. Castaño de Sosa is only consistent in that his league measured either 2.6 or 4.0 miles and not some other value. Oñate used the long league of 4.0 miles. For a discussion of the Spanish land league as used in North America see Roland Chardon, "The Linear League in North America," *Annals of the Association of American Geographers* 70 (1980): 147–51.

2. Jan V. Biella, "Changing Residential Patterns among the Anasazi, A.D. 725–1525" in vol. 4 of *Archeological Investigations in Cochiti Reservoir, New Mexico,* ed. by Jan V. Biella and Richard C. Chapman (Albuquerque: Office of Contract Archeology, University of New Mexico, 1979), 122, 123–25, 128, 132–33, 137; Rosalind Hunter-Anderson, "Explaining Residential Aggregation in the Northern Rio Grande: A Competitive Reduction Model," in volume 4 of *Archeological Investigations in Cochiti Reservoir, New Mexico,* ed. by Jan V. Biella and Richard C. Chapman (Albuquerque: Office of Contract Archeology, University of New Mexico, 1979), 172; Mark T. Lycett, *Archeological Implications of European Contact: Demography, Settlement, and Land Use in the Middle Rio Grande Valley, New Mexico,* Ph.D. dissertation (Albuquerque: University of New Mexico, 1996), 356, 398–99, 407–8; Michael L. Elliott, ed., *Archeological Investigations at Small Sites in the Jemez Mountains, New Mexico,* Cultural Resources Document 6 (Santa Fe, N.Mex.: Santa Fe National Forest, U.S. Department of Agriculture, 1988), 43, 45; Dietrich Fliedner, "Pre-Spanish Pueblos in New Mexico," *Annals of the Association of American Geographers* 65 (1975): 365–69; Kurt F. Anschuetz, *Not Waiting for the Rain: Integrated Systems of Water Management by Pre-Columbian Pueblo Farmers in North Central New Mexico,* Ph.D. dissertation (Ann Arbor: University of Michigan, 1998), 416–19; Robert W. Preucel, Jr., *Seasonal Circulation and Dual Residence in the Pueblo Southwest: A Prehistoric Example from the Pajarito Plateau, New Mexico* (New York: Garland Publishing, Inc., 1990), 177–79.

3. Biella, "Changing Residential Patterns," 124, 125, 128.

4. George P. Winship, ed., *The Coronado Expedition, 1540–1542,* Fourteenth Annual Report of the U.S. Bureau of American Ethnology for the Years 1892–1893 (Washington, D.C.: Smithsonian Institution, 1896), 454, 525; George P. Hammond and Agapito Rey, eds. and trans., *Narratives of the Coronado Expedition, 1540–1542,* Coronado Cuarto Centennial Publications II (Albuquerque: University of New Mexico Press, 1940), 259.

5. Hammond and Rey, *The Rediscovery,* 172.

6. Ibid., 164.

7. Ibid., 181–82.

8. George P. Hammond and Agapito Rey, eds. and trans., *Obregón's History of Sixteenth Century Explorations in Western America Entitled: Chronicle, Commentary, or Relation of the Ancient and Modern Discoveries in New Spain and New Mexico, 1584* (Los Angeles: Wetzel Publishing Company, Inc., 1928), 325.

9. Winship, *The Coronado Expedition,* 525; Hammond and Rey, *Narratives,* 259.

10. Winship, *The Coronado Expedition,* 519; Hammond and Rey, *Narratives,* 253.

11. Hammond and Rey, *The Rediscovery,* 102–8.

12. His chronicler, Diego Pérez de Luxán, mentions that they found seven thousand to eight thousand Indians who had fled to the *sierra* from the thirteen pueblos of Coronado's Tiguex province in the northern Albuquerque-Belen Basin, but these were undoubtedly only part of that population. He also reports that Pecos had two thousand warriors (Hammond and Rey, *The Rediscovery,* 177, 206).

13. Ibid., 219, 222–24, 228, 229, 340–41. Obregón claims to have interviewed returned members of the Coronado, Chamuscado, and Espejo expeditions (Hammond and Rey, *Obregón's History*). Some of his data on numbers of pueblos and people support what is found in the documents of these expeditions, but some seem exaggerated or otherwise not useful and, in general, are not cited in this work.

14. George P. Hammond and Agapito Rey, eds. and trans., *Don Juan de Oñate: Colonizer of New Mexico, 1595–1628,* Coronado Cuarto Centennial Publications V and VI (Albuquerque: University of New Mexico Press, 1953), 483, 619.

15. Ibid., 625.

16. Ibid., 851, 863.

17. Ibid., 702, 706, 708, 711, 720, 724, 727, 733, 736.

18. Ibid., 633, 644, 659, 695, 838, 1012, 1095.

19. See part II for further discussion of the impact of epidemics.

20. Winship, *The Coronado Expedition,* 567, 569; Hammond and Rey, *Narratives,* 309.

21. Hammond and Rey, *The Rediscovery,* 84, 103–7.

22. Ibid., 221.

23. Ibid., 129, 130.

24. Winship, *The Coronado Expedition,* 566, 569; Hammond and Rey, *Narratives,* 309.

25. Hammond and Rey, *Don Juan,* 625, 633, 644, 851.

26. Winship, *The Coronado Expedition,* 446–47, 512; Hammond and Rey, *Narratives,* 246.

27. Winship, *The Coronado Expedition,* 445, 511, 575, 595; Hammond and Rey, *Narratives,* 244, 288–89.

28. Winship, *The Coronado Expedition,* 452, 523, 567, 570, 575, 587; Hammond and Rey, *Narratives,* 256–57, 289, 310. The figure of fifty houses is probably a mistake for five hundred houses in the *Relación Postrera de Cíbola,* in Winship, *The Coronado Expedition,* 567, 570; Hammond and Rey, *Narratives,* 310.

29. Hammond and Rey, *The Rediscovery,* 105, 130, 206.

30. Ibid., 277–78.

31. Hammond and Rey, *Don Juan*, 321.

32. Winship, *The Coronado Expedition*, 439, 503, 587; Hammond and Rey, *Narratives*, 233, 300.

33. Hammond and Rey, *The Rediscovery*, 105, 180, 223.

34. Winship, *The Coronado Expedition*, 430, 491, 560, 569, 575, 587, 594; Hammond and Rey, *Narratives*, 173, 182, 218, 288, 299, 309.

35. Hammond and Rey, *The Rediscovery*, 107, 120, 224.

36. Hammond and Rey, *Don Juan*, 394, 485.

37. Ibid., 614–15; Juan de Montoya, *New Mexico in 1602, Juan de Montoya's Relation of the Discovery of New Mexico*, eds. and trans. George P. Hammond and Agapito Rey, eds. and trans., Quivira Society Publications VIII (Albuquerque: University of New Mexico Press, 1938), 47–48.

38. Hammond and Rey, *The Rediscovery*, 105.

39. Ibid., 107; Hammond and Rey, *Don Juan*, 322.

40. Hammond and Rey, *The Rediscovery*, 105–6.

41. Ibid., 106.

42. Ibid., 206.

43. Ibid., 107.

44. Hammond and Rey, *Don Juan*, 393.

45. Hammond and Rey, *The Rediscovery*, 103.

46. Ibid., 173.

47. Henri D. Grissino-Mayer, "A 2129-Year Reconstruction of Precipitation for Northwestern New Mexico, USA," in *Tree Rings, Environment, and Humanity: Proceedings of the International Conference*, ed. by J. S. Dean, D. M. Meko, and T. W. Swetnam (Tucson: Radiocarbon, Dept. of Geosciences, University of Arizona, 1996), 199 fig. 4, 202; Henri D. Grissino-Mayer, Thomas W. Swetnam, and Rex K. Adams, "The Rare, Old-aged Conifers of El Malpais—Their Role in Understanding Climate Change in the American Southwest," *New Mexico Bureau of Mines & Mineral Resources Bulletin* 156 (1997): 158 fig. 8, 160; Rosanne D'Arrigo and Gordon C. Jacoby, "A Tree-ring Reconstruction of New Mexico Winter Precipitation and Its Relation to El Niño/Southern Oscillation Events," in *El Niño: Historical and Paleoclimate Aspects of the Southern Oscillation*, ed. by Henry F. Diaz and Vera Markgraf (Cambridge: Cambridge University Press, 1992), 243; Connie A. Woodhouse and Jonathon T. Overpeck, "2000 Years of Drought Variability in the Central United States," *Bulletin of the American Meteorological Society* 79 (1998): 2699, 2703; Martin R. Rose, Jeffrey S. Dean, and William J. Robinson, *The Past Climate of Arroyo Hondo, New Mexico, Reconstructed from Tree Rings*, Arroyo Hondo Archaeological Series 4 (Santa Fe, N.Mex.: School of American Research, 1981), 102–5.

48. Jean M. Grove, *The Little Ice Age* (London: Methuen, 1988), 1; H. H. Lamb, *Climatic History and the Future* (New Haven, Conn.: Princeton University Press, 1985), 461, 463.

49. For an additional discussion of climate related to historical events of the contact period see Dan Scurlock, *From the Rio to the Sierra: An Environmental History of the Middle Rio Grande Basin* (Fort Collins, Colo.: Rocky Mountain Research Station, Forest Service, U.S. Department of Agriculture, 1998), 23–24.

50. Hammond and Rey, *The Rediscovery*, 206.

51. Hammond and Rey, *Don Juan*, 696.

52. Ibid., 610, 684.

53. Ibid., 626, 634, 656, 660.

54. Hammond and Rey, *The Rediscovery*, 107, 109, 183, 185, 266, 282, 283, 288; Hammond and Rey, *Don Juan*, 394, 395, 610, 851.

55. Winship, *The Coronado Expedition*, 487, 492, 494, 497, 500, 503, 558, 566, 567, 576,

579, 586, 595; Hammond and Rey, *Narratives*, 171, 184, 213, 220, 222–23, 227, 230, 233–34, 290, 294, 298, 308, 309.

56. Hammond and Rey, *The Rediscovery*, 280, 285; Hammond and Rey, *Don Juan*, 645, 660.

57. Hammond and Rey, *Don Juan*, 626, 634, 645, 656, 660.

Chapter Two

1. Winship, *The Coronado Expedition*, 445, 511; Hammond and Rey, *Narratives*, 245.

2. Hammond and Rey, *The Rediscovery*, 102–3, 115–16.

3. Ibid., 171–74.

4. Although Gallegos and Luxán each gives evidence for nine occupied pueblos, Obregón, writing in 1584 after interviewing returned members of the Chamuscado expedition, reports twelve Piro pueblos, and Espejo himself reports ten (Hammond and Rey, *Obregón's History*, 290, 340; Hammond and Rey, *The Rediscovery*, 219). Castaño de Sosa, who led an expedition into New Mexico via the Pecos River in 1591, did not explore or report on the Piro province.

5. Wilcox equates San Felipe Pueblo with the east-side San Pascual site (LA 487) as the southernmost Piro pueblo but, in doing so, ignores Senecu and Tiffany pueblos located farther south (David R. Wilcox, "Changing Contexts of Pueblo Adaptations, A.D. 1250–1600," in *Farmers, Hunters, and Colonists: Interaction between the Southwest and the Southern Plains*, ed. by Katherine A. Spielmann [Tucson: University of Arizona Press, 1991], 135, 139–40). The site of Senecu is no longer identifiable. It is thought to have been opposite Black Mesa, also known as Mesa de Senecú, but on the west side of the river where it is shown on a map published in 1776 (Michael P. Marshall and Henry J. Walt, *Rio Abajo: Prehistory and History of a Rio Grande Province* [Santa Fe: New Mexico Historic Preservation Division, New Mexico Office of Cultural Affairs, 1984], 239). The mission was called "San Antonio de Senecú," leading to a later mistaken identification with the San Antonio site (LA 760), located some distance north near the village of San Antonio (Frederick Webb Hodge, ed., *Handbook of American Indians North of Mexico*, vol. 2, Bureau of American Ethnology Bulletin 30 [Washington, D.C.: Smithsonian Institution, 1910], 508). For other interpretations of Piro settlements see Lloyd J. Mecham, "The Second Spanish Expedition to New Mexico," *New Mexico Historical Review* 1 (1926): map, and Albert H. Schroeder, "Pueblos Abandoned in Historic Times," in *Southwest*, vol. 9 of *Handbook of North American Indians*, ed. by Alfonso Ortiz (Washington, D.C.: Smithsonian Institution, 1979), 240.

6. One league in the journal of Luxán consistently measures about three miles, slightly more than the standard 2.6 miles.

7. Hammond and Rey, *The Rediscovery*, 173, 219.

8. Ibid., 103. Wilcox, by locating San Felipe on the east side of the river, gives Gallegos's large Piña Pueblo a west-side location at the Pilabo site (Wilcox, "Changing Contexts," 134, 140). Pilabo was an important pueblo and mission in the early Spanish colonial period but, because this site lies under the modern city of Socorro, its size and state of occupancy in the 1580s are unknown (Harry P. Mera, *Population Changes in the Rio Grande Glaze Paint Area*, New Mexico Archeological Survey, Technical Series Bulletin 9 [Santa Fe: Laboratory of Anthropology, Museum of New Mexico, 1940], 8; Marshall and Walt, *Rio Abajo*, 248, 345). Pilabo was probably one of the ruined pueblos reported by Luxán in 1583, making it more likely that Piña Pueblo occupied the large Las Cañas site on the east side of the river (Hammond and Rey, *The Rediscovery*, 173).

9. The site of Alamillo Pueblo cannot be located today, but is thought to be south of

Alamillo Arroyo on the east side of the Rio Grande (Marshall and Walt, *Rio Abajo*, 254–55).

10. An alternate interpretation puts the location of El Término de Puala farther north in Tiwa territory at the Ladera del Sur site (LA 50257), too far north to account for the other pueblos that Luxán ascribed to that province (David H. Snow, "Initial Entradas and Explorations: 1540–1593," in *The North Central Regional Overview, vol. 1, Historic Overview of North Central New Mexico*, ed. by Boyd C. Pratt and David H. Snow [Santa Fe: New Mexico Historic Preservation Division, New Mexico Office of Cultural Affairs, 1988], 102, 103).

11. Hammond and Rey, *Don Juan*, 1: 314, 317–18.

12. San Pascual (LA 487) is the largest Piro site, but neither Gallegos nor Luxán considered it large when they reported the size of pueblos through which they travelled, indicating that only a small part of it was occupied in the contact period (Hammond and Rey, *The Rediscovery*, 103, 173; Marshall and Walt, *Rio Abajo*, 182).

13. In the colonial period the name "Socorro" came to be attached to the west-side pueblo of Pilabo and nearby Spanish settlement, but originally it was applied to the pueblo of Teypama, located about 3.5 miles south (Marshall and Walt, *Rio Abajo*, 248, 250).

14. Hammond and Rey, *Don Juan*, 318.

15. Ibid., 346; Snow, "Initial Entradas," 104–5.

16. Marshall and Walt, *Rio Abajo*, 252.

17. Ibid., 135.

18. Hammond and Rey, *The Rediscovery*, 82.

19. Ibid., 219.

20. ARMS site files for Magdalena (LA 284), Bear Mountain (LA 285), and Silver Creek (LA 20954); Marshall and Walt, *Rio Abajo*, 136, 140, 213–17, 341, 345.

21. Mera, *Population Changes*, 6–10; John Montgomery and Kathleen Bowman, *Archeological Reconnaissance of the Chupadera Arroyo Drainage, Central New Mexico*, Agency for Conservation Archeology Report (Portales: Eastern New Mexico University, 1989), 118; Stuart J. Baldwin, *A Tentative Occupation Sequence for Abo Pass, Central New Mexico*, Ms. on file, Laboratory of Anthropology (Santa Fe: Museum of New Mexico, 1983), 20, n7; Joseph A. Tainter and Frances Levine, *Cultural Resources Overview, Central New Mexico* (Washington, D.C.: U.S. Government Printing Office, 1987), 44; Richard C. Chapman, personal communication; Katherine A. Spielmann, "Rio Abajo and Eastern Border Pueblos," in *The Prehistoric Pueblo World, A.D. 1150–1350*, ed. by Michael A. Adler (Tucson: University of Arizona Press, 1996), 81.

22. Winship, *The Coronado Expedition*, 451, 454, 519, 525; Hammond and Rey, *Narratives*, 253–54, 259; Mera, *Population Changes*, 22.

23. ARMS site file for Quarai (LA 95).

24. Hammond and Rey, *The Rediscovery*, 106–7, 131–32.

25. Erik K. Reed, *History of Quarai* (Santa Fe, N.Mex.: National Park Service, U.S. Department of the Interior, 1940), 3; Warren, "Glaze Paint Wares," 191. According to Hayes, et al., Quarai was not occupied at this time (Alden C. Hayes, J. N. Young, and A. H. Warren, *Excavation of Mound 7, Gran Quivira National Monument*, vol. 16 of Publications in Archeology [Washington, D.C.: National Park Service, U.S. Department of the Interior, 1981], 2).

26. Hammond and Rey, *The Rediscovery*, 107, 137; Mera, *Population Changes*, 14, 16.

27. Las Humanas Pueblo is part of the site known as Gran Quivira (LA 120).

28. Hammond and Rey, *The Rediscovery*, 106.

29. Ibid., 174–76.

30. Ibid., 222; Hammond and Rey, *Obregón's History*, 322; Stuart J. Baldwin, *Preliminary*

Report on the 1982 Excavations at the Pueblo of Abo, Salinas National Monument, Ms. on file, Laboratory of Anthropology (Santa Fe: Museum of New Mexico, 1982), 12.

31. Hammond and Rey, *Don Juan*, 324, 345, 393–94; France V. Scholes and H. P. Mera, *Some Aspects of the Jumano Problem*, Contributions to American Anthropology and History 34, Carnegie Institution of Washington Publication 523 (Washington, D.C., 1940), 276–78.

32. According to Hayes, et al., the pottery at Pueblo Colorado indicates that it was abandoned by the early 1500s and that Pueblo Pardo was the third pueblo; however, Mera holds that there were four "Jumano" pueblos in the contact period, and they probably included Colorado and Pardo in addition to Las Humanas and Blanco (Hayes, Young, and Warren, *Excavation of Mound 7*, 7; Mera, *Population Changes*, 15–17; ARMS site files for Pueblo Colorado (LA 476) and Pueblo Pardo (LA 83); Scholes and Mera, *Some Aspects*, 296–97; Linda S. Cordell, "Prehistory: Eastern Anasazi," in *Southwest*, vol. 9 of *Handbook of North American Indians*, ed. by Alfonso Ortiz [Washington, D.C.: Smithsonian Institution, 1979], 146).

33. Hammond and Rey, *Don Juan*, 345, 351.

34. Even more so than in the Piro province farther south in the Socorro Basin, the disturbance of Tiwa lands in the Albuquerque-Belen Basin by intensive agricultural and urban development as well as by periodic flooding and channel shifting has made identification of pueblo sites and their temporal placement especially difficult (Curtis F. Schaafsma, "Tiguex Province Revisited," in *Secrets of a City: Papers on Albuquerque Area Archeology in Honor of Richard A. Bice*, ed. by Anne V. Poore and John L. Montgomery, Papers of the Archeological Society of New Mexico 13 [Santa Fe, N.Mex.: Ancient City Press, 1987], 10). The basic work of site identification has been done by Adolph F. A. Bandelier (*Final Report of Investigations among the Indians of the Southwestern United States Carried on Mainly in the Years from 1880 to 1885*, Papers of the Archaeological Institute of America, American Series 3 and 4 [Cambridge, Mass.: John Wilson & Son, 1890 and 1892]; Reginald G. Fisher, *Second Report of the Archeological Survey of the Pueblo Plateau: Santa Fe Sub-Quadrangle A*, University of New Mexico Bulletin 1 [Albuquerque: University of New Mexico Press, 1931]; Mera, *Population Changes*; and Michael P. Marshall and Henry J. Walt, *Archeological Investigations of Colonial and Mexican Period Cultural Properties in the Rio Medio Province of New Mexico*, Ms. on file, New Mexico Historic Preservation Division [Santa Fe: New Mexico Office of Cultural Affairs, 1985].

35. Winship, *The Coronado Expedition*, 594; Hammond and Rey, *Narratives*, 183.

36. Winship, *The Coronado Expedition*, 430, 431, 490, 491; Hammond and Rey, *Narratives*, 218, 219.

37. Winship, *The Coronado Expedition*, 432, 492–93; Hammond and Rey, *Narratives*, 220–21.

38. Carroll L. Riley, *Rio del Norte, People of the Upper Rio Grande from Earliest Times to the Pueblo Revolt* (Salt Lake City: University of Utah Press, 1995), 170.

39. Winship, *The Coronado Expedition*, 432, 434–47, 451–52, 454, 492, 495–501, 519–20, 525, 567, 569, 576, 594; Hammond and Rey, *Narratives*, 183, 220, 224–31, 253–54, 259, 290, 309, 326, 347–49, 351, 352–62; *Relación sacada de la probanza . . . que trata con Dn. García Ramírez de Cárdenas*, Archivo General de Indias, Justicia, legajo 1021, pieza 3, 1546–1548 (from transcript in Bolton research papers, Bancroft Library, University of California, Berkeley); *Información contra Francisco Vázquez de Coronado*, Archivo General de Indias, Justicia, legajo 1021, pieza 4, 1544 (from transcript in Bolton research materials, Bancroft Library, University of California, Berkeley); Antonio Tello, *Libro Segundo de la crónica miscelanea, en que se trata de la conquista espiritual y temporal de la Santa provincia de Xalisco* (Guadalajara, Mexico, 1891), 419–22, 425;

40. For a summary of some site correlations see Dan Scurlock, "An Historical Overview

of Bernalillo, New Mexico and Site LA 677," in *Excavations at Nuestra Señora de Dolores Pueblo (LA 677), A Prehistoric Settlement in the Tiguex Province,* ed. by Michael P. Marshall, Project # 185-58a, 176–82 (Albuquerque: Office of Contract Archeology, University of New Mexico, 1982), 180.

41. Riley suggests that Arenal might have been the east-side pueblo Puaray (LA 717) (Carroll L. Riley, "Puaray and Coronado's Tiguex," In *Collected Papers in Honor of Erik K. Reed,* ed. by A. H. Schroeder, Papers of the Archeological Society of New Mexico 6 [Albuquerque, 1981], 206, 210, and *Rio del Norte,* 170. Flint postulates that another east-side pueblo, Watche (LA 677), could have been Pueblo de la Alameda (Richard Flint, *Greater Cruelties Have Been Reported, The 1544 Investigation of the Coronado Expedition,* Ph.D. dissertation [Albuquerque: University of New Mexico, 1999], 278).

42. Snow, "Initial Entradas," 106–12.

43. Albert H. Schroeder, "Vásquez de Coronado and the Southern Tiwa Pueblos," in *Archeology, Art, and Anthropology: Papers in Honor of J. J. Brody,* ed. by Meliha S. Duran and David T. Kirkpatrick, Papers of the Archeological Society of New Mexico 18 (Santa Fe, N.Mex.: Ancient City Press, 1992), 189.

44. Gordon Vivian, *Restudy of the Province of Tiguex,* M.A. thesis (Albuquerque: University of New Mexico, 1932), 67; Joseph C. Winter, "Life in Old Bernalillo in the Fifteenth Century," in *Excavations at Nuestra Señora de Dolores Pueblo (LA 677), A Prehistoric Settlement in the Tiguex Province,* ed. by Michael P. Marshall, et al. (Albuquerque: Office of Contract Archeology, University of New Mexico, 1982), 185; Bradley J. Vierra, "The Tiguex Province: A Tale of Two Cities," in *Secrets of a City: Papers on Albuquerque Area Archeology in Honor of Richard A. Bice,* ed. by Anne V. Poore and John L. Montgomery, Papers of the Archeological Society of New Mexico 13 (Santa Fe, N.Mex., 1987), 81; Riley, *Rio del Norte,* 177.

45. Bradley J. Vierra and Stanley M. Hordes, "Let the Dust Settle: A Review of the Coronado Campsite in the Tiguex Province," in *To Tierra Nueva: The Route of the Coronado Expedition in the Southwest,* ed. by Richard Flint and Shirley Cushing Flint (Niwot: University Press of Colorado, 1997), 249–50, 256, 257.

46. Flint, *Greater Cruelties,* 274–77; Tello, *Libro Segundo,* 422.

47. Hammond and Rey, *The Rediscovery,* 103–5, 116–17, 176–77, 203; *Relación sacada,* pieza 3; *Información contra,* pieza 4.

48. See Mecham ("The Second Spanish Expedition" [map]) for another interpretation of the pueblos encountered by the Chamuscado expedition and Schroeder ("Pueblos Abandoned," 243) for a comparison of the Southern Tiwa pueblos of the Chamuscado and Espejo expeditions.

49. Mera, *Population Changes,* 17–18; Wilcox, "Changing Contexts," 132–33; Marshall and Walt, *Archaeological Investigations,* maps; Riley, *Rio del Norte,* 230; Hammond and Rey, *Obregón's History,* 290; Hammond and Rey, *The Rediscovery,* 82, 221, 303.

50. ARMS site file for San Francisco (LA 778); Mera, *Population Changes,* 8; Marshall and Walt, *Rio Abajo,* 211, 345.

51. ARMS site file for Abo Confluence (LA 50241); Marshall and Walt, *Archaeological Investigations,* n.p.; Michael P. Marshall and Cristina L. Marshall, *Investigations in the Middle Rio Grande Conservancy District: A Cultural Resource Survey of Irrigation and Drainage Canals in the Isleta-South to La Joya Area, Phase II Survey* (Albuquerque, N.Mex.: Bureau of Reclamation, U.S. Department of the Interior, 1992), 75.

52. ARMS site file for Ladera Pueblo (LA 50259); Marshall and Walt, *Archaeological Investigations,* n.p.; Marshall and Marshall, *Investigations in the Middle Rio Grande,* 40.

53. There are two large west-side pueblo sites in the general area but neither is opposite the Abo Confluence site: Abeytas (LA 780) five miles to the south and Los Trujillos (LA 50271) eight miles north; neither shows evidence of contact-period occupation (ARMS site files for LA 780 and LA 50271).

54. Because the late ceramics (Glazes E and F) found at the Valencia site (LA 953) in the 1930s were not found in the survey of the 1980s, there is some doubt about the occupation of this site in the contact period, but it has not been ruled out (ARMS site file for LA 953; Mera, *Population Changes,* 20; Marshall and Walt, *Archaeological Investigations,* n.p.; National Register of Historic Places Inventory Nomination Form for LA 953 [Santa Fe, N.Mex.: National Park Service, U.S. Department of the Interior]; Hayward H. Franklin, *Valencia Pueblo Ceramics,* Ms. on file, Office of Contract Archeology [Albuquerque: University of New Mexico, 1994], 75, 88).

55. There has been much difference of opinion over the identification of these pueblos in the northern Albuquerque Basin. One analysis of the Pueblo settlement pattern there is presented by Vivian (*Restudy,* 14–77). A listing of different interpretations by various scholars is found in Scurlock ("An Historical Overview," 180).

56. Hammond and Rey, *The Rediscovery,* 203.

57. Ibid., 104–5.

58. ARMS site files for Sandia (LA 294), Watche (LA 677), Maigua (LA 716), and Puaray (LA 717); Mera, *Population Changes,* 18–19; Winter, "Life in Old Bernalillo," 183–85; Scurlock, "An Historical Overview," 179–82.

59. Alameda Pueblo (LA 421) was reported on the west side of the Rio Grande in Spanish chronicles and on maps as late as 1701 (Charles W. Hackett, "The Location of the Tigua Pueblos of Alameda, Puaray, and Sandia in 1680–81," *Old Santa Fe* 2 (1915): 383–84; Mecham, "The Second Spanish Expedition," 277; Guillaume Delisle, *Carte des Environs du Missisipi par G. de l'Isle Geogr. donne par Mr d'Iberville en 1701,* discussed in Wheat, *Mapping,* 1: 56–57). Subsequent reports, maps, and archeological investigations show its location on the east side. A shift in the river's channel has been considered a possible explanation for this phenomenon. The river might have reoccupied, for a time, the more easterly channel it had established in an earlier era, but recent attempts to ascertain if this could have been the case have given inconclusive results (David P. Staley, *Changes in the Morphology of the Rio Grande from Bernalillo to Isleta, New Mexico,* Ms. on file, Office of Contract Archeology [Albuquerque: University of New Mexico, 1981], 24; Gregory Martínez, Mary Davis, and Kathryn Sargeant, "Paleochannel Analysis in the North Valley of Albuquerque," in *An Archeological and Historical Survey of the Village of Los Ranchos,* Kathryn Sargeant and Mary Davis, Ms. on file, New Mexico Historic Preservation Division [Santa Fe: New Mexico Office of Cultural Affairs, 1985], 4.33–4.34, 4.6; Kathryn Sargeant, "Coping with the River: Settlements in Albuquerque's North Valley," in *Secrets of a City: Papers on Albuquerque Area Archeology in Honor of Richard A. Bice,* ed. by Anne V. Poore and John L. Montgomery, Papers of the Archeological Society of New Mexico 13 [Santa Fe, N.Mex.: Ancient City Press, 1987], 38–39, 41–44; Vincent C. Kelley, *Albuquerque: Its Mountains, Valley, Water, and Volcanoes,* vol. 9 of *Scenic Trips to the Geologic Past* [Socorro: New Mexico Bureau of Mines and Mineral Resources, 1969], 15; Scurlock, *From the Rio to the Sierra,* 33). A major flood in 1735 or 1736 might have caused the river to shift to the more westerly channel it still occupies (Martínez, Davis, and Sargeant, "Paleochannel Analysis," 4.7). The Miera y Pacheco map of 1758 shows Alameda on the east side of the river (John L. Kessell, *Kiva, Cross and Crown: The Pecos Indians and New Mexico, 1540–1840* [Washington, D.C.: National Park Service, U.S. Department of the Interior, 1979], 385, endpapers). If the river did alter its course, nearby Chamisal Pueblo (LA 22765), which was also located in the floodplain, was probably

affected, and it too is considered a west-side pueblo in the contact period.

60. Hammond and Rey, *The Rediscovery*, 109.

61. Ibid., 177.

62. Ibid., 178.

63. Fisher, *Second Report*, n.p.; Vivian, *Restudy*, 59, 63; David H. Snow, "The Identification of Puaray Pueblo," in *Collected Papers in Honor of Florence Hawley Ellis*, ed. by Theodore R. Frisbie, Papers of the Archeological Society of New Mexico 2 (Norman, Okla.: Hooper Publishing Co., 1975), 463–80; Riley, "Puaray and Coronado's Tiguex," 210; Scurlock, "An Historical Overview," 180; Hammond and Rey, *The Rediscovery*, 293, and *Don Juan*, 319.

64. Hammond and Rey, *The Rediscovery*, 293.

65. Hammond and Rey, *Don Juan*, 319.

66. Gaspar Pérez de Villagrá, *History of New Mexico by Gaspar Pérez de Villagrá Acalá 1610*, trans. by Gilberto Espinosa (Los Angeles: Quivira Society, 1933), 142.

67. Snow, "The Identification of Puaray Pueblo," 464; Carroll L. Riley, *The Frontier People: The Greater Southwest in the Protohistoric Period* (Albuquerque: University of New Mexico Press, 1987), 227.

68. Hammond and Rey, *The Rediscovery*, 204.

69. Ibid., 292.

70. Ibid., 291–92; Snow, "Initial Entradas," 95–97. For an alternate interpretation involving an approach from the north end of the Sandias, see Albert H. Schroeder and Dan S. Matson, *A Colony on the Move: Gaspar Castaño de Sosa's Journal, 1590–1591* (Santa Fe, N.Mex.: The School of American Research, 1965), 168–70.

71. Watche, the LA 677 site, also known as Nuestra Señora de Dolores, has been built over and much disturbed by a church and school complex that has prevented excavation adequate to determine precisely when it was occupied (Scurlock, "An Historical Overview," 179–82). Ceramic collection at the site in the 1930s yielded the full range of glaze types, indicating occupation throughout the Classic Period, including the contact years, but trenching in part of the site in 1982 yielded only early glaze types predating Spanish exploration (ARMS site file for LA 677; Mera, *Population Changes*, 19; Winter, "Life in Old Bernalillo," 183–85; Michael P. Marshall, et al., *Excavations at Nuestra Señora de Dolores Pueblo (LA 677), A Prehistoric Settlement in Tiguex Province* [Albuquerque: Office of Contract Archeology, University of New Mexico, 1982], 2, 4).

72. ARMS site file for Piedras Marcadas (LA 290); Michael P. Marshall, *An Archeological Survey of the Mann-Zuris Pueblo Complex, Phase II* (Santa Fe and Albuquerque: New Mexico Historic Commission and Miller-Brown Land Co., 1988), 13.

73. Hammond and Rey, *Don Juan*, 346.

74. Ibid., 319. The earlier Casa Colorado site, LA 50249, might have been the one referred to by Espejo (Marshall and Marshall, *Investigations in the Middle Rio Grande*, 58, 89).

75. ARMS site files for Pur-e Tu-ay (LA 489), Isleta (LA 724), Bei-jui Tu-ay (LA 81), Valencia (LA 953), Laderà del Sur (LA 50257), Casa Colorado (LA 50249), and Abo Confluence (LA 50241); National Register of Historic Places Inventory Nomination Form for Pur-e Tu-ay (LA 489); Marshall and Walt, *Archaeological Investigations*, n.p.

76. Richard I. Ford, Albert H. Schroeder, and Stewart L. Peckham, "Three Perspectives on Pueblan Prehistory," in *New Perspectives on the Pueblos*, ed. by Alfonso Ortiz (Albuquerque: University of New Mexico Press, 1972), 29, 33, 34–35; Joseph A. Tainter and David "A" Gillio, *Cultural Resources Overview, Mount Taylor Area, New Mexico* (Washington, D.C.: U.S. Government Printing Office, 1980), 63; Riley, *Rio del Norte*, 102.

77. Winship, *The Coronado Expedition*, 430–31, 454, 490–91, 524, 560, 566, 569, 575, 587,

594; Hammond and Rey, *Narratives*, 173, 182, 218, 259, 288, 299, 309; Hammond and Rey, *Obregón's History*, 16, 324; Hammond and Rey, *The Rediscovery*, 107, 182, 224; Hammond and Rey, *Don Juan*, 346, 354, 394.

78. Hammond and Rey, *The Rediscovery*, 181–82.

79. Tainter and Gillio, *Cultural Resources Overview*, 53–54; Mark Wimberly and Peter Eidenbach, *Reconnaissance Study of the Archeological and Related Resources of the Lower Puerco and Salado Drainages, Central New Mexico* (Tularosa, N.Mex.: Human Systems Research, Inc., 1980), 227; Marshall and Walt, *Rio Abajo*, 186; Marshall and Walt, *Archaeological Investigations*, n.p.

80. Winship, *The Coronado Expedition*, 439, 503; Hammond and Rey, *Narratives*, 233.

81. Hammond and Rey, *The Rediscovery*, 105.

82. Ibid., 180.

83. Ibid., 223.

84. Hammond and Rey, *Don Juan*, 337, 338, 346; Snow, "Initial Entradas," 104.

85. Mera, *Population Changes*, 27; Bandelier, *Final Report*, 1: 126; Laura W. Bayer, *Santa Ana: The People, the Pueblo, and the History of Tamaya* (Albuquerque: University of New Mexico Press, 1994), 11, 259–65.

86. Bayer, et al., *Santa Ana*, 11.

87. Ibid., 293–94 n20.

88. Winship, *The Coronado Expedition*, 439, 451, 454, 503, 519, 525; Hammond and Rey, *Narratives*, 233, 254, 259.

89. Hodge, *Handbook*, 2: 462.

90. Hammond and Rey, *The Rediscovery*, 105–06, 130–31.

91. Ibid., 58–59.

92. Hammond and Rey suggest that Talaván was LA 35, Cañada Pueblo, which has yielded Glaze A–E ceramics but which is located in inaccessible canyon country northwest of Cochiti—unlike La Bajada (Glazes A–F), which is located on the open plain east of Cochiti (Hammond and Rey, *The Rediscovery*, 59; ARMS site file for La Bajada (LA 7).

93. Albert H. Schroeder, "Tunque Pueblo—Who Lived There?" in *Clues to the Past: Papers in Honor of William M. Sundt*, ed. by Meliha S. Duran and David T. Kirkpatrick, Papers of the Archeological Society of New Mexico 16 (Santa Fe, N.Mex.: Ancient City Press, 1990), 259.

94. Hammond and Rey, *The Rediscovery*, 179, 204, 223.

95. Tipolti has been interpreted as Santa Ana Pueblo, but evidence from Oñate and the 1602 map would indicate that La Bajada might be a better match (Hammond and Rey, *The Rediscovery*, 204; Riley, *Rio del Norte*, 235).

96. Hammond and Rey, *The Rediscovery*, 179–80.

97. Sieharan has been interpreted as Zia Pueblo, but Luxán and Espejo place Zia in their Punames province and note that Sieharan was a "Quires" pueblo (Riley, *Rio del Norte*, 235; Hammond and Rey, *The Rediscovery*, 180, 204, 223).

98. Hammond and Rey, *The Rediscovery*, 286; " . . . había quatro pueblos a vista unos de otros" (*Colección de documentos inéditos relativos al descubrimiento, conquista, y organización de las antiguas posesiones españolas en América y Oceanía, sacados de los archivos del reino, y muy especialmente del de Indias*, xv [Madrid, 1871], 342).

99. Schroeder and Matson, *A Colony on the Move*, 140–42; Snow, "Initial Entradas," 94–95; David H. Snow, *Archeological Excavations at Pueblo del Encierro, LA 70*, Laboratory of Anthropology Note 78 (2) (Santa Fe: Museum of New Mexico, 1976), B115–16; Stewart Peckham, "The Anasazi of the Northern Rio Grande Rift," in *Rio Grande Rift: Northern New Mexico*, Guidebook, 35th field Conference (Socorro: New Mexico Geological Society,

1984), 280; ARMS site file for Pueblo Encierro, LA 70.

100. This site, which Castaño de Sosa named Santo Domingo, has not been identified but is thought to have been located near the present site (LA 1281), which dates from about 1700 (ARMS site file for LA 1281; Bandelier, *Final Report,* 2: 184, 185–86; Hodge, *Handbook,* 2: 462). Virtual absence of sixteenth-century ceramics at the present Cochiti site (LA 126) suggests a similar history of displacement by flooding and loss of the contact-period site (ARMS site file for LA 126; Warren, "Glaze Paint Wares," 191; Snow, *Archeological Excavations,* B116).

101. Hammond and Rey, *The Rediscovery,* 289–90; Schroeder and Matson, *A Colony on the Move,* 157–58, 160.

102. Hammond and Rey, *The Rediscovery,* 294; Schroeder and Matson, *A Colony on the Move,* 175. In this instance Castaño de Sosa seems to have used the standard league of 2.6 miles. The La Vega site is about three miles south of Santo Domingo Pueblo, whereas San Felipe is seven miles away, or almost two long leagues. In other instances Castaño de Sosa uses the long league, which measures about four miles.

103. Hammond and Rey, *Don Juan,* 337, 345; Snow, "Initial Entradas," 104. A sixth pueblo was listed, the pueblo of the "ciénaga of Carabajal," which might be construed to be La Ciénega Pueblo (LA 44) except that the site yields only post-contact pottery.

104. Hammond and Rey, *The Rediscovery,* 204; John P. Harrington, *The Ethnography of the Tewa Indians,* Twenty-Ninth Annual Report of the Bureau of American Ethnology for the Years 1907–1908 (Washington, D.C.: Smithsonian Institution, 1916), 470–71.

105. ARMS site file for La Bajada (LA 7); Mera, *Population Changes,* 24; David E. Stuart and Rory P. Gauthier, *Prehistoric New Mexico, Background for Survey* (Albuquerque: University of New Mexico Press, 1996), 99.

106. Hammond and Rey, *Don Juan,* 345, 393; Schroeder and Matson, *A Colony on the Move,* 162.

107. A. Helene Warren, "Tonque," *El Palacio* 76 (1969): 37; Schroeder, "Tunque Pueblo," 260–61. There is a medium-sized pueblo on the Arroyo del Tuerto about two miles north-west of Tunque Pueblo that archeologists have named Pueblo Tuerto (LA 38928), but it was abandoned by 1500 (National Register of Historic Places Inventory Nomination Form for Tunque Pueblo, LA 240).

108. Warren, "Tonque," 36–37.

109. Hammond and Rey, *Don Juan,* 348.

110. Winship, *The Coronado Expedition,* 451, 454, 519, 524, 525; Hammond and Rey, *Narratives,* 253–54, 258, 259; Nels C. Nelson, "Pueblo Ruins of the Galisteo Basin, New Mexico," *Anthropological Papers of the American Museum of Natural History* 15 (1914): 19, 22; Erik K. Reed, "The Southern Tewa in the Historic Period," *El Palacio* 50 (1943): 255; Schroeder, "Tunque Pueblo," 259; Mera, *Population Changes,* 29–30; Cordell, "Prehistory: Eastern Anasazi," 146; Linda S. Cordell, *Tijeras Canyon, Analyses of the Past* (Albuquerque: University of New Mexico Press, 1980), 4–5.

111. Marshall and Walt, *Archaeological Investigations,* n.p.; Michael P. Marshall, Nancy Atkins, and Joseph Winter, *Cultural Resources Monitoring and Data Recovery for the Cortez CO2 Pipeline in the Las Huertas Valley Area* (Albuquerque: Office of Contract Archeology, University of New Mexico, 1986), 147; Curtis F. Schaafsma, *Archeological Reconnaissance of the Proposed MAPCO Pipeline from Bloomfield to Hobbs,* Ms. on file, Laboratory of Anthropology (Santa Fe: Museum of New Mexico, 1972), n.p.

112. Winship, *The Coronado Expedition,* 453–54, 523–24; Hammond and Rey, *Narratives,* 257–58; Marjorie F. Lambert, *Paa-ko: Archeological Chronicle of an Indian Village in North Central*

New Mexico, School of American Research Monograph 19 (Albuquerque: University of New Mexico Press, 1954), 5, 174; Nelson, "Pueblo Ruins," 22; Warren, "Glaze Paint Wares," 191.

113. Hammond and Rey, *Obregón's History,* 17.

114. Hammond and Rey, *The Rediscovery,* 106.

115. Ibid.

116. Ibid., 228.

117. Ibid., 291–92; Schroeder and Matson, *A Colony on the Move,* 162.

118. Hammond and Rey, *Don Juan,* 348, 393–94.

119. An alternate view holds that Oñate went back to the Rio Grande via the east side of the Sandias and that Portezuelo was Paa-ko, but Oñate knew Paa-ko by that name because "Paaco" appears on one of his lists (Reed, *History of Quarai,* 7; Hammond and Rey, *Don Juan,* 348). The Silva Site (LA 12924) is another pueblo site for which ceramic evidence to support its occupation in the contact period is not clear (mainly Glaze F), but neither can such occupation be ruled out (ARMS site file for LA 12924; National Register of Historic Places Inventory Nomination Form for LA 12924; Marshall and Walt, *Archaeological Investigations,* n.p.).

120. Ford, Schroeder, and Peckham, "Three Perspectives," 35; Schroeder and Matson, *A Colony on the Move,* 10; Schroeder, "Tunque Pueblo," 262; Stewart Peckham and Bart Olinger, "Postulated Movements of the Tano or Southern Tewa, A.D. 1300–1700," in *Clues to the Past; Papers in Honor of William M. Sundt,* ed. by Meliha S. Durand and David T. Kirkpatrick, Papers of the Archeological Society of New Mexico 16 (Santa Fe, N.Mex.: Ancient City Press, 1990), 208–10, 212; Warren, "Tonque," 37. San Marcos might have been one of Coronado's seven Quirix (Keres) pueblos.

121. Winship, *The Coronado Expedition,* 453–54, 523–24, 567, 570; Hammond and Rey, *Narratives,* 257–58, 310; Albert H. Schroeder, "Querechos, Vaqueros, Cocoyes, and Apaches," in *Collected Papers in Honor of Charlie R. Steen, Jr.,* Papers of the Albuquerque Archeological Society 8 (Albuquerque, N.Mex., 1983), 159–60; Nancy P. Hickerson, *The Jumanos: Hunters and Traders of the Southern Plains* (Austin: University of Texas Press, 1994), 24–27; Reed, "The Southern Tewa," 257.

122. Winship, *The Coronado Expedition,* 595; Hammond and Rey, *Narratives,* 183.

123. Nelson, "Pueblo Ruins," 16–22; Nels C. Nelson, "Chronology of the Tano Ruins, New Mexico," *American Anthropologist* 18 (1916): 179; Reed, "The Southern Tewa," 255; Richard W. Lang, *Archeological Survey of the Upper San Cristobal Arroyo Drainage, Galisteo Basin, Santa Fe County, New Mexico* (Santa Fe, N.Mex.: School of American Research Contract Program, 1977), 27.

124. Nelson, "Pueblo Ruins," 20–22; Reed, "The Southern Tewa," 258.

125. Winship, *The Coronado Expedition,* 439, 454, 503, 525; Hammond and Rey, *Narratives,* 233, 259.

126. Nelson, "Pueblo Ruins," 25; Hammond and Rey, *The Rediscovery,* 86–87, 106; Reed, "The Southern Tewa," 259, 260.

127. A. Helene Warren and Frances Joan Mathien, "Prehistoric and Historic Turquoise Mining in the Cerrillos District: Time and Place," in *Southwestern Culture History: Collected Papers in Honor of Albert H. Schroeder,* ed. by Charles H. Lange, Papers of the Archeological Society of New Mexico, 10 (Santa Fe, N.Mex.: Ancient City Press, 1985), 98, 121; Garmon Harbottle and Phil C. Weigand, "Turquoise in Pre-Columbian America," *Scientific American* 26 (1992): 58, 59, 62.

128. Reed's designation of Piedrahita as Pecos is countered by the more likely proposal that

another pueblo named in the Chamuscado report, "Tlaxcala," was Pecos (Reed, "The Southern Tewa," 260; Hammond and Rey, *The Rediscovery*, 61, 105–6, 130, 135; Riley, *Río del Norte*, 231).

129. Hammond and Rey, *The Rediscovery*, 205–6; 228–29; Hammond and Rey, *Obregón's History*, 334, 340; Nelson, "Pueblo Ruins," 23; Reed, "The Southern Tewa," 261–62.

130. A mining site called Santa Catalina was also mentioned by members of the Chamuscado expedition, but it was described as five leagues (thirteen miles) from San Marcos (their Malpartida). They could have been referring to mines in Arroyo del Tuerto in the San Pedro Mountains east of the Sandia Mountains that are known to have been worked in precontact times (Hammond and Rey, *Obregón's History*, 301, 334; A. Helene Warren, "Indian and Spanish Mining in the Galisteo and Hagan Basins," *Special Publications* 8 [Socorro: New Mexico Geological Society, 1979], 9).

131. Hammond and Rey, *The Rediscovery*, 278.

132. Ibid., 286, 288; Nelson, "Pueblo Ruins," 24–26; Reed, "The Southern Tewa," 263; Schroeder and Matson, *A Colony on the Move*, 142–48, 154–55; *Colección de Documentos Inéditos*, xv: 251.

133. ARMS site files for San Lázaro (LA 91 and LA 92); National Register of Historic Places Inventory Nomination Form for San Lazaro, LA 91 and LA 92; Mera, *Population Changes*, 30; Lambert, *Paa-ko*, 177; Lycett, *Archeological Implications*, 315; Warren, "Glaze Paint Wares," 191.

134. Nelson holds that this pueblo was La Ciénega (LA 44), but Glaze F ceramics indicate that it was probably not established until after 1600 (Nelson, "Pueblo Ruins," 24, 25, 26; Mera, *Population Changes*, 29).

135. Hammond and Rey, *Don Juan*, 321.

136. Nelson, "Pueblo Ruins," 24; Ralph E. Twitchell, *The Leading Facts of New Mexican History* vol. 1 (Cedar Rapids, Iowa: The Torch Press), 313.

137. Reed, "The Southern Tewa," 263, 264.

138. Hammond and Rey, *The Rediscovery*, 291–92.

139. Winship, *The Coronado Expedition*, 453, 523; Hammond and Rey, *Obregón's History*, 18; Hammond and Rey, *Narratives*, 256, 257.

140. See note 128.

141. Hammond and Rey, *The Rediscovery*, 206.

142. Hammond and Rey, *Don Juan*, 321; Harrington, *The Ethnography*, 476.

143. Ford, Schroeder, and Peckham, "Three Perspectives," 25, 29, 33; Riley, *Río del Norte*, 102. Some scholars doubt that the language spoken at Pecos was Towa, or even a Tanoan language (Irvine Davis, "The Kiowa-Tanoan, Keresan, and Zuñi Languages," in *The Languages of Native America*, ed. by Lyle Campbell and Marianne Mithun [Austin: University of Texas Press, 1979], 419). However, when Pecos Pueblo was abandoned by its few remaining survivors in 1838, they joined their linguistic relatives at Jemez Pueblo, where their descendants still live (Harrington, *The Ethnography*, 477–78; Hodge, *Handbook*, 2: 220–21).

144. ARMS site files for Unshagi (LA 123), Nanishagi (LA 541), Guisewa (LA 679), Kiatsukwa (LA 132), Seshukwa (LA 303), Amoxiumqua (LA 481), Kwastiyukwa (LA 482), LA 484, and Tavokwa (LA 483); Elliott, *Archeological Investigations at Small Sites*, 32, 54–55; Michael L. Elliott, *Large Pueblo Sites near Jemez Springs, New Mexico*, Cultural Resources Report 3 (Santa Fe, N.Mex.: U.S. Forest Service, Department of Agriculture, 1982), 89. When it becomes available, *The Chronological History of the Ancestral Jemez Domain*, by William Whatley and Robert W. Delaney with contributions by the people of the Jemez Pueblo, might reveal other pueblos that were occupied in the 1540–98 contact period.

145. Winship, *The Coronado Expedition*, 445, 451, 454, 510, 519, 525; Hammond and Rey,

Narratives, 244, 254, 259.

146. ARMS site files for Guisewa (LA 679), Unshagi (LA 123), and Nanishagi (LA 541); Elliott, *Archeological Investigations at Small Sites,* 32.

147. Hammond and Rey, *The Rediscovery,* 107; Elliott, *Archeological Investigations at Small Sites,* 32–33; Michael L. Elliott, *The Jemez Falls Campground Project: Archeological Investigations at Four Small Sites in the Jemez Mountains, New Mexico,* Archeological Report 89-2, Prepared for the Santa Fe National Forest, Santa Fe, New Mexico (Albuquerque, N.Mex.: Jemez Mountains Research Center, 1991), 22.

148. Hammond and Rey, *The Rediscovery,* 224; Elliott, *Archeological Investigations at Small Sites,* 33.

149. Hammond and Rey, *Don Juan,* 322, 337, 345; Elliott, *Archeological Investigations at Small Sites,* 33; Snow, "Initial Entradas," 104–5.

150. Elliott, *Archeological Investigations at Small Sites,* 34.

151. ARMS site files for Puye (LA 47) and Tsirege (LA 170); National Register of Historic Places Inventory Nomination Form for Puye, LA 47; Harry P. Mera, *A Survey of the Biscuit Ware Area in Northern New Mexico,* New Mexico Archeological Survey, Technical Series Bulletin 6 (Santa Fe: Laboratory of Anthropology, Museum of New Mexico, 1934), 18; Terah L. Smiley, Stanley A. Stubbs, and Bryant Bannister, *A Foundation for the Dating of Some Late Archeological Sites in the Rio Grande Area, New Mexico: Based on Studies in Tree-Ring Methods and Pottery Analysis,* Laboratory of Tree-Ring Research Bulletin 6 (Tucson: University of Arizona, 1953), 19, 24; Charles R. Steen, *Pajarito Plateau Archeological Surveys and Excavations,* Los Alamos Scientific Laboratories Report No. 77-4 (Los Alamos, N.Mex.: 1977), 8; Linda S. Cordell, *A Cultural Resources Overview, Middle Rio Grande Valley, New Mexico* (Washington, D.C.: United States Government Printing Office, 1979), 64; Peckham and Olinger, "Postulated Movements," 211; William J. Robinson and Catherine M. Cameron, *A Directory of Tree-Ring Dated Prehistoric Sites in the American Southwest,* Laboratory of Tree-Ring Research (Tucson: University of Arizona Press, 1991), 20.

152. ARMS site files for Sankawi'i (LA 211), Potsuwi'i (LA 169), and Tyuonyi (LA 82); Mera, *Survey of the Biscuit Ware Area,* 14; Mera, *Population Changes,* 24; Warren, "Glaze Paint Wares," 190–91; A. Helene Warren, *New Dimension in the Study of Prehistoric Pottery, A Preliminary Report Relating to the Excavation at Cochiti Dam, 1964–1966,* Laboratory of Anthropology Note 90 (Santa Fe: Museum of New Mexico, 1973), n.p.; Riley, *The Frontier People,* 343; Riley, *Rio del Norte,* 222; Peckham and Olinger, "Postulated Movements," 210–11.

153. ARMS site file for Kuapa (LA 3444); Peckham, *An Archeological Sites Inventory,* 2; Warren, *New Dimension,* n.p.; Warren, "Glaze Paint Wares," 190.

154. ARMS site files for San Ildefonso (LA 6188), Santa Clara (LA 925), and Cochiti (LA 126); Nancy S. Arnon and W. W. Hill, "Santa Clara Pueblo," *Southwest,* vol. 9 of *Handbook of North American Indians,* ed. by Alfonso Ortiz (Washington, D.C.: Smithsonian Institution, 1979), 296; Sandra A. Edelman, "San Ildefonso Pueblo," in *Southwest,* vol. 9 of *Handbook of North American Indians,* ed. by Alfonso Ortiz (Washington, D.C.: Smithsonian Institution, 1979), 312; Peckham and Olinger, "Postulated Movements," 211.

155. Hewett, *Pajarito Plateau,* 50; Schaafsma, personal communication.

156. Peckham, "The Anasazi," 279; Peckham and Olinger, "Postulated Movements," 208; D. Bruce Dickson, Jr., *Prehistoric Pueblo Settlement Patterns: The Arroyo Hondo, New Mexico, Site Survey,* vol. 2 of the Arroyo Hondo Archeological Series (Santa Fe, N.Mex.: School of American Research Press, 1979), 120–25; Mera, *A Survey of the Biscuit Ware Area,* 15–16; Mera, *Population Changes,* maps following page 31.

157. Mera, *A Survey of the Biscuit Ware Area,* 19; Wilcox, "Changing Contexts," 142–43.

158. Stephan F. de Borhegyi, "The Evolution of a Landscape," *Landscape, Magazine of Human Geography* 4 (1954): 25–26; Peckham, "The Anasazi," 279; Mera, *A Survey of the Biscuit Ware Area*, 11–12; Donald J. Usner, *The Plaza del Cerro in Chimayó: Settlement and Function*, M.A. thesis (Albuquerque: University of New Mexico, 1991), 27.

159. Hammond and Rey, *The Rediscovery*, 280–83; Schroeder and Matson, *A Colony on the Move*, 110–18.

160. The pottery at Jacona (LA 1065), Tewa Polychrome, is generally attributed to the postcontact period, but, if its beginning date is accepted as 1550 rather than 1600, this pueblo might have been the one Castaño de Sosa visited; otherwise that site might have been eroded beyond recognition (Breternitz, *An Appraisal of Tree-Ring Dated Pottery*, 97). It is not likely that nearby Jaconita (LA 63) was the site because its Glaze A ceramics are not late enough to place it in the contact period (ARMS site files for LA 63 and LA 1065; Mera, *A Survey of the Biscuit Ware Area*, 12). Ceramic dating of the other Pojoaque drainage area pueblos in the contact period is based on ARMS site files for the pueblos listed in table 10 and related National Register of Historic Places Inventory Nomination Forms; Mera, *A Survey of the Biscuit Ware Area*, 12–13; and Florence Hawley Ellis and J. J. Brody, "Ceramic Stratigraphy and Tribal History at Taos Pueblo," *American Antiquity* 30 (1964): 34.

161. Hammond and Rey, *The Rediscovery*, 285; Schroeder and Matson, *A Colony on the Move*, 133–34.

162. Hammond and Rey, *Don Juan*, 320, 346; Snow, "Initial Entradas," 104.

163. ARMS site file for Pioge (LA 144).

164. Winship, *The Coronado Expedition*, 445, 510–11; Hammond and Rey, *Narratives*, 244.

165. Hammond and Rey, *The Rediscovery*, 283, 285; Schroeder and Matson, *A Colony on the Move*, 121, 128–29.

166. Hammond and Rey, *Don Juan*, 320, 322–23.

167. Ibid., 639; Myra E. Jenkins, "Oñate's Administration and the Pueblo Indians," in *When Cultures Meet: Remembering San Gabriel del Yunge Oweenge*, Papers from the October 20, 1984 conference held at San Juan Pueblo, New Mexico (Santa Fe, N.Mex.: Sunstone Press, 1987), 63; Florence Hawley Ellis, "The Long Lost 'City,' of San Gabriel del Yungue, Second Oldest European Settlement in the United States," in *When Cultures Meet: Remembering San Gabriel del Yunge Oweenge*, Papers from the October 20, 1984 conference held at San Juan Pueblo, New Mexico (Santa Fe, N.Mex.: Sunstone Press, 1987), 17.

168. Hammond and Rey, *Don Juan*, 346; Snow, "Initial Entradas," 104.

169. Winship, *The Coronado Expedition*, 445, 454, 510–11, 525; Hammond and Rey, *Narratives*, 244, 259.

170. John D. Beal, *Foundations of the Rio Grande Classic: Lower Rio Chama 1300–1500*, Ms. on file, New Mexico Historic Preservation Division (Santa Fe: New Mexico Office of Cultural Affairs, 1987), 148; Schroeder, "Pueblos Abandoned," 250; Frank E. Wozniak, *The Ethnohistory of the Abiquiu Reservoir Area: A Study of the Native American Utilization of the Piedra Lumbre Valley (1500–1890)*, Archeological and Historical Research at Abiquiu Reservoir, Rio Arriba County, New Mexico vol. 3, ed. by Kenneth J. Lord and Nancy S. Sella (Albuquerque, N.Mex.: Chambers Consultants and Planners, 1987), 13:41–13:42.

171. Mera, *A Survey of the Biscuit Ware Area*, 19; Beal, *Foundations of the Rio Grande Classic*, 19; Cordell, *A Cultural Resources Overview*, 51–53; Kurt F. Anschuetz, Timothy D. Maxwell, and John A. Ware, *Testing Report and Research Design for the Medanales North Project, Rio Arriba County, New Mexico*, Laboratory of Anthropology Note 347 (Santa Fe: Museum of New Mexico, 1985), 13–14.

172. Hammond and Rey, *The Rediscovery*, 285; Schroeder and Matson, *A Colony on the*

Move, 129–33."

173. Hammond and Rey, *Don Juan,* 346; Snow, "Initial Entradas," 104.

174. Winship, *The Coronado Expedition,* 445, 511, 575, 595; Hammond and Rey, *Narratives,* 183–84, 244, 288–89.

175. Some scholars doubt that Alvarado visited Taos (Riley, *Rio del Norte,* 166–67). To reach it from Pecos, which is located at the southern end of the Sangre de Cristo Mountains, he would have had to follow a very circuitous route, and there are no clues to indicate what route he might have taken.

176. Hammond and Rey, *The Rediscovery,* 283; Schroeder and Matson, *A Colony on the Move,* 123–26.

177. Hammond and Rey, *Don Juan,* 320–21.

178. Neither the Chamuscado nor the Espejo expedition reached the Far North subregion. A pueblo called Nueva Tlaxcala by Gallegos, chronicler of the Chamuscado expedition, has been identified as Taos by some scholars, but subsequent opinion has settled on Pecos as a more likely candidate (Hammond and Rey, *The Rediscovery,* 106; Mecham, "The Second Spanish Expedition," 281; Myra E. Jenkins, "Taos Pueblo and Its Neighbors, 1540–1847," *New Mexico Historical Review* 41 [1966]: 87).

PART TWO
Chapter Three

1. Hammond and Rey, *Don Juan,* 337–51.

2. Ibid., 393–94.

3. For the seventeenth century, either Glaze F (commonly dated 1650–1700 but probably begun earlier) or a combination of Glaze E (1515–1650) and Glaze F is considered diagnostic, but these dates are subject to some controversy (Breternitz, *An Appraisal of Tree-Ring Dated Pottery,* 105–7; Warren, "Glaze Paint Wares," 193).

4. Hammond and Rey, *Don Juan,* 346.

5. ARMS files for Old Zia (LA 384), Chackham (LA 374), and Corn Clan Zia (LA 241).

6. Hammond and Rey, *Don Juan,* 322.

7. Michael L. Elliott, personal communication; Elliott, *Archeological Investigations at Small Sites,* 32, 54–55; Elliott, *The Jemez Falls Campground Project,* 22–23.

8. ARMS files for Magdalena (LA 284) and Bear Mountain (LA 285).

9. Fray Gerónimo de Zárate Salmerón, *Relaciones: An Account of things seen and learned by Father Jerónimo de Zárate Salmerón from the Year 1538 to Year 1626,* trans. by Alicia Ronstadt Milich (Albuquerque, N.Mex.: Horn & Wallace Publishers, 1966), 26; France V. Scholes, "Notes on the Jemez Missions in the Seventeenth Century," *El Palacio* 44 (1938): 64.

10. A more complete listing of pueblos was ascribed to him at one time, but evidence discovered subsequently showed that the listing was a later work (France V. Scholes, "Documents for the History of the New Mexican Missions in the Seventeenth Century," *New Mexico Historical Review* 4 [1929]: 45; France V. Scholes, "Correction," *New Mexico Historical Review* 19 [1944]: 243; Stuart J. Baldwin, "A Reconsideration of the Dating of a Seventeenth Century New Mexican Document," *New Mexico Historical Review* 59 [1984]: 411, 412; James E. Ivey, "Another Look at Dating the Scholes Manuscript: A Research Note," *New Mexico Historical Review* 64 [1989]: 346–47; Zárate Salmerón, *Relaciones,* 17).

11. Zárate Salmerón, *Relaciones,* 26, 56, 92, 93; Schroeder, "Pueblos Abandoned," 251. Schroeder identifies Quiumziqua as Guisewa.

12. Zárate Salmerón, *Relaciones,* 56.

13. Scholes, "Notes on the Jemez Missions," 69–70; Alonso de Benavides, *The Memorial of Fray Alonso de Benavides, 1630,* trans. by Mrs. Edward E. Ayer, annotated by Frederick Webb Hodge and Charles Fletcher Lummis (Chicago: privately printed, 1916; Reprinted, Albuquerque; N.Mex.: Horn & Wallace Publishers, 1965), 24; Alonso de Benavides, *Fray Alonso de Benavides' Revised Memorial of 1634,* ed. by Frederick Webb Hodge, George P. Hammond, and Agapito Rey (Albuquerque: University of New Mexico Press, 1945), 69; Joe S. Sando, *Nee Hemish, a History of Jemez Pueblo* (Albuquerque: University of New Mexico Press, 1982), 13. The possibility that the name "San Diego de la Congregación" was given to the mission at Guisewa when it was rebuilt in the latter 1620s is discussed in Robin Elizabeth Farwell, *An Architectural History of the Seventeenth Century Mission Church of San José de Guisewa, Jemez National Monument, New Mexico,* M.A. thesis (Albuquerque: University of New Mexico, 1991), 16–31.

14. France V. Scholes and Lansing B. Bloom, "Friar Personnel and Mission Chronology, 1598–1629," *New Mexico Historical Review* 20 (1945): 63–68.

15. Zárate Salmerón, *Relaciones,* 95. It is unclear if this figure includes the Zuni and Hopi pueblos that are outside the scope of this study.

16. Benavides, *The Memorial of . . . 1630;* Benavides, *Revised Memorial of 1634.*

17. For an analysis of Benavides's memorials see Daniel T. Reff, "Contextualizing Missionary Discourse: The Benavides Memorials of 1630 and 1634," *Journal of Anthropological Research* 50 (1994): 62.

18. ARMS files for Tsirege (LA 170), Yunque (LA 59), Tsama (LA 980).

19. Tsama is on the 1602 map and is mentioned by Zárate Salmerón, but Tsirege is never mentioned. It is assumed that a symbol on the map on what could be the Pajarito Plateau is Tsirege, because it is known as the last pueblo in that area to be abandoned.

20. Warren, "Tonque," 37.

21. Benavides, *The Memorial of . . . 1630,* 24–25; Zárate Salmerón, *Relaciones,* 26; Benavides, *Revised Memorial of 1634,* 69.

22. Joe Sando, historian and member of the Jemez nation, names eleven pueblos occupied as late as 1680 (Joe S. Sando, "Jemez Pueblo," in *Southwest,* vol. 9 of *Handbook of North American Indians,* ed. by Alfonso Ortiz (Washington, D.C.: Smithsonian Institution, 1979), 419). Archeologist Albert Schroeder lists six prerevolt seventeenth-century settlements (excluding Walatowa) (Schroeder, "Pueblos Abandoned," 251). Archeologist Michael Elliott, who has investigated Jemez pueblo sites extensively, is of the opinion that four pueblos were occupied in the seventeenth century after 1630: Walatowa, Boletsakwa, Patokwa, and Astialakwa, while a few families might have continued to live in Guisewa (Elliott, *Archeological Investigations at Small Sites,* 24). Jeremy Kulisheck, an archeologist currently studying protohistoric Jemez sites, suggests that after the congregations of the 1620s there might have been seven non-mission and non-refuge pueblos occupied by the Jemez: Boletsakwa, Seshukwa, and Kiatsukwa east of the Jemez River and Amoxiumqua, Kwastiyukwa, Tovakwa, and Cerro Colorado (LA 2048) west of the river (Jeremy Kulisheck, *Settlement Patterns, Population, and Congregación on the 17th Century Jemez Plateau,* Society of American Archaeology, 61st Annual Meeting [New Orleans, La.: 1996], 6–7, 14). Historian France Scholes, noting that Boletsakwa has mid-seventeenth-century tree-ring dates, writes that this pueblo, and perhaps others such as the abandoned San José mission at Guisewa, were served by lay brothers from the San Diego mission because the friars found it impossible to congregate all of the Jemez in one pueblo. These visits must have been very sporadic because no such "visitas" were ever reported, but Scholes does open the possibility of other pueblos occupied by the Jemez besides the San Diego mission-pueblo

(Scholes, "Notes on the Jemez Missions," 94). According to Fray Agustín de Vetancurt, who was writing in the 1690s, the number of Jemez pueblos was reduced from five to one after the 1680 revolt (Fray Agustín de Vetancurt, *Teatro Mexicano; descripción breve de los sucesos ejemplares, históricos, politicos, militares, y religiosos del nuevo mundo occidental de las Indias. Crónica de la provincia del Santo Evangelio de México,* facsimile edition, Mexico, 1971, 319). An unpublished manuscript commissioned by the Jemez authorities, *The Chronological History of the Ancestral Jemez Domain,* by William Whatley and Robert W. Delaney with Contributions by the People of the Pueblo of Jemez, might shed further light on this matter when it becomes available.

23. Benavides, *The Memorial of . . . 1630,* 19; Benavides, *Revised Memorial of 1634,* 64.

24. ARMS files for Watche (LA 677), Calabacillas (LA 289), and Piedras Marcadas (LA 290).

25. Benavides, *The Memorial of . . . 1630,* 19.

26. ARMS files for Pueblo de Arena (LA 31717), El Barro (LA 283), Pueblito Point (LA 31751), Pilabo (no LA number), and Plaza Montoya (31744).

27. Benavides, *The Memorial of . . . 1630,* 20; Benavides, *Revised Memorial of 1634,* 65.

28. See note 10 for references that discuss the dating of this document. Its author is unknown, and in this study it will be referred to as the "Marquez" report because the only extant copy, dated May 24, 1664, was signed by Fray Bartolomé Marquez, Secretary-General of the Indies. For abandonment of the San José mission, (Scholes, "Notes on the Jemez Missions," 98 n29).

29. Pacheco reports forty-three pueblos, excluding those in Zuni province but apparently including the five Hopi pueblos reported in 1641 (Scholes, "Correction," 246). By excluding the Hopi settlements, the remaining thirty-eight are assumed to be those of the Rio Grande Pueblo Region.

30. Vetancurt, *Teatro Mexicano,* 4: 309–24—reference to the 1660 *padrón* is on page 314. It is Bandelier's opinion that the prerevolt data are from the 1660 census (Bandelier, *Final Report,* I: 122n).

31. Scholes, "Documents for the History," 51–55.

32. Charles W. Hackett, *Historical Documents Relating to New Mexico, Nueva Viscaya, and Approaches Thereto to 1773, Collected by Adolph F. A. Bandelier and Fanny R. Bandelier* (Washington, D.C.: Carnegie Institution, 1923–37), 3: 264.

33. The number of Hopi and Zuni pueblos is that reported by Vetancurt, *Teatro Mexicano,* 4: 320, 321.

34. Hackett, *Historical Documents,* 3: 297–99.

35. *National Register of Historic Places Inventory Nomination Form for Pueblo Blanco / Tabira (LA 51),* 3. Fray Silvestre Vélez de Escalante, reporting from Santa Fe in 1778, lists Tabira as one of the six Estancia Basin pueblos destroyed (*Documentos para la historia de México,* series 3 [Mexico, 1856], 1: 116).

36. Hackett, *Historical Documents,* 3: 297–99.

37. Villagutierre y Sotomayor was a member of Spain's Council of the Indies, who, about 1702, wrote a history of New Mexico from contemporary records. The thirty-two pueblos he mentions are drawn from the detailed table of contents of this history that can be found in Otto P. Maase, *Misiones de Nuevo Méjico: Documentos del Archivo General de Indias (Sevilla) publicadas por primera vez y anotadas* (Madrid, 1929), X–LVI.

38. Charles Wilson Hackett, ed. and Charmion Clair Shelby, trans. *Revolt of the Pueblo Indians of the Pueblo Indians of New Mexico and Otermín's Attempted Reconquest, 1680–1682* (Albuquerque: University of New Mexico Press, 1942), 1: 3–111 passim. The treasury official

Martín de Solís de Miranda, writing from Mexico City on January 7, 1681, mentions the need to recover the thirty-four lost pueblos, but there is no way to know if this figure includes Hopi and Zuni pueblos (Hackett and Shelby, *Revolt of the Pueblo Indians,* 231).

39. The reduction from seventy-one pueblos (Benavides's figure) to thirty-seven yields a loss of 48 percent, whereas using my adjusted Benavides figure of seventy-nine gives a loss of 53 percent. Stodder and Martin, noting the epidemic of 1636–40, state that as many as one half of the Rio Grande pueblos were abandoned between 1600 and 1643 (Ann L. W. Stodder and Debra L. Martin, "Health and Disease in the Southwest Before and After Spanish Contact," in *Disease and Demography in the Americas,* ed. by John W. Verano and Douglas H. Ubelaker [Washington, D.C.: Smithsonian Institution Press, 1992], 66.)

40. Bandelier, *Final Report,* 1: 122n.

41. Hackett, *Historical Documents,* 3: 108

42. France V. Scholes, "Church and State in New Mexico, 1610–1650," *New Mexico Historical Review* 11 (1936): 324.

43. Preucel, *Seasonal Circulation and Dual Residence,* 40.

Chapter Four

1. Lycett, *Archeological Implications,* 526–27; Hackett and Shelby, *Revolt of the Pueblo Indians,* 2: 299–300.

2. Hackett, *Historical Documents,* 3: 111; Benavides, *The Memorial of . . . 1630,* 17; Benavides, *Revised Memorial of 1634,* 64; Amy C. Earls, "Raiding, Trading, and Population Reduction Among the Piro Pueblos, A.D. 1540–1680," in *Current Research on the Late Prehistory and Early History of New Mexico,* ed. by Bradley J. Vierra and Clara Gualtieri (Albuquerque: New Mexico Archeological Council, 1992), 14; H. Allen Anderson, "The Encomienda in New Mexico, 1598–1680," *New Mexico Historical Review* 60 (1985): 371.

3. Scholes, "Documents for the History," 50; Hackett, *Historical Documents,* 3: 264; Jack D. Forbes, "The Appearance of the Mounted Indian in Northern Mexico and the Southwest to 1680," *Southwestern Journal of Anthropology* 25 (1959): 200. Some writers have located El Cuartelejo in southeastern Colorado (Alfred Barnaby Thomas, *After Coronado, Spanish Exploration Northeast of New Mexico, 1696–1727; Documents from the Archives of Spain, Mexico, and New Mexico* [Norman: University of Oklahoma Press, 1935], 16, 262 n6, 264 n23, map following page 260; Donald J. Blakeslee, *Along Ancient Trails: The Mallet Expedition of 1739* [Niwot: University Press of Colorado, 1995], 14). El Cuartelejo has also been located in Scott County in western Kansas (Benavides, *The Memorial of . . . 1630,* 245–46 33n; Phil Carson, *Across the Northern Frontier, Spanish Explorations in Colorado* [Boulder, Colo.: Johnson Books, 1998], 33, 65 map).

4. Charles Gibson, *The Aztecs Under Spanish Rule, A History of the Indians of the Valley of Mexico, 1519–1810* (Stanford, Calif.: Stanford University Press, 1964), 282–83.

5. Hammond and Rey, *Don Juan,* 1089.

6. Benavides, *The Memorial of . . . 1630,* 24; Benavides, *Revised Memorial of 1634,* 69–70.

7. Ibid.

8. Hammond and Rey, *The Rediscovery,* 84, 130, 221, 222, 223; Lycett, *Archeological Implications,* 503, 506; Earls, *The Organization of Piro Pueblo Subsistence,* 152; Earls, "Raiding, Trading," 15.

9. Scholes, *Documents for the History,* 48.

10. Lycett, *Archeological Implications,* 524–25.

11. France V. Scholes, "Civil Government and Society in New Mexico in the Seventeenth Century," *New Mexico Historical Review* 10 (1935): 81; Hackett, *Historical Documents,* 3: 109; Hammond and Rey, *Don Juan,* 509; David H. Snow, "A Note on Encomienda Economics

in Seventeenth-Century New Mexico," in *Hispanic Arts and Ethnohistory in the Southwest, Papers Inspired by the Work of E. Boyd,* ed. by Marta Weigle (Santa Fe, N.Mex.: Ancient City Press, 1983); Anderson, "The Encomienda."

12. Hackett, *Historical Documents,* 3: 110, 120; Benavides, *Revised Memorial of 1634,* 170.

13. Snow, "A Note on Encomienda," 349; Anderson, "The Encomienda," 365.

14. Hammond and Rey, *Don Juan,* 1089.

15. Gibson, *The Aztecs,* 223, 235.

16. Lansing B. Bloom, "A Glimpse of New Mexico in 1620," *New Mexico Historical Review* 3 (1928): 366–67; Scholes, "Church and State," 149, 169–70 n17.

17. Bloom, "A Glimpse of New Mexico," 368; Scholes, "Civil Government," 81–82, 86; Scholes, "Church and State," 300; France V. Scholes, *Troublous Times in New Mexico: 1659–1670,* Publications in History 11 (Albuquerque: Historical Society of New Mexico, 1942), 47–48; Anderson, "The Encomienda," 364.

18. Scholes, "Civil Government," 105–6; Anderson, "The Encomienda," 363–64; Hammond and Ray, 1953: 630, 667.

19. Scholes, "Civil Government," 106; Hackett, *Historical Documents,* 3: 131; Silvio A. Závala, *De encomiendas y propiedad territorial en algunas regiones de la América española* (Mexico, 1940), 52; Anderson, "The Encomienda," 262–63; Myra E. Jenkins, "Spanish Land Grants in the Tewa Area," *New Mexico Historical Review* 47 (1972): 114; Marc Simmons, "New Mexico's Colonial Agriculture," *El Palacio* 89 (1983): 5; *Recopilación de Leyes de los Reynos de las Indias,* Edición facsimilar de la cuarta impresión hecha en Madrid el año 1791 (Madrid, 1943), lib. 6, tít. 3, leyes 21–22.

20. Scholes, "Civil Government," 107.

21. Elinore M. Barrett, "Indian Community Lands in the *Tierra Caliente* of Michoacán," *Jahrbuch für Geschichte von Staat, Wirtschaft und Gesellschaft Lateinamerikas* 11 (1974): 98; Scholes, *Troublous Times,* 42–43; *Recopilación,* lib. 4, tít. 12, leyes 7, 9, 12; lib. 6, tít. 3, ley 20.

22. Hackett, *Historical Documents,* 3: 131.

23. Scholes, "Civil Government," 105–6, 107; Scholes, "Notes on the Jemez Missions," 77; Hackett, *Historical Documents,* 3: 71, 113; John P. Wilson, "Quarai, Living Mission to Monument," *El Palacio* 78 (1973): 20.

24. Bloom, "A Glimpse of New Mexico," 368–69.

25. *Recopilación,* lib. 4, tít. 17, ley 10.

26. Scholes, "Civil Government," 96n; Lycett, *Archeological Implications,* 527–28.

27. Scholes, "Documents for the History," 46–49, 52–56.

28. James E. Ivey, "The Greatest Misfortune of All: Famine in the Province of New Mexico, 1667–1672," *Journal of the Southwest* 36 (1994): 78.

29. Hackett, *Historical Documents,* 3: 119.

30. Lycett, *Archeological Implications,* 528–30; Marc Simmons, "Settlement Patterns and Village Plans in Colonial New Mexico," *Journal of the West* 8 (1969): 10.

31. Hackett and Shelby, 1942(2): 380.

32. Gibson, *The Aztecs,* 282; José M. Ots Capdequí, *España en América, El régimen de tierras en la época colonial* (Mexico, 1959), 30; G. Emlen Hall, "The Pueblo Grant Labyrinth," in *Land, Water, and Culture: New Perspectives on Hispanic Land Grants,* ed. by Charles L. Briggs and John R. Van Ness (Albuquerque: University of New Mexico Press, 1987), 75; Ivey, "The Greatest Misfortune," 78; *Recopilación,* lib. 4, tít. 12, ley 14; lib. 6, tít. 3, ley 9. *Mercedes* were the principal means by which Spaniards could obtain land, although acquisition through purchase from or by marriage to a native person was not proscribed. Unfortunately, New Mexico land acquisition records for the period prior to 1680 are not available (Jenkins, "Spanish Land

Grants," 114; Malcom Ebright, "New Mexican Land Grants: The Legal Background," in *Land, Water, and Culture: New Perspectives on Hispanic Land Grants,* ed. by Charles L. Briggs and John R. Van Ness (Albuquerque: University of New Mexico Press, 1987), 21–22).

33. *Recopilación,* lib. 6, tít. 1, ley 30.

34. Gibson, *The Aztecs,* 283; *Recopilación,* lib. 6, tít. 3, leyes 8, 9, 14.

35. Katherine A. Spielmann, "Colonists, Hunters, and Farmers: Plains-Pueblo Interaction in the Seventeenth Century," in *Archeological and Historical Perspectives on the Spanish Borderlands West,* ed. by David Hurst Thomas, *Columbian Consequences* (Washington, D.C.: Smithsonian Institution Press, 1989), 107.

36. Scholes, "Civil Government," 108; Hackett, *Historical Documents,* 3: 113, 164, 191, 204; Ivey, "The Greatest Misfortune," 82.

37. Spielmann, "Colonists, Hunters, and Farmers," 103.

38. Scholes, "Civil Government," 84; Spielmann, "Colonists, Hunters, and Farmers," 107, 109.

39. Ralph E. Twitchell, ed. and trans., *The Spanish Archives of New Mexico* (Cedar Rapids, Iowa: Torch Press, 1914), 2: 2; Jack D. Forbes, *Apache, Navaho, and Spaniard* (Norman: University of Oklahoma Press, 1960), 158–59.

40. Forbes, *Apache, Navaho, and Spaniard,* 139.

41. Scholes, *Troublous Times,* 17.

42. Scholes, "Juan Martínez," 340; Forbes, "The Appearance," 199; Dolores A. Gunnerson, *The Jicarilla Apaches: A Study in Survival* (Dekalb: Northern Illinois University Press, 1974), 72.

43. Scholes, "Juan Martínez," 340.

44. Hammond and Rey, *Don Juan,* 1059; Donald E. Worcester, "The Beginnings of the Apache Menace in the Southwest," *New Mexico Historical Review* 16 (1941): 5; Forbes, *Apache, Navaho, and Spaniard,* 110.

45. Forbes, "The Appearance," 198–200; Frank D. Reeve, "Seventeenth Century Navaho-Spanish Relations," *New Mexico Historical Review* 32 (1957): 45.

46. Benavides, *The Memorial of . . . 1630,* 24–25.

47. Benavides, *Revised Memorial of 1634,* 86, 89; Reeve, "Seventeenth Century," 39.

48. Benavides, *Revised Memorial of 1634,* 64.

49. Hackett, *Historical Documents,* 3: 110.

50. Scholes, "Church and State," 323–24.

51. Hammond and Rey, *Don Juan,* 1089; Scholes, "Church and State," 28; Reeve, "Seventeenth Century," 38.

52. Hackett and Shelby, *Revolt of the Pueblo Indians,* 2: 266; Reeve, "Seventeenth Century," 44.

53. Hackett and Shelby, *Revolt of the Pueblo Indians,* 2: 299; Worcester, "The Beginnings," 9.

54. Scholes, *Troublous Times,* 17.

55. Ibid.

56. Hackett, *Historical Documents,* 3: 220; Scholes, *Troublous Times,* 29; Forbes, *Apache, Navaho, and Spaniard,* 149.

57. France V. Scholes, "Supply Service of the New Mexico Missions of the Seventeenth Century," *New Mexico Historical Review* 5 (1930): 401; Scholes, "Civil Government," 91; Frank D. Reeve, "Seventeenth Century Navaho-Spanish Relations," New Mexico Historical Review 32 (1957): Forbes, *Apache, Navaho, and Spaniard,* 164.

58. Forbes, *Apache, Navaho, and Spaniard,* 158, 164.

59. Hackett, *Historical Documents,* 3: 271–72; Worcester, "The Beginnings," 12; Scholes and Mera, *Some Aspects,* 283.

60. Hackett, *Historical Documents,* 3: 292, 297–98, 302; Ivey, "The Greatest Misfortune,"

90–91; Wilson, "Quarai," 19, 25–26; John P. Wilson, "Before the Pueblo Revolt: Populations Trends, Apache Relations, and Pueblo Abandonments in Seventeenth Century New Mexico," in *Prehistory and History in the Southwest,* ed. by Nancy L. Fox, Papers of the Archeological Society of New Mexico 11 (Santa Fe, N.Mex.: Ancient City Press, 1985), 115–17; Scholes, "Supply Service," 402; Forbes, *Apache, Navaho, and Spaniard,* 166–68, 172–75.

61. Hackett and Shelby, *Revolt of the Pueblo Indians,* 1: 62.

62. Schroeder, "Pueblos Abandoned," 241; Forbes, *Apache, Navaho, and Spaniard,* 174–75; James E. Ivey, *In the Midst of Loneliness, The Architectural History of the Salinas Missions, Salinas Missions National Monument Historic Structure Report,* Southwest Cultural Resources Center Professional Papers No. 15 (Santa Fe, N.Mex.: National Park Service, U.S. Department of the Interior, 1988), 229–35.

63. Ivey, "The Greatest Misfortune," 91; Hackett, *Historical Documents,* 3: 298.

64. Forbes, *Apache, Navaho, and Spaniard,* 173–74.

65. 1950–95 data are from the Midwestern Climate Center, a cooperative project of the National Climate Data Center and the Illinois State Water Survey, Champaign, Illinois.

66. Harold C. Fritts, *Reconstructing Large-Scale Climatic Patterns from Tree-Ring Data, A Diagnostic Analysis* (computerized appendix) (Tucson: University of Arizona Press, 1991), xix, 176, 190.

67. See Dan Scurlock for a discussion relating climate to historical events in the seventeenth century (Scurlock, *From the Rio to the Sierra,* 24–25).

68. Hammond and Rey, *Don Juan,* 696.

69. Forbes, *Apache, Navaho and Spaniard,* 97.

70. Benavides, *The Memorial of . . . 1630,* 24.

71. Scholes, "Church and State," 324.

72. Hackett, *Historical Documents,* 3: 186, 187, 191–92.

73. Twitchell, *The Spanish Archives,* 2: 2; Forbes, *Apache, Navaho, and Spaniard,* 158–59.

74. Hackett, *Historical Documents,* 3: 272; Ivey, "The Greatest Misfortune," 76–77.

75. Ivey, writing about the 1667–72 famine, notes that its causes are never stated in the available documents, but he concludes that shortage of rainfall was probably the principal cause (Ivey, "The Greatest Misfortune," 98 n25).

76. Ibid., 82.

77. Spielmann, "Colonists, Hunters, and Farmers," 107.

78. Hackett, *Historical Documents,* 3: 302; France V. Scholes, "Royal Treasury Records Relating to the Province of New Mexico, 1596–1683," *New Mexico Historical Review* 50 (1975): 149.

79. This disease might have been smallpox, according to Dobyns (Henry F. Dobyns, *Their Number Become Thinned: Native American Population Dynamics in Eastern North America* [Knoxville: University of Tennessee Press, 1983], 315; Henry F. Dobyns, "Native American Trade Centers as Contagious Disease Foci," in *Disease and Demography in the Americas,* ed. by John W. Verano and Douglas H. Ubelaker [Washington, D.C.: Smithsonian Institution Press, 1992], 217–18).

80. Hackett, *Historical Documents,* 3: 108.

81. Gibson, *The Aztecs,* 448; Daniel T. Reff, *Disease, Depopulation, and Culture Change in Northwestern New Spain, 1518–1764* (Salt Lake City: University of Utah Press, 1991), 127.

82. Scholes, "Church and State," 324. This peste was possibly smallpox (Daniel T. Reff, *The Demographic and Cultural Consequences of Old World Disease in the Greater Southwest, 1520–1660* [Ann Arbor: University of Michigan Microfilms, 1985], 258; Dobyns, *Their Number*

Become Thinned, 315).

83. For a discussion of differential survival between northern upland and southern lowland pueblos, see Ann F. Ramenofsky, "The Problem of Introduced Infectious Diseases in New Mexico: 1540–1680," *Journal of Anthropological Research* 54 (1996).

84. Kessell, *Kiva, Cross, and Crown,* 170; Frances Levine and Anna LaBauve, "Examining the Complexity of Historic Population Decline: A Case Study of Pecos Pueblo, New Mexico," *Ethnohistory* 44 (1997): 84.

85. Scholes, "Supply Service," 186.

86. Daniel T. Reff, "The Introduction of Smallpox in the Greater Southwest," *American Anthropologist* 89 (1987): 704; Reff, *Disease, Depopulation, and Culture,* 167, 172.

87. Dobyns, *Their Number Become Thinned,* 11; Steadman Upham, "Smallpox and Climate in the American Southwest," *American Anthropologist* 88 (1986): 118.

88. Dobyns, *Their Number Become Thinned,* 12–13, 15. For a contrary view, see Ann M. Palkovich, "Historic Epidemics of the American Pueblos," in *In the Wake of Contact: Biological Responses to Conquest,* ed. by Clark Spenser Larsen and George R. Miller (New York: Wiley-Liss, Inc., 1994), 87.

89. Upham, "Smallpox and Climate," 125; Dobyns, *Their Number Become Thinned,* 14.

90. Daniel T. Reff, "Old World Diseases and the Dynamics of Indian and Jesuit Relations in Northwestern New Spain, 1520–1660," in *Ejidos and Regions of Refuge in Northwestern Mexico,* ed. by N. Ross Crumrine and Phil C. Weigand, Anthropological Papers of the University of Arizona No. 46 (Tucson: University of Arizona Press, 1987), 85–88.

91. Dobyns, *Their Number Become Thinned,* 13; Upham, "Smallpox and Climate," 125; Reff, *Disease, Depopulation, and Culture,* 229. The question of the size of the pre-Hispanic Pueblo population and the impact of European contact on it, especially in the form of epidemic diseases, has been the subject of conflicting views for a long time. Some scholars contend that no major population change took place before the seventeenth century (Riley, *Rio del Norte,* 224; Earls, *The Organization of Piro Pueblo Subsistence,* 138, 140–41, 156; Frank Zoretich, "Paths Not Taken: Jonathan Haas Studies Pueblo Political Life Before the Spanish," Santa Fe Institute, *Bulletin* [summer 1997]: 4–5). Others hold the position that European diseases diffused into New Mexico in advance of contact, perhaps as early as the 1520–24 pandemic, and that there were subsequent epidemics during the sixteenth-century contact period for which no records have yet been found (Dobyns, *Their Number Become Thinned,* 17; Upham, "Smallpox and Climate," 124–25; Steadman Upham, "Population and Spanish Contact in the Southwest," in *Disease and Demography in the Americas,* ed. by John W. Verano and Douglas H. Ubelaker [Washington, D.C.: Smithsonian Institution Press, 1992], 232–33).

PART THREE
Introduction

1. Andrew L. Knaut, *The Pueblo Revolt: Conquest and Resistance in Seventeenth-Century New Mexico* (Norman: University of Oklahoma Press, 1995), 180.

2. Hackett and Shelby, *Revolt of the Pueblo Indians,* 2: 235.

3. Diego de Vargas, *Blood on the Boulders, The Journals of don Diego de Vargas, New Mexico, 1694–1697,* ed. by John L. Kessell, Rick Hendricks, and Meredith D. Dodge (Albuquerque: University of New Mexico Press, 1998), 915.

Chapter Five

1. Diego de Vargas, *By Force of Arms, The Journals of don Diego de Vargas, 1691–1693,* ed. by John L. Kessell and Rick Hendricks (Albuquerque: University of New Mexico Press, 1992), 524, 600; Vargas, *Blood,* 31, 184, 258.

2. For 1690s and seventeenth-century data that pertain to Santa Fe, New Mexico, see Fritts, R*econstructing Large-Scale Climatic Patterns.* Data are from the computer file related to Fritts's volume and made available through the courtesy of Louis A. Scuderi, Department of Geography, University of New Mexico. Data for 1950–95 are from the Midwestern Climatic Center, a cooperative project of the National Climatic Data Center and the Illinois State Water Survey, Champaign, Illinois.

3. Vargas, *Blood,* 862. The term "catarrh" could have referred to a number of upper respiratory infections such as the common cold or flu, which ordinarily do not cause death but might do so among a population in which the viruses were not endemic and which was weakened by environmental and dietary stress (Ann Ramenofsky, personal communication).

4. More than 800 of the 959 who answered the muster at El Paso on January 2, 1693, were joined by recruits from New Spain, who numbered about 300, including 100 soldiers and 50 families (Diego de Vargas, *To The Royal Crown Restored, The Journals of don Diego de Vargas, 1692–1694,* ed. by John L. Kessell, Rick Hendricks, and Meredith D. Dodge [Albuquerque: University of New Mexico Press, 1995], 65, 349, 355, 383). Families were converted to persons using a factor of four. Twenty-two priests were also part of the expedition that journeyed north toward Santa Fe (Vargas, *To the Royal Crown Restored,* 224, 351).

5. Vargas, *Blood,* 281, 626. The Mexico City group consisted of sixty and one half families and the Zacatecas group forty-four families, both converted to persons using a factor of four.

6. Fray Francisco de Vargas, the New Mexico missionary custodian, reporting in March 1696 on the inadequate number of soldiers to protect his missionaries, notes that some soldiers had died in an epidemic the previous year (Vargas, *Blood,* 675). Governor Vargas asks the viceroy not only to send 276 families to fill out the complement of 500 originally agreed upon, but to replace the loss in 1695 of 52 soldiers and settlers who died in the fighting or as a result of the epidemic. He further notes that this loss does not include fugitives who had fled the colony since his entrada in 1693 (Ibid., 699). The fiscal in Mexico City, in a document dated September 20, 1696, states there were more than 1,200 Spaniards and more than 2,000 peaceful Indians—probably meaning Pueblo allies (Ibid., 915).

7. The population in 1680 is based on estimates made by Fray Francisco de Ayeta, the New Mexico missionary custodian: seventeen thousand in 1678 and sixteen thousand in 1681 for forty-six pueblos (Hackett, *Historical Documents,* 1: 252). Six of these pueblos were the ones in the Estancia Basin, which was by then abandoned. The eleven Hopi and Zuni pueblos were subtracted using an average population calculated for the forty remaining pueblos. The 1706 data are from the report of Fray Juan Álvarez, New Mexico missionary custodian, whose estimates of the population of each of the eighteen inhabited pueblos totaled 7,340, with additional people still returning from their places of refuge (Hackett, *Historical Documents,* 3: 373–76). For evidence of the return of Puebloans who had sought refuge with Navajos, see Roque Madrid, *The Navajos in 1705, Roque Madrid's Campaign Journal,* ed. and trans. by Rick Hendricks and John P. Wilson (Albuquerque: University of New Mexico Press, 1996), 92–93.

8. Vargas, *To the Royal Crown,* 442.

9. Ibid., 404, 408; Vargas, *Blood,* 53.

10. Vargas, *To the Royal Crown,* 409, 412, 426, 440, 442, 447, 449, 451, 456, 461, 465,

475, 478, 481, 484.

11. Ibid., 427.

12. Ibid., 464, 485. The amounts sent by Pecos were given in fanegas converted at the rate of 2.6 bushels to one fanega (Manuel Carrera Stampa, "The Evolution of Weights and Measures in New Spain," *Hispanic American Historical Review* 29 [1949]: 15). Various measures such as *fanega, arroba, carga,* and sack were used, making it difficult or impossible to compare the different amounts cited.

13. Vargas, *To the Royal Crown,* 520.

14. Ibid., 537, 563; Vargas, *Blood,* 53, 74. Vargas states in one instance that they found in the villa 3,000 to 4,000 arrobas of maize and in another 4,000 fanegas, the first of which could be converted to 51 tons (2,000 pounds to the ton) and the second to 10,400 bushels at 2.6 bushels to one fanega (Carrera Stampa, "The Evolution of Weights and Measures," 13, 15).

15. Vargas, *To the Royal Crown,* 426, 444.

16. Vargas, *Blood,* 233, 288, 379.

17. Ibid., 176, 252.

18. Ibid., 378, 382.

19. Ibid., 204.

20. Ibid., 235, 340.

21. Ibid., 209–10, 327, 336, 369.

22. Ibid., 286.

23. Ibid., 290, 296.

24. Ibid., 298, 361.

25. Ibid., 365.

26. According to Vargas, Jemez women brought down from the peñol 110 sacks of maize in the ear each day for nine days, which he estimates to be a total of 420 fanegas (1,092 bushels) and which when shelled (also by Jemez women) amounted to 240 fanegas (624 bushels) (Vargas, *Blood,* 327, 329, 330, 334–35, 340–41, 369). In addition, Keres allies brought down 55 sacks each of five days for themselves, a total of 275 sacks, converted to bushels at 1.1 bushel to the sack, making a total of 303 bushels (Vargas, *Blood,* 336).

27. Ibid., 378, 379, 382, 384–85, 389.

28. Ibid., 217, 221.

29. Ibid., 250, 258–59.

30. Ibid., 211, 278.

31. Ibid., 394–95, 418, 428, 445, 550, 666–67, 683, 695, 700, 812, 814–15, 859, 860, 916, 917, 946–47, 974, 1131, 1132, 1138, 1158.

32. Ibid., 624–43, 649, 1076.

33. Ibid., 676.

34. Ibid., 289, 290, 393.

35. Ibid., 9, 90, 993, 1017, 1023–25, 1032, 1034–35.

36. Ibid., 737, 768, 770, 775–76, 780, 793, 817, 821–23, 825, 842, 973, 975, 977, 998, 999.

37. Ibid., 1004.

38. Ibid., 1013, 1050.

39. Ibid., 981, 987, 988–90, 993.

40. Ibid., 1017, 1019, 1022, 1025, 1032.

41. Ibid., 1034–35.

42. Ibid., 860, 1028, 1037, 1055–56, 1062.

43. Ibid., 860.

44. Ibid., 974.
45. Ibid., 852–54.
46. Ibid., 854.
47. Ibid., 803.
48. Ibid., 1003, 1004, 1014, 1016, 1019, 1022.
49. *Documentos,* 3(1): 187.

Chapter Six

1. Hackett and Shelby, *Revolt of the Pueblo Indians,* 2: 234; Knaut, *The Pueblo Revolt,* 14.
2. Hackett and Shelby, *Revolt of the Pueblo Indians,* 2: 234, 1: 70–71; Charles Wilson Hackett, "The Retreat of the Spaniards from New Mexico in 1680 and the Beginnings of El Paso," *Southwestern Historical Quarterly* 16 (1912): 138, 140.
3. Hackett and Shelby, *Revolt of the Pueblo Indians,* 2: 203, 205, 206, 207, 208.
4. Ibid., 2: 356.
5. Ibid., 2: 227, 329, 339.
6. Ibid., 1: 159.
7. Hackett, "The Retreat of the Spaniards," 275.
8. Anne Eugenia Hughes, *The Beginnings of Spanish Settlement in the El Paso District,* Publications in History 1 (Berkeley: University of California Press, 1914, reprint 1935), 323; J. Walter Fewkes, "The Pueblo Settlements Near El Paso, Texas," *American Anthropologist* 4 (1902): 57; Fray Silvestre Vélez de Escalante, "Carta del Padre Fray Silvestre Vélez de Escalante escrita en 2 de abril de 1778 años, Santa Fe," *Documentos para la historia de México,* series 3, vol. 1 (Mexico, 1856): 120–21.
9. Hughes, *The Beginnings of Spanish Settlement,* 329; Vélez de Escalante, "Carta del Padre Fray Silvestre," 121.
10. Hughes, *The Beginnings of Spanish Settlement,* 366–68.
11. Hackett, *Historical Documents,* 3: 460–61.
12. Fewkes, "The Pueblo Settlements," 58, 74–75; Nicolas P. Houser, "Tigua Pueblo," in *Southwest,* vol. 9 of *Handbook of North American Indians,* ed. by Alfonso Ortiz (Washington, D.C.: Smithsonian Institution, 1979), 337.
13. Vargas, *By Force,* 373, 374, 375.
14. Vargas, *To the Royal Crown,* 114.
15. Hackett and Shelby, *Revolt of the Pueblo Indians,* 1: 73, 2: 330.
16. Ibid., 1: 27, 73, 81.
17. Ibid., 1: 27.
18. Ibid., 1: 26.
19. Ibid., 2: 208.
20. Ibid., 2: 222, 226, 236, 361, 394; Bayer, et al., *Santa Ana,* 70.
21. Hackett and Shelby, *Revolt of the Pueblo Indians,* 2: 220, 228–31, 356.
22. Ibid., 2: 393–94.
23. Hughes, *The Beginnings of Spanish Settlement,* 320.
24. Vélez de Escalante, "Carte de Padre Fray Silvestre," 121; Hughes, *The Beginnings of Spanish Settlement,* 323, 366–68.
25. Houser, "Tigua Pueblo," 339, 341; Hughes states that Spanish refugees occupied a settlement called La Isleta, at least for a time (Hughes, *The Beginnings of Spanish Settlement,* 388).
26. Houser, "Tigua Pueblo," 341.
27. Fewkes, "The Pueblo Settlements," 59.

28. Houser, "Tigua Pueblo," 337.

29. Vargas, *By Force*, 376, 383, 531–32; Vargas, *To the Royal Crown*, 391.

30. Florence Hawley Ellis, "Isleta Pueblo," in *Southwest*, vol. 9 of *Handbook of North American Indians*, ed. by Alfonso Ortiz (Washington, D.C.: Smithsonian Institution, 1979), 354; Elizabeth A. Brandt, "Sandia Pueblo," in *Southwest*, vol. 9 of *Handbook of North American Indians*, ed. by Alfonso Ortiz (Washington, D.C.: Smithsonian Institution, 1979), 345.

31. Hodge, *Handbook*, 2: 218; Vargas, *By Force*, 564.

32. Joe S. Sando, *Pueblo Nations: Eight Centuries of Pueblo Indian History* (Santa Fe, N.Mex.: Clear Light Publishers, 1991), 252; Hackett, *Historical Documents*, 3: 375.

33. Sando, *Pueblo Nations*, 252.

34. Benito Crespo, "Documents Concerning Bishop Crespo's Visitation, 1730," ed. and trans. by Eleanor B. Adams, *New Mexico Historical Review* 28 (1953): 224, 227.

35. Hackett, *Historical Documents*, 3: 388–90.

36. Ibid., 472.

37. Ibid.

38. Pedro Tamarón y Romeral, *Bishop Tamarón's Visitation of New Mexico, 1760*, Publications in History 15, ed. by Eleanor B. Adams (Albuquerque: Historical Society of New Mexico, 1954), 44.

39. Donald C. Cutter, ed., "An Anonymous Statistical Report on New Mexico in 1765," *New Mexico Historical Review* 50 (1975): 350.

40. Carlos de Sigüenza y Góngora, *The Mercurio Volante of don Carlos de Sigüenza y Góngora, An Account of the First Expedition of don Diego de Vargas into New Mexico in 1692*, ed. and trans. by Irving Albert Leonard (Los Angeles: The Quivira Society, 1932), 58; Vina E. Walz, *History of the El Paso Area, 1680–1692*, Ph.D. dissertation (Albuquerque: University of New Mexico, 1951), 226–27; Forbes, *Apache, Navaho, and Spaniard*, 208.

41. Sigüenza y Góngora, *The Mercurio Volante*, 58; Walz, *History of the El Paso Area*, 246–47, 250; Forbes, *Apache, Navaho, and Spaniard*, 217; Vélez de Escalante, "Carta del Padre Fray Silvestre," 123; Vargas, *Blood*, 914.

42. Walz, *History of the El Paso Area*, 248; Vargas, *To the Royal Crown*, 401, 403.

43. Vargas, *To the Royal Crown*, 401.

44. Ibid., 552–53 61n.

45. Bayer, et al., *Santa Ana*, 63, 264; ARMS site files for Canjillon Pueblo (LA 2049) and Santa Ana Pueblo (LA 8975); Marshall and Walt, *Archeological Investigations*, n.p.; Bandelier, *Final Report of Investigations*, 2: 195–96.

46. Hackett and Shelby, *Revolt of the Pueblo Indians*, 2: 236; Bayer, et al., *Santa Ana*, 68.

47. Pauline Turner Strong, "Santa Ana Pueblo," in *Southwest*, vol. 9 of *Handbook of North American Indians*, ed. by Alfonso Ortiz (Washington, D.C.: Smithsonian Institution, 1979), 405; Bayer, et al., *Santa Ana*, 70–71; Marshall and Walt, *Archaeological Investigations*, n.p.

48. Vargas, *By Force*, 517, 518, 523, 557, 609; Vargas, *To the Royal Crown*, 201, 203, 408; Vélez de Escalante, "Carta del Padre Fray Silvestre," 131; E. Adamson Hoebel, "Zia Pueblo," in *Southwest*, vol. 9 of *Handbook of North American Indians*, ed. by Alfonso Ortiz (Washington, D.C.: Smithsonian Institution, 1979), 408.

49. Strong, "Santa Ana Pueblo," 405; Vargas, *To the Royal Crown*, 429, 433–34; Bayer, et al., *Santa Ana*, 72. The present site, LA 8975, is now mainly of ceremonial importance and most Santa Anans live at Ranchitos near their fields on the west side of the Rio Grande north of Bernalillo.

50. Vargas, *To the Royal Crown*, 429, 434–35.

51. Ibid., 501; Vargas, *Blood*, 213.

52. Vargas, *Blood,* 728, 752, 778–79, 786, 802, 806, 857, 882, 900.

53. Ibid., 323–24, 979.

54. According to Jemez historian and elder Joe S. Sando, Tovakwa (LA 483) is properly spelled Tu-va-kwa and is also known as "Kwnn-stiyu-kwa," meaning pine beetle place (personal communication). The name "Kwastiyukwa" is used by the Laboratory of Anthropology to refer to LA 482.

55. Hackett and Shelby, *Revolt of the Pueblo Indians,* 2: 236.

56. *Documentos* 3(1): 131; Vargas, *By Force,* 520, 609; Vargas, *To the Royal Crown,* 201–2; Lansing B. Bloom and Lynne B. Mitchell, "The Chapter Elections in 1672," *New Mexico Historical Review* 13 (1938): 98–99; Sando, "Jemez Pueblo," 419–20; Sando, *Nee Hemish,* 119.

57. Bloom and Mitchell, "The Chapter Elections," 99.

58. Vargas, *To the Royal Crown,* 404, 441–42.

59. Ibid., 444.

60. Vargas, *Blood,* 35.

61. Ibid., 236.

62. Ibid., 324; Sando, "Jemez Pueblo," 420–21; Sando, *Nee Hemish,* 120.

63. Vargas, *Blood,* 325, 327, 337.

64. Ibid., 332.

65. Bloom and Mitchell, "The Chapter Elections," 103; Scholes, "Notes on the Jemez Missions," 101–2; Vargas, *Blood,* 405.

66. Vargas, *To the Royal Crown,* 416; Vargas, *Blood,* 332, 402–3.

67. According to archeologist Jeremy Kulisheck, both pueblos, located in the Guadalupe drainage west of the Jemez River, contain refugee-style roomblocks (Kulisheck, *Settlement Patterns,* 6).

68. Vargas, *Blood,* 402.

69. Archeologist Michael L. Elliott suggests that while some Jemez sought refuge at Asti-alakwa on the peñol of San Diego Mesa after the 1680 revolt, others moved to Boletsakwa, located in the Vallecitos drainage east of the Jemez River, where they might have established themselves on San Juan Mesa (Elliott, *The Jemez Falls Campground Project,* 24). Historian Joe S. Sando concurs in this location of the San Juan Jemez group (personal communication).

70. Bloom and Mitchell, "The Chapter Elections," 104; Vargas, *Blood,* 406, 586.

71. Bloom and Mitchell, "The Chapter Elections," 103–5; Scholes, "Notes on the Jemez Missions," 100; Vargas, *Blood,* 681, 685, 688, 696.

72. Vargas, *Blood,* 690.

73. Bloom and Mitchell, "The Chapter Elections," 105–7; *Documentos* 3(1): 171; Vargas, *Blood,* 36, 748, 750–51; Sando, "Jemez Pueblo," 421–22; Sando, *Nee Hemish,* 121.

74. Vargas, *Blood,* 778, 802.

75. Ibid., 792, 795, 796.

76. Ibid., 977–78, 982, 984, 1004, 1064, 1102; *Documentos* 3(1): 197; Sando, *Nee Hemish,* 121–22.

77. Hackett, *Historical Documents,* 3: 376.

78. Velma Garcia-Mason, "Acoma Pueblo," in *Southwest,* vol. 9 of *Handbook of North American Indians,* ed. by Alfonso Ortiz (Washington, D.C.: Smithsonian Institution, 1979), 454; *National Register of Historic Places Inventory Nomination Form for Acoma Pueblo (LA 112),* 5; Walz, *History of the El Paso Area,* 24; Velez de Escalante, "Carta del Padre Fray Silvestre," 177.

79. Hackett and Shelby, *Revolt of the Pueblo Indians,* 1: 111.

80. Vargas, *By Force,* 534–40; Vargas, *Blood,* 985–90; *Documentos* 3(1): 132, 172–73.

81. Vargas, *Blood,* 679, 698, 751.

82. Ibid., 736, 798–99, 802, 875, 877, 881.

83. Ibid., 969, 981–84, 1057; Vélez de Escalante, "Carta del Padre Fray Silvestre," 177.

84. Vargas, *Blood*, 984, 1057.

85. Vélez de Escalante, "Carta del Padre Fray Silvestre," 177; Ellis, "Laguna Pueblo," 438.

86. Vélez de Escalante, "Carta del Padre Fray Silvestre," 177.

87. Hackett, *Historical Documents*, 3: 376.

88. At one time La Cieneguilla Pueblo (LA 16) was thought to be the seventeenth-century pueblo called La Cienega but the former is a prehistoric pueblo. La Cienega Pueblo was also thought to be the site LA 44 but that has been identified as a Hispanic rancho. The seventeenth-century pueblo of La Cienega was probably created by the Spanish authorities as a reducción to which families from various pueblos were relocated to provide a convenient source of labor for the citizens of the villa of Santa Fe and owners of rural properties in the Santa Fe River Valley. The site of La Cienega Pueblo has not been identified but is most likely in the vicinity of present La Cienega in the Santa Fe River Valley. Personal communications: C.T. Snow and D. H. Snow.

89. Hackett and Shelby, *Revolt of the Pueblo Indians*, 2: 236, 254, 260; Bandelier, *Final Report*, 2: 188–90 and notes. The distance is actually about seven miles.

90. ARMS site file for San Felipe Pueblo (LA 3137); Vargas, *By Force*, 384, 513, 515, 620 n4; Vargas, *To the Royal Crown*, 200. Potrero Viejo was located adjacent to the larger refuge-pueblo called Old Kotyiti (LA 295) (Vargas, *Blood*, 448 n9).

91. Vargas, *By Force*, 385, 515.

92. Strong, "Santa Ana Pueblo," 393; Vargas, *To the Royal Crown*, 401, 405, 451; Bandelier, *Final Report*, 2: 191.

93. Vargas, *Blood*, 185; *Documentos* 3(1): 155.

94. Hackett and Shelby, *Revolt of the Pueblo Indians*, 2: 263, 297, 302.

95. Vargas, *Blood*, 728, 786, 806, 808, 979.

96. Ibid., 819, 875.

97. Ibid., 968; Strong, "Santa Ana Pueblo," 393; Hackett, *Historical Documents*, 3: 375.

98. Hackett and Shelby, *Revolt of the Pueblo Indians*, 1: 13, 25, 68.

99. Ibid., 2: 236.

100. Ibid., 2: 263, 297, 302.

101. Vargas, *By Force*, 382, 384, 386, 512.

102. Ibid., 557, 609.

103. Ibid., 448 n9, 514–15, 609; *Documentos* 3(1): 131.

104. Vargas, *To the Royal Crown*, 111, 438; Vargas, *Blood*, 186, 319, 582; *Documentos* 3(1): 167.

105. Vargas, *To the Royal Crown*, 416, 445.

106. Ibid., 425.

107. Ibid., 426.

108. Vargas, *Blood*, 192–93.

109. Ibid., 210.

110. Ibid., 226, 320.

111. Ibid., 406–7.

112. Ibid., 585, 681.

113. Ibid., 582, 871. There is no further information in the Vargas documents about the people of La Cieneguilla Pueblo as a distinct group, but the pueblo continued to be mentioned as abandoned and as a possible place to resettle dispossessed Puebloans such as those taken in battle.

114. Ibid., 983.

115. Hackett and Shelby, *Revolt of the Pueblo Indians,* 2: 236; Vargas, *By Force,* 557, 609.

116. Vargas, *Blood,* 173, 328, 339, 586; *Documentos* 3(1): 131.

117. Vargas, *Blood,* 396, 402–3, 406.

118. Ibid., 585, 586.

119. Bloom and Mitchell, "The Chapter Elections," 104 46n; Vargas, *Blood,* 695–96.

120. Vargas, *Blood,* 767–78, 819.

121. Ibid., 820–25.

122. Ibid., 978, 981, 982.

123. Ibid., 1056–57, 1062.

124. Hackett and Shelby, *Revolt of the Pueblo Indians,* 1: 13, 25, 98.

125. Ibid., 1: 16, 17–18.

126. Ibid., 2: 339.

127. Vargas, *By Force,* 418, 444, 445; Vargas, *To the Royal Crown,* 194, 199, 495; Vargas, *Blood,* 45, 51, 67, 607; *Documentos* 3(1): 127, 129, 131.

128. *Documentos* 3(1): 127.

129. Vargas, *To the Royal Crown,* 553.

130. Ibid., 535–36; Vargas, *Blood,* 35, 53; *Documentos* 3(1): 168.

131. Vargas, *Blood,* 47, 56.

132. Ford, Schroeder, and Peckham, "Three Perspectives," 32; Michael B. Stanislawski, "Hopi-Tewa," in *Southwest,* vol. 9 of *Handbook of North American Indians,* ed. by Alfonso Ortiz (Washington, D.C.: Smithsonian Institution, 1979), 600.

133. Stanislawski, "Hopi-Tewa," 587.

134. Vargas, *By Force,* 444–46.

135. Borhegyi, "The Evolution of a Landscape," 26; Donald J. Usner, *Sabino's Map, Life in Chimayó's Old Plaza* (Santa Fe: Museum of New Mexico Press, 1995), 29–30, 43; Harrington, *The Ethno-Geography,* 1916: 254–55.

136. Vargas, *Blood,* 288, 392.

137. Ibid., 413.

138. Ibid., 605–7.

139. Ibid., 607–8.

140. Ibid., 616.

141. Ibid., 608–9, 612.

142. Ibid., 615.

143. Ibid., 624–25.

144. Ibid., 281, 618, 620–21; *Documentos* 3(1): 168.

145. Vargas, *Blood,* 626.

146. Usner, *Sabino's Map,* 45.

147. Vargas, *Blood,* 678.

148. Espinosa, *The Pueblo Indian Revolt of 1696,* 177.

149. Vargas, *Blood,* 688, 690.

150. Ibid., 698.

151. Ibid., 698, 842.

152. Ibid., 776, 783; *Documentos* 3(1): 172.

153. Vargas, *Blood,* 116, 450 n69, 783.

154. Ibid., 833.

155. Ibid., 842.

156. Ibid., 969, 992, 995, 1003, 1020, 1048.

157. Ibid., 1050.

158. Ibid., 1051, 1053–55.

159. Ibid., 1064, 1089.

160. Usner, *Sabino's Map*, 47.

161. J. Manuel Espinosa, *Crusaders of the Rio Grande: The Story of Don Diego de Vargas and the Reconquest and Refounding of New Mexico* (Chicago: Institute of Jesuit History, 1942), 303; *Documentos* 3(1): 174.

162. Stanislawski, "Hopi-Tewa," 600, 601; Hodge, *Handbook*, 1: 531; Edward P. Dozier, *Hano: A Tewa Indian Community* (New York: Holt, Rinehart, and Winston, 1966), 13–14, 17–19.

163. Hackett, *Historical Documents*, 3: 375; Bloom, "Alburquerque and Galisteo," 49.

164. Hackett, *Historical Documents*, 3: 380; *Documentos* 3(1): 193.

165. Tamarón y Romeral, *Bishop Tamarón's Visitation*, 53; Alfred Barnaby Thomas, *The Plains Indians and New Mexico, 1751–1778, A Collection of Documents Illustrative of the History of the Eastern Frontier of New Mexico* (Albuquerque: University of New Mexico Press, 1940), 183, 212.

166. Francisco Atanasio Domínguez, *The Missions of New Mexico, 1776, A Description by Fray Francisco Atanasio Domínguez with Other Contemporary Documents*, trans. and annotated by Eleanor B. Adams and Fray Angélico Chávez (Albuquerque: University of New Mexico Press, 1956), 216.

167. Ibid., 217.

168. Simmons, "New Mexico's Smallpox Epidemic," 322.

169. Alfred Barnaby Thomas, *Forgotten Frontiers: A Study of the Spanish Indian Policy of don Juan Bautista de Anza, Governor of New Mexico, 1777–1787; from the Original Documents in the Archives of Spain, Mexico, and New Mexico* (Norman: University of Oklahoma Press, 1932), 93; Conde de Revilla Gigedo (Juan Vicente Güemes Pacheco de Padilla Horcasitas y Aguayo), *Informe sobre las Misiones, 1793, e Instrucción Reservada al Marqués de Branciforte, 1794* (Mexico, 1966), 56–57.

170. Domínguez, *The Missions of New Mexico*, 217 n3.

171. Kessell, *Kiva, Cross, and Crown*, 232; Vargas, *To the Royal Crown*, 501.

172. Hackett and Shelby, *Revolt of the Pueblo Indians*, 1: 13, 25, 98; Vargas, *By Force*, 423–34, 458.

173. Diego de Vargas, *First Expedition of Vargas into New Mexico, 1692*, ed. and trans. by J. Manuel Espinosa (Albuquerque: University of New Mexico Press, 1940), 168–70; Kessell, *Kiva, Cross, and Crown*, 248–49; Vargas, *By Force*, 434.

174. Vargas, *To the Royal Crown*, 404, 406, 548 n30.

175. Ibid., 432–33, 437, 450, 461, 464, 473–74, 485.

176. Ibid., 529; Vargas, *Blood*, 378.

177. Vargas, *By Force*, 426; Vargas, *To the Royal Crown*, 112; Kessell, *Kiva, Cross, and Crown*, 262–63.

178. Kessell, *Kiva, Cross, and Crown*, 170.

179. Vargas, *By Force*, 458; Vargas, *Blood*, 786; Kessell, *Kiva, Cross, and Crown*, 276–77.

180. Vargas, *Blood*, 677, 748–49, 809.

181. Ibid., 830, 836, 995.

182. Ibid., 730.

183. Ibid., 780, 817, 837, 1015, 1060.

184. Kessell, *Kiva, Cross, and Crown*, 282, 295.

185. *Documentos* 3(1): 180; Kessell, *Kiva, Cross, and Crown*, 295.

186. Thomas, *The Plains Indians*, 7–8, 16, 17, 18; Hackett, *Historical Documents*, 3: 465, 490.

187. Kessell, *Kiva, Cross, and Crown*, 357, 410.

188. Levine and LaBauve, "Examining the Complexity," 84, 87, 92–93; Kessell, *Kiva, Cross, and Crown,* 378; Palkovich, "Historic Epidemics," 92–93.

189. Kessell, *Kiva, Cross, and Crown,* 439–45.

190. Ibid., 457; Albert H. Schroeder, "Pecos Pueblo," in *Southwest,* vol. 9 of *Handbook of North American Indians,* ed. by Alfonso Ortiz (Washington, D.C.: Smithsonian Institution, 1979), 432.

191. Kessell, *Kiva, Cross, and Crown,* 458–59; Sando, *Pueblo Nations,* 253.

192. Hackett and Shelby, *Revolt of the Pueblo Indians,* 2: 270, 271.

193. Vargas, *By Force,* 435–43.

194. Vargas, *To the Royal Crown,* 462, 474, 502.

195. Ibid., 539.

196. Vargas, *Blood,* 39; *Documentos* 3(1): 148.

197. Vargas, *Blood,* 47, 56.

198. Ibid., 118, 450 n69.

199. Ibid., 149–50.

200. Ibid., 230.

201. Ibid., 165.

202. Ibid., 388–89, 391.

203. Ibid., 392–93, 408–12.

204. Ibid., 687–88.

205. Ibid., 727.

206. Ibid., 731–32.

207. Ibid., 817, 857, 881–82, 1015–16.

208. Ibid., 771–75.

209. Ibid., 729.

210. Ibid., 752.

211. Ibid., 780, 784, 829, 836–37, 881.

212. Ibid., 842.

213. Ibid., 784, 829.

214. Ibid., 843–45.

215. Ibid., 1003.

216. Ibid., 1028.

217. Ibid., 978; *Documentos* 3(1): 172.

218. Vargas, *Blood,* 1041, 1042, 1047.

219. Ibid., 783, 833, 1001, 1002.

220. Ibid., 1062.

221. Ibid., 1020, 1024, 1050. For Cuartelejo see chapter 4, note 3.

222. Ibid., 1064.

223. Thomas, *After Coronado,* 20.

224. Hackett, *Historical Documents,* 3: 374–75.

225. Vargas, *Blood,* 1056, 1059.

226. Ibid., 1058.

227. Bandelier, *Final Report,* 2: 85 n1 and n2.

228. Hackett, *Historical Documents,* 3: 380; *Documentos* 3(1): 193–94.

229. Marjorie F. Lambert, "Pojoaque Pueblo," in *Southwest,* vol. 9 of *Handbook of North American Indians,* ed. by Alfonso Ortiz (Washington, D.C.: Smithsonian Institution, 1979), 326, 327.

230. Hackett and Shelby, *Revolt of the Pueblo Indians,* 1: 55–56, 57, 61, 98, 110.

231. Ibid., 1: 13, 14. 15. 20.
232. *Documentos* 3(1): 127.
233. Vargas, *By Force,* 447–48, 449.
234. Ibid., 450.
235. Ibid., 451–52.
236. Vargas, *Blood,* 289, 290; *Documentos* 3(1): 156.
237. Vargas, *Blood,* 296–300.
238. Ibid., 898; *Documentos* 3(1): 169.
239. Vargas, *Blood,* 687.
240. Ibid., 830, 995.
241. Ibid., 827, 833.
242. Ibid., 1001, 1003, 1016.
243. Ibid., 1017–20.
244. Ibid., 1019–34.
245. Ibid., 996.
246. Ibid., 1002.
247. Ibid., 1013, 1020, 1033.
248. Ibid., 1042, 1044.
249. Ibid., 1050–55, 1061.
250. Vargas, *Blood,* 1063.
251. Thomas, *After Coronado,* 21, 74, 76.

WORKS CITED

Anderson, H. Allen. "The Encomienda in New Mexico, 1598–1680." *New Mexico Historical Review* 60(1985): 353–77.

Anschuetz, Kurt F. *Not Waiting for the Rain: Integrated Systems of Water Management by Pre-Columbian Pueblo Farmers in North Central New Mexico.* 2 vols. Ph.D. Dissertation. Ann Arbor: University of Michigan, 1998.

Anschuetz, Kurt F., Timothy D. Maxwell, and John A. Ware. *Testing Report and Research Design for the Medanales North Project, Rio Arriba County, New Mexico.* Laboratory of Anthropology Note 347. Santa Fe: Museum of New Mexico, 1985.

Arnon, Nancy S. and W. W. Hill. "Santa Clara Pueblo." In *Southwest*, volume 9 of *Handbook of North American Indians.* Edited by Alfonso Ortiz, 296–307. Washington, D.C.: Smithsonian Institution, 1979.

Baldwin, Stuart J. *Preliminary Report on the 1982 Excavations at the Pueblo of Abo, Salinas National Monument.* Ms. on file, Laboratory of Anthropology. Santa Fe: Museum of New Mexico, 1982.

———. *A Tentative Occupation Sequence for Abo Pass, Central New Mexico.* Ms. on file, Laboratory of Anthropology. Santa Fe: Museum of New Mexico, 1983.

———. "A Reconsideration of the Dating of a Seventeenth Century New Mexican Document." *New Mexico Historical Review* 59(1984): 411–13.

Bandelier, Adolph F. A. *Final Report of Investigations Among the Indians of the Southwestern United States Carried on Mainly in the Years from 1880 to 1885.* 2 vols. Papers of the Archaeological Institute of America, American Series 3 and 4. Cambridge, Mass.: John Wilson & Son, 1890 and 1892.

Barrett, Elinore M. "Indian Community Lands in the *Tierra Caliente* of Michoacán." *Jahrbuch für Geschichte von Staat, Wirtschaft und Gesellschaft Lateinamerikas* 11(1974): 78–120.

Bayer, Laura W., with Floyd Montoya and the Pueblo of Santa Ana. *Santa Ana: The People, the Pueblo, and the History of Tamaya.* Albuquerque: University of New Mexico Press, 1994.

Beal, John D. *Foundations of the Rio Grande Classic: The Lower Rio Chama 1300–1500.* Ms. on file, New Mexico Historic Preservation Division. Santa Fe: New Mexico Office of Cultural Affairs, 1987.

Benavides, Alonso de. *The Memorial of Fray Alonso de Benavides, 1630.* Translated by Mrs. Edward E. Ayer. Annotated by Frederick Webb Hodge and Charles fletcher Lummis. Chicago: privately printed, 1916 (Reprinted: Albuquerque, N.Mex.: Horn and Wallace Publishers, 1965.)

———. *Fray Alonso de Benavides' Revised Memorial of 1634.* Edited by Frederick Webb Hodge, George P. Hammond, and Agapito Rey. Albuquerque: University of New Mexico Press, 1945.

Biella, Jan V. "Changing Residential Patterns among the Anasazi, A.D. 725–1525." In volume 4 of *Archeological Investigations in Cochiti Reservoir, New Mexico.* Edited by Jan V. Biella and Richard C. Chapman, 103–44. Albuquerque: Office of Contract Archeology, University of New Mexico, 1979.

Blakeslee, Donald J. *Along Ancient Trails: The Mallet Expedition of 1739.* Niwot: University Press of Colorado, 1995.

Bloom, Lansing B. "Alburquerque and Galisteo: Certificate of their Founding, 1706." *New Mexico Historical Review* 10(1935): 48–50.

———. "A Glimpse of New Mexico in 1620." *New Mexico Historical Review* 3(1928): 357–80.

———. "The West Jemez Culture Area." *New Mexico Historical Review* 21 (1946): 120–26.

Bloom, Lansing B., and Lynn B. Mitchell. "The Chapter Elections in 1672." *New Mexico Historical Review* 13(1938): 85–119.

Bolton, Herbert E. *Coronado, Knight of Pueblos and Plains.* Albuquerque: University of New Mexico Press, 1990.

Borhegyi, Stephan F. de. "The Evolution of a Landscape." *Landscape, Magazine of Human Geography* 4(1954): 24–30.

Brandt, Elizabeth A. "Sandia Pueblo." In *Southwest,* volume 9 of *Handbook of North American Indians.* Edited by Alfonso Ortiz, 343–50. Washington, D.C.: Smithsonian Institution, 1979.

Breternitz, David A. *An Appraisal of Tree-Ring Dated Pottery in the Southwest.* Volume 10 of Anthropological Papers of the University of Arizona. Tucson: University of Arizona, 1966.

Carrera Stampa, Manuel. "Evolution of Weights and Measures in New Spain." *Hispanic American Historical Review* 29(1949): 2–24.

Carson, Phil. *Across the Northern Frontier, Spanish Explorations in Colorado.* Boulder, Colo.: Johnson Books, 1998.

Chardon, Roland. "The Linear League in North America." *Annals of the Association of American Geographers* 70(1980): 129–53.

Colección de documentos inéditos relativos al descubrimiento, conquista, y organización de las antiguas posesiones españolas en América y Oceanía, sacados de los archivos del reino, y muy especialmente del de Indias. Vol. Madrid, 1871.

Cordell, Linda S. *A Cultural Resources Overview, Middle Rio Grande Valley, New Mexico.* Washington, D.C.: U.S. Government Printing Office, 1979.

———. "Prehistory: Eastern Anasazi." In *Southwest,* volume 9 of *Handbook of North American Indians.* Edited by Alfonso Ortiz, 131–11. Washington, D.C.: Smithsonian Institution, 1979.

———. *Tijeras Canyon, Analyses of the Past.* Albuquerque: University of New Mexico Press, 1980.

———. *Prehistory of the Southwest.* Orlando, Fla.: Academic Press, Inc., 1984.

———. "Northern and Central Rio Grande." In *Dynamics of Southwest Prehistory,* 293–335. Linda S. Cordell and George J. Gumerman, eds. Washington, D.C.: Smithsonian Institution Press, 1989.

Crespo, Benito. "Documents Concerning Bishop Crespo's Visitation, 1730." Edited and translated by Eleanor B. Adams. *New Mexico Historical Review* 28(1953): 222–33.

Cutter, Donald C., ed. "An Anonymous Statistical Report on New Mexico in 1765." *New Mexico Historical Review* 50(1975): 347–52.

D'Arrigo, Rosanne, and Gordon C. Jacoby. "A Tree-ring Reconstruction of New Mexico Winter Precipitation and its Relation to El Niño/Southern Oscillation Events." In *El Niño: Historical and Paleoclimate Aspects of the Southern Oscillation.* Edited by Henry F. Diaz and Vera Markgraf. Cambridge, U.K.: Cambridge University Press, 1992.

Davis, Irvine. "The Kiowa-Tanoan, Keresan, and Zuñi Languages." In *The Languages of Native America.* Edited by Lyle Campbell and Marianne Mithun, 390–443. Austin: University of Texas Press, 1979.

Dean, Jeffrey S., and William J. Robinson. *Dendroclimatic Variability in the American Southwest,* A.D. *680 to 1970.* Tucson: Laboratory of Tree-Ring Research, University of Arizona, 1977.

Delisle, Guillaume. *Carte des Environs du Missisipi par G. de 1'Isle Geogr. donne par Mr d'Iberville en 1701.* Copy in New Mexico State Historical Library, Santa Fe, N.Mex.

Dickson, D. Bruce, Jr. *Prehistoric Pueblo Settlement Patterns: The Arroyo Hondo, New Mexico, Site Survey.* Volume 2 of the Arroyo Hondo Archeological Series. Santa Fe, N.Mex.: School of American Research Press, 1979.

Dobyns, Henry F. "Disease Transfer at Contact." *Annual Review of Anthropology* 22(1993): 273–91.

———. "Native American Trade Centers as Contagious Disease Foci." In *Disease and Demography in the Americas.* Edited by John W. Verano and Douglas H. Ubelaker, 215–22. Washington, D.C.: Smithsonian Institution Press, 1992

———. *Their Number Become Thinned: Native American Population Dynamics in Eastern North America.* Knoxville: University of Tennessee Press, 1983.

Documentos para la historia de México. Series 3, vol. 1. Mexico, 1856.

Domínguez, Francisco Atanasio. *The Missions of New Mexico, 1776, A Description by Fray Francisco Atanasio Domínguez with Other Contemporary Documents.* Translated and annotated by Eleanor B. Adams and Fray Angélico Chávez. Albuquerque: University of New Mexico Press, 1956.

Dozier, Edward P. *Hano: A Tewa Indian Community.* New York: Holt, Rinehart, and Winston, 1966.

Earls, Amy C. *The Organization of Piro Pueblo Subsistence, A.D. 1300–1680.* Ph.D. Dissertation. Albuquerque: University of New Mexico, 1985.

———. "Raiding, Trading, and Population Reduction Among the Piro Pueblos, A.D. 1540–1680." In *Current Research on the Late Prehistory and Early History of New Mexico.* Edited by Bradley J. Vierra and Clara Gualtieri, 11–19. Albuquerque: New Mexico Archeological Council, 1992.

Ebright, Malcolm. "New Mexican Land Grants: The Legal Background." In *Land, Water, and Culture: New Perspectives on Hispanic Land Grants.* Edited by Charles L. Briggs and John R. Van Ness, 15–64. Albuquerque: University of New Mexico Press, 1987.

Edelman, Sandra A. "San Ildefonso Pueblo." In *Southwest,* volume 9 of *Handbook of North American Indians.* Edited by Alfonso Ortiz, 308–16. Washington, D.C.: Smithsonian Institution, 1979.

Elliott, Michael L. *The Jemez Falls Campground Project: Archeological Investigations at Four Small Sites in the Jemez Mountains, New Mexico.* Archeological Report 89–2. Prepared for the Santa Fe National Forest, Santa Fe, New Mexico. Albuquerque: N.Mex.: Jemez Mountains Research Center, 1991.

———. *Large Pueblo Sites near Jemez Springs, New Mexico.* Cultural Resources Report 3. Santa Fe, N.Mex.: U.S. Forest Service, U.S. Department of Agriculture, 1982.

———, ed. *Archeological Investigations at Small Sites in the Jemez Mountains, New Mexico.* Cultural Resources Document 6. Santa Fe, N.Mex.: Santa Fe National Forest, U.S. Department of Agriculture, 1988.

Ellis, Florence Hawley. "Isleta Pueblo." In *Southwest,* volume 9 of *Handbook of North American Indians.* Edited by Alfonso Ortiz, 351–65. Washington, D.C.: Smithsonian Institution, 1979.

———. "Laguna Pueblo." In *Southwest,* volume 9 of *Handbook of North American Indians.* Edited by Alfonso Ortiz, 438–39. Washington, D.C.: Smithsonian Institution, 1979.

———. "The Long Lost 'City' of San Gabriel del Yungue, Second Oldest European Settlement in the United States." In *When Cultures Meet: Remembering San Gabriel del Yunge Oweenge*. Papers from the October 20, 1984, conference held at San Juan Pueblo, New Mexico, 10–38. Santa Fe, N.Mex.: Sunstone Press, 1987.

———. "Small Structures Used by Historic Pueblo Peoples and Their Immediate Ancestors." In *Limited Activity and Occupation Sites: A Collection of Conference Papers*. Edited by Albert E. Ward, 59–68. Albuquerque, N.Mex.: Center for Anthropological Studies, 1978.

Ellis, Florence Hawley, and J. J. Brody. "Ceramic Stratigraphy and Tribal History at Taos Pueblo." *American Antiquity* 30(1964): 34–42.

Espinosa, J. Manuel. *Crusaders of the Rio Grande: The Story of Don Diego de Vargas and the Reconquest and Refounding of New Mexico*. Chicago: Institute of Jesuit History, 1942.

———, ed. and trans. *The Pueblo Revolt of 1696 and the Franciscan Missions in New Mexico: Letters of the Missionaries and Related Documents*. Norman: University of Oklahoma Press, 1988.

Farwell, Robin Elizabeth. *An Architectural History of the Seventeenth Century Mission Church of San José de Guisewa, Jemez National Monument, New Mexico*. M.A. Thesis. Albuquerque: University of New Mexico, 1991.

Fewkes, J. Walter. "The Pueblo Settlements Near El Paso, Texas." *American Anthropologist* 4(1902): 57–75.

Fisher, Reginald G. *Second Report of the Archeological Survey of the Pueblo Plateau: Santa Fe Sub-Quadrangle A*. University of New Mexico Bulletin 1. Albuquerque: University of New Mexico Press, 1931.

Fliedner, Dietrich. "Pre-Spanish Pueblos in New Mexico." *Annals of the Association of American Geographers* 65(1975): 363–77.

Flint, Richard. *Greater Cruelties Have Been Reported, The 1544 Investigation of the Coronado Expedition*. Ph.D. Dissertation. Albuquerque: University of New Mexico, 1999.

Forbes, Jack D. "The Appearance of the Mounted Indian in Northern Mexico and the Southwest to 1680." *Southwestern Journal of Anthropology* 25(1959): 189–212.

———. *Apache, Navaho, and Spaniard*. Norman: University of Oklahoma Press, 1960.

Ford, Richard I., Albert H. Schroeder, and Stewart L. Peckham. "Three Perspectives on Pueblan Prehistory." In *New Perspectives on the Pueblos*. Edited by Alfonso Ortiz, 19–39. Albuquerque: University of New Mexico Press, 1972.

Franklin, Hayward H. *Valencia Pueblo Ceramics*. Ms. on file, Office of Contract Archeology. Albuquerque: University of New Mexico, 1994.

Fritts, Harold C. *Tree-Rings and Climate*. London, 1979.

———. *Reconstructing Large-Scale Climatic Patterns from Tree-Ring Data, A Diagnostic Analysis* (computerized appendix). Tucson: University of Arizona Press, 1991.

Garcia-Mason, Velma. "Acoma Pueblo." In *Southwest*, volume 9 of *Handbook of North American Indians*. Edited by Alfonso Ortiz, 450–66. Washington, D.C.: Smithsonian Institution, 1979.

Gibson, Charles. *The Aztecs Under Spanish Rule, A History of the Indians of the Valley of Mexico, 1519–1810*. Stanford, Calif.: Stanford University Press, 1964.

Grissino-Mayer, Henri D. "A 2129-Year Reconstruction of Precipitation for Northwestern New Mexico, USA." In *Tree Rings, Environment, and Humanity*. Edited by J. S. Dean, D. M. Meko, and T. W. Swetnam, 191–204. *Radiocarbon,* 1996.

———. "El Malpais Tree-Ring Record." Edited by Henri D. Grissino-Mayer and Harold C. Fritts. In *International Tree-Ring Data Bank*. Boulder, Colo.: IGPB Pages/World Data Center-A for Paleoclimatology. NOAA/NGDC Paleoclimatology Program, 1998.

Grissino-Mayer, Henri D., Thomas W. Swetnam, and Rex K. Adams. "The Rare, Old-age Conifers of El Malpais—Their Role in Understanding Climate Change in the American Southwest." *New Mexico Bureau of Mines & Mineral Resources Bulletin* 156(1997): 155–61.

Grissino-Mayer, Henri D., Christopher H. Baisan, and Thomas W. Swetnam. *A 1,373 Year Reconstruction of Annual Precipitation for the Southern Rio Grande Basin.* Fort Bliss, Tex.: Department of the Army, Directorate of Environment, Natural Resources Division, 1997.

Grove, Jean M. *The Little Ice Age.* London: Methuen, 1988.

Gunnerson, Dolores A. *The Jicarilla Apaches: A Study in Survival.* Dekalb: Northern Illinois University Press, 1974.

Hackett, Charles Wilson. "The Location of the Tigua Pueblos of Alameda, Puaray, and Sandia in 1680–81." *Old Santa Fe* 2(1915): 381–91.

———. "The Retreat of the Spaniards from New Mexico in 1680 and the Beginnings of El Paso." *Southwestern Historical Quarterly* 16(1912): 137–68 and 16(1913): 259–76.

———, ed. *Historical Documents Relating to New Mexico, Nueva Viscaya, and Approaches Thereto to 1773, Collected by Adolph F. A. Bandelier and Fanny R. Bandelier.* 3 vols. Washington, D.C.: Carnegie Institution, 1923–37.

Hackett, Charles Wilson, and Charmion Clair Shelby, eds.and trans. *Revolt of the Pueblo Indians of New Mexico and Otermín's Attempted Reconquest, 1680–1682.* 2 vols. Albuquerque: University of New Mexico Press, 1942.

Hall, G. Emlen. "The Pueblo Grant Labyrinth." In *Land, Water, and Culture: New Perspectives on Hispanic Land Grants.* Edited by Charles L. Briggs and John R. Van Ness, 67–138. Albuquerque: University of New Mexico Press, 1987.

Hammond, George P., and Agapito Rey, eds.and trans. *Obregón's History of Sixteenth Century Explorations in Western America Entitled: Chronicle, Commentary, or Relation of the Ancient and Modern Discoveries in New Spain and New Mexico, 1584.* Los Angeles: Wetzel Publishing Company, Inc., 1928.

———. *Narratives of the Coronado Expedition, 1540–1542.* Coronado Cuarto Centennial Publications II. Albuquerque: University of New Mexico Press, 1940.

———. *Don Juan de Oñate: Colonizer of New Mexico, 1595–1628.* 2 vols. Coronado Cuarto Centennial Publications V and VI. Albuquerque: University of New Mexico Press, 1953.

———. *The Rediscovery of New Mexico, 1580–1594.* Coronado Cuarto Centennial Publications III. Albuquerque: University of New Mexico Press, 1966.

Harbottle, Garmon, and Phil C. Weigand. "Turquoise in Pre-Columbian America." *Scientific American* 26(1992): 56–62.

Harrington, John P. *The Ethnography of the Tewa Indians.* Twenty-Ninth Annual Report of the Bureau of American Ethnology for the Years 1907–1908. Washington, D.C.: Smithsonian Institution, 1916.

Hayes, Alden C., J. N. Young, and A. H. Warren. *Excavation of Mound 7, Gran Quivira National Monument.* Volume 16 of Publications in Archeology. Washington, D.C.: National Park Service, U.S. Department of the Interior, 1981.

Hewett, Edgar L. *Pajarito Plateau and Its Ancient People.* Albuquerque: University of New Mexico Press, 1938.

Hickerson, Nancy P. *The Jumanos: Hunters and Traders of the Southern Plains.* Austin: University of Texas Press, 1994.

Hodge, Frederick Webb, ed. *Handbook of American Indians North of Mexico*. 2 vols. Bureau of American Ethnology Bulletin 30. Washington, D.C.: Smithsonian Institution, 1907 and 1910.

Hoebel, E. Adamson. "Zia Pueblo." In *Southwest,* volume 9 of *Handbook of North American Indians*. Edited by Alfonso Ortiz, 407–17. Washington, D.C.: Smithsonian Institution, 1979.

Houser, Nicolas P. "Tigua Pueblo." In *Southwest,* volume 9 of *Handbook of North American Indians*. Edited by Alfonso Ortiz, 336–42. Washington, D.C.: Smithsonian Institution, 1979.

Hughes, Anne Eugenia. *The Beginnings of Spanish Settlement in the El Paso District*. Publications in History 1: 295–392. Berkeley: University of California Press, 1914, reprint 1935.

Hunter-Anderson, Rosalind. "Explaining Residential Aggregation in the Northern Rio Grande: A Competition Reduction Model." In volume 4 of *Archeological Investigations in Cochiti Reservoir, New Mexico*. Edited by Jan V. Biella and Richard C. Chapman, 169–75. Albuquerque: Office of Contract Archeology, University of New Mexico, 1979.

Información contra Francisco Vázquez de Coronado. Archivo General de Indias, Justicia, legajo 1021, pieza 4, 1544 (from transcript in Bolton research materials, Bancroft Library, University of California, Berkeley).

Ivey, James E. "Another Look at Dating the Scholes Manuscript: A Research Note." *New Mexico Historical Review* 64(1989): 341–47.

———. "The Greatest Misfortune of All: Famine in the Province of New Mexico, 1667–1672." *Journal of the Southwest* 36(1994): 76–100.

———. *In the Midst of Loneliness, The Architectural History of the Salinas Missions, Salinas Missions National Monument Historic Structure Report*. Southwest Cultural Resources Center Professional Papers No. 15. Santa Fe, N.Mex.: National Park Service, U.S. Department of the Interior, 1988.

Jenkins, Myra E. "Taos Pueblo and its Neighbors, 1540–1847." *New Mexico Historical Review* 41(1966): 85–114.

———. "Oñate's Administration and the Pueblo Indians." In *When Cultures Meet: Remembering San Gabriel del Yunge Oweenge*. Papers from the October 20, 1984, conference held at San Juan Pueblo, New Mexico, 63–72. Santa Fe, N.Mex.: Sunstone Press, 1987.

———. "Spanish Land Grants in the Tewa Area." *New Mexico Historical Review* 47(1972): 113–34.

Kelley, N. Edmund. *The Contemporary Ecology of Arroyo Hondo, New Mexico*. Volume 1 of Arroyo Hondo Archeological Series. Santa Fe, N.Mex.: School of American Research, 1980.

Kelley, Vincent C. *Albuquerque: Its Mountains, Valley, Water, and Volcanoes*. Volume 9 of *Scenic Trips to the Geologic Past*. Socorro: New Mexico Bureau of Mines and Mineral Resources, 1969.

Kessell, John L. *Kiva, Cross, and Crown: The Pecos Indians and New Mexico, 1540–1840*. Washington, D.C.: National Park Service, U.S. Department of the Interior, 1979.

Knaut, Andrew L. *The Pueblo Revolt: Conquest and Resistance in Seventeenth-Century New Mexico*. Norman: University of Oklahoma Press, 1995.

Kulisheck, Jeremy. *Settlement Patterns, Population, and Congregación on the 17th Century Jemez Plateau*. Society of American Archaeology, 61st Annual Meeting, New Orleans, La., 1996.

Lamb, H. H. *Climatic History and the Future*. New Haven, Conn.: Princeton University Press, 1985.

Lambert, Marjorie F. *Paa-ko: Archeological Chronicle of an Indian Village in North Central New Mexico*. School of American Research Monograph 19. Albuquerque: University of New Mexico Press, 1954.

———. "Pojoaque Pueblo." In *Southwest*, volume 9 of *Handbook of North American Indians*. Edited by Alfonso Ortiz, 324–29. Washington, D.C.: Smithsonian Institution, 1979.

Lang, Richard W. *Archeological Survey of the Upper San Cristobal Arroyo Drainage, Galisteo Basin, Santa Fe County, New Mexico*. 3 vols. Santa Fe, N.Mex.: School of American Research Contract Program, 1977.

Levine, Frances, and Anna LaBauve. "Examining the Complexity of Historic Population Decline: A Case Study of Pecos Pueblo, New Mexico." *Ethnohistory* 44(1997): 75–112.

Lycett, Mark T. *Archeological Implications of European Contact: Demography, Settlement, and Land Use in the Middle Rio Grande Valley, New Mexico*. Ph.D. Dissertation. Albuquerque: University of New Mexico, 1996.

Maase, Otto P., ed. *Misiones de Nuevo Méjico: Documentos del Archivo General de Indias (Sevilla) publicadas por primera vez y anotadas*. Madrid, 1929.

Madrid, Roque. *The Navajos in 1705, Roque Madrid's Campaign Journal*. Edited and translated by Rick Hendricks and John P. Wilson. Albuquerque: University of New Mexico Press, 1996.

Marshall, Michael P. *An Archeological Survey of the Mann-Zuris Pueblo Complex, Phase II*. Santa Fe and Albuquerque: New Mexico Historic Commission and Miller-Brown Land Co., 1988.

Marshall, Michael P., et al. *Excavations at Nuestra Señora de Dolores Pueblo (LA 677), A Prehistoric Settlement in Tiguex Province*. Albuquerque: Office of Contract Archeology, University of New Mexico, 1982.

Marshall, Michael P., Nancy Atkins, and Joseph Winter. *Cultural Resources Monitoring and Data Recovery for the Cortez Co2 Pipeline in the Las Huertas Valley Area*. Albuquerque: Office of Contract Archeology, University of New Mexico, 1986.

Marshall, Michael P., and Cristina L. Marshall. *Investigations in the Middle Rio Grande Conservancy District: A Cultural Resource Survey of Irrigation and Drainage Canals in the Isleta-South to La Joya Area, Phase II Survey*. Albuquerque, N.Mex.: Bureau of Reclamation, U.S. Department of the Interior, 1992.

Marshall, Michael P., and Henry J. Walt. *Rio Abajo: Prehistory and History of a Rio Grande Province*. Santa Fe: New Mexico Historic Preservation Division, New Mexico Office of Cultural Affairs, 1984.

———. *Archeological Investigations of Colonial and Mexican Period Cultural Properties in the Rio Medio Province of New Mexico*. 2 vols. Ms. on file, New Mexico Historic Preservation Division. Santa Fe: New Mexico Office of Cultural Affairs, 1985.

Martínez, Gregory, Mary Davis, and Kathryn Sargeant. "Paleochannel Analysis in the North Valley of Albuquerque." In *An Archeological and Historical Survey of the Village of Los Ranchos*. Kathryn Sargeant and Mary Davis. Ms. on file, New Mexico Historic Preservation Division. Santa Fe: New Mexico Office of Cultural Affairs, 1985.

Mecham, J. Lloyd. "The Second Spanish Expedition to New Mexico." *New Mexico Historical Review* 1(1926): 265–91.

Mera, Harry P. *A Survey of the Biscuit Ware Area in Northern New Mexico*. New Mexico Archeological Survey, Technical Series Bulletin 6. Santa Fe: Laboratory of Anthropology, Museum of New Mexico, 1934.

———. *Population Changes in the Rio Grande Glaze Paint Area*. New Mexico Archeological Survey, Technical Series Bulletin 9. Santa Fe: Laboratory of Anthropology, Museum of New Mexico, 1940.

Midwestern Climatic Data Center, a cooperative program of the National Climate Data Center and the Illinois State Water Survey, Champaign, Illinois.

Montgomery, John, and Kathleen Bowman. *Archeological Reconnaissance of the Chupadera Arroyo Drainage, Central New Mexico.* Agency for Conservation Archeology Report. Portales: Eastern New Mexico University, 1989.

Montoya, Juan de. *New Mexico in 1602, Juan de Montoya's Relation of the Discovery of New Mexico.* Edited and translated by George P. Hammond and Agapito Rey. Quivira Society Publications VIII. Albuquerque: University of New Mexico Press, 1938.

National Register of Historic Places Inventory. Reports prepared for nomination to the National Register of Historic Places Inventory. Santa Fe, N.Mex.: National Park Service, U.S. Department of the Interior.

Nelson, Nels C. "Pueblo Ruins of the Galisteo Basin, New Mexico." *Anthropological Papers of the American Museum of Natural History* 15(1914): 1–33.

———. "Chronology of the Tano Ruins, New Mexico." *American Anthropologist* 18(1916): 159–80.

Ots Capdequí, José M. *España en América, El régimen de tierras en la época colonial.* Mexico, 1959.

Palkovich, Ann M. "Historic Epidemics of the American Pueblos." In *In the Wake of Contact: Biological Responses to Conquest.* Edited by Clark Spenser Larsen and George R. Miller. New York: Wiley-Liss, Inc., 1994.

Peckham, Stewart. *An Archeological Sites Inventory of New Mexico, Part 1.* Ms. on file, Laboratory of Anthropology. Santa Fe: Museum of New Mexico, 1969.

———. "The Anasazi of the Northern Rio Grande Rift." In *Rio Grande Rift: Northern New Mexico,* 275–81. Guidebook, 35th field Conference. Socorro: New Mexico Geological Society, 1984.

Peckham, Stewart, and Bart Olinger. "Postulated Movements of the Tano or Southern Tewa, A.D. 1300–1700." In *Clues to the Past: Papers in Honor of William M. Sundt.* Edited by Meliha S. Durand and David T. Kirkpatrick. Papers of the Archeological Society of New Mexico 16: 203–16. Santa Fe: Ancient City Press, 1990.

Preucel, Robert W., Jr. *Seasonal Circulation and Dual Residence in the Pueblo Southwest: A Prehistoric Example from the Pajarito Plateau, New Mexico.* New York: Garland Publishing, Inc., 1990.

Ramenofsky, Ann F. "The Problem of Introduced Infectious Diseases in New Mexico: 1540–1680." *Journal of Anthropological Research* 54(1996): 161–84.

Recopilación de Leyes de los Reynos de las Indias. Edición facsimilar de la cuarta impresión hecha en Madrid el año 1791. 3 vols. Madrid, 1943.

Reed, Erik K. *History of Quarai.* Santa Fe, N.Mex.: National Park Service, U.S. Department of the Interior, 1940.

———. "The Southern Tewa in the Historic Period." *El Palacio* 50 (1943): 254–64, 279–88.

Reeve, Frank D. "Early Navajo Geography." *New Mexico Historical Review* 31(1956): 290–309.

———. "Seventeenth Century Navaho-Spanish Relations." *New Mexico Historical Review* 32(1957): 36–52.

Reff, Daniel T. *The Demographic and Cultural Consequences of Old World Disease in the Greater Southwest, 1520–1660.* Ann Arbor: University of Michigan Microfilms, 1985.

———. "The Introduction of Smallpox in the Greater Southwest." *American Anthropologist* 89(1987): 704–8.

———. "Old World Diseases and the Dynamics of Indian and Jesuit Relations in Northwestern New Spain, 1520–1660." In *Ejidos and Regions of Refuge in Northwestern Mexico.* Edited by N. Ross Crumrine and Phil C. Wiegand. Anthropological Papers of the University of Arizona No. 46. Tucson: University of Arizona Press, 1987.

———. *Disease, Depopulation, and Culture Change in Northwestern New Spain, 1518–1764.* Salt Lake City: University of Utah Press, 1991.

———. "Contextualizing Missionary Discourse: The Benavides Memorials of 1630 and 1634." *Journal of Anthropological Research* 50(1994): 51–67.

Relación sacada de la probanza . . . que trata con Dn. García Ramírez de Cárdenas. Archivo General de Indias, Justicia, legajo 1021, pieza 3, 1546–1548 (from transcript in Bolton research papers, Bancroft Library, University of California, Berkeley).

Revilla Gigedo, Conde de (Juan Vicente Güemes Pacheco de Padilla Horcasitas y Aguayo). *Informe sobre las Misiones, 1793, e Instrucción Reservada al Marqués de Branciforte, 1794.* Mexico, 1966.

Riley, Carroll L. "Puaray and Coronado's Tiguex." In *Collected Papers in Honor of Erik K. Reed.* Edited by A. H. Schroeder. Papers of the Archeological Society of New Mexico 6: 197–213. Albuquerque, 1981.

———. *The Frontier People: The Greater Southwest in the Protohistoric Period.* Albuquerque: University of New Mexico Press, 1987.

———. *Rio del Norte, People of the Upper Rio Grande from Earliest Times to the Pueblo Revolt.* Salt Lake City: University of Utah Press, 1995.

Robinson, William J., and Catherine M. Cameron. *A Directory of Tree-Ring Dated Prehistoric Sites in the American Southwest.* Laboratory of Tree-Ring Research. Tucson: University of Arizona Press, 1991.

Rose, Martin R., Jeffrey S. Dean, and William J. Robinson. *The Past Climate of Arroyo Hondo, New Mexico, Reconstructed from Tree-Rings.* Arroyo Hondo Archaeological Series 4. Santa Fe, N.Mex.: School of American Research, 1981.

Salzer, Matthew W. *Dendroclimatology in the San Francisco Peaks Region of Northern Arizona, USA.* Ph.D. Dissertation, University of Arizona. Ann Arbor: University of Michigan Microfilms International, 2000.

Sando, Joe S. "Jemez Pueblo." In *Southwest*, volume 9 of *Handbook of North American Indians.* Edited by Alfonso Ortiz, 418–29. Washington, D.C.: Smithsonian Institution, 1979.

———. *Nee Hemish, A History of Jemez Pueblo.* Albuquerque: University of New Mexico Press, 1982.

———. *Pueblo Nations: Eight Centuries of Pueblo Indian History.* Santa Fe, N.Mex.: Clear Light Publishers, 1991.

Sargeant, Kathryn. "Coping with the River: Settlements in Albuquerque's North Valley." In *Secrets of a City: Papers on Albuquerque Area Archeology in Honor of Richard A. Bice.* Edited by Anne V. Poore and John L. Montgomery. Papers of the Archeological Society of New Mexico 13: 31–47. Santa Fe, N.Mex.: Ancient City Press, 1987.

Schaafsma, Curtis F. *Archeological Reconnaissance of the Proposed MAPCO Pipeline from Bloomfield to Hobbs.* Ms. on file, Laboratory of Anthropology. Santa Fe: Museum of New Mexico, 1972.

———. "Tiguex Province Revisited." In *Secrets of a City: Papers on Albuquerque Area Archeology in Honor of Richard A. Bice.* Edited by Anne V. Poore and John L. Montgomery. Papers of the Archeological Society of New Mexico 13: 6–13. Santa Fe, N.Mex.: Ancient City Press, 1987.

Scholes, France V. "Church and State in New Mexico, 1610–1650." *New Mexico Historical Review* 11(1936): 9–76, 145–78, 283–94, 297–349; 12(1937): 78–106.

———."Civil Government and Society in New Mexico in the Seventeenth Century." *New Mexico Historical Review* 10(1935): 71–111.

———. "Correction." *New Mexico Historical Review* 19(1944): 243–46.

———. "Documents for the History of the New Mexican Missions in the Seventeenth Century." *New Mexico Historical Review* 4(1929): 45–58.

———. "Juan Martínez de Montoya, Settler and Conquistador of New Mexico." *New Mexico Historical Review* 19 (1944a): 337–42.

———. "Notes on the Jemez Missions in the Seventeenth Century." *El Palacio* 44(1938): 61–71 and 93–102.

———. "Royal Treasury Records Relating to the Province of New Mexico, 1596–1683." *New Mexico Historical Review* 50(1975): 5–23 and 139–64.

———. "Supply Service of the New Mexico Missions of the Seventeenth Century." *New Mexico Historical Review* 5(1930): 93–114, 186–209, and 386–404.

———. *Troublous Times in New Mexico: 1659–1670.* Publications in History 11. Albuquerque: Historical Society of New Mexico, 1942.

Scholes, France V., and Lansing B. Bloom. "Friar Personnel and Mission Chronology, 1598–1629." *New Mexico Historical Review* 20(1945): 58–82.

Scholes, France V., and H. P. Mera. *Some Aspects of the Jumano Problem.* Contributions to American Anthropology and History 34, Carnegie Institution of Washington Publication 523. Washington, D.C., 1940.

Schroeder, Albert H. "Pecos Pueblo." In *Southwest,* volume 9 of *Handbook of North American Indians.* Edited by Alfonso Ortiz, 430–37. Washington, D.C.: Smithsonian Institution, 1979.

———. "Protohistoric Pueblo Demographic Changes." In *Current Research in the Late Prehistory and Early History of New Mexico.* Edited by Bradley J. Vierra and Clara Gualtieri, 29–35. Albuquerque: New Mexico Archeological Council, 1992.

———. "Pueblos Abandoned in Historic Times." In *Southwest,* volume 9 of *Handbook of North American Indians.* Edited by Alfonso Ortiz, 236–54. Washington, D.C.: Smithsonian Institution, 1979.

———. "Querechos, Vaqueros, Cocoyes, and Apaches." In *Collected Papers in Honor of Charlie R. Steen, Jr.* Papers of the Albuquerque Archeological Society 8: 159–66. Albuquerque, N.Mex., 1983.

———. "Rio Grande Ethnohistory." In *New Perspectives on the Pueblos.* Edited by Alfonso Ortiz. A School of American Research Book. Albuquerque: University of New Mexico Press, 1972.

———. "Tunque Pueblo—Who Lived There?" In *Clues to the Past: Papers in Honor of William M. Sundt.* Edited by Meliha S. Duran and David T. Kirkpatrick. Papers of the Archeological Society of New Mexico 16: 259–64. Santa Fe, N.Mex.: Ancient City Press, 1990.

———. "Vasquez de Coronado and the Southern Tiwa Pueblos." In *Archeology, Art, and Anthropology: Papers in Honor of J. J. Brody.* Edited by Meliha S. Duran and David T. Kirkpatrick. Papers of the Archeological Society of New Mexico 18: 185–91. Santa Fe, N.Mex.: Ancient City Press, 1992.

Schroeder, Albert H., and Dan S. Matson. *A Colony on the Move: Gaspar Castaño de Sosa's Journal, 1590–1591.* Santa Fe, N.Mex.: The School of American Research, 1965.

Scurlock, Dan. "An Historical Overview of Bernalillo, New Mexico and Site LA 677." In *Excavations at Nuestra Señora de Dolores Pueblo (LA 677), A Prehistoric Settlement in the Tiguex Province*. Michael P. Marshall, et al., Project #185–58a, 176–82. Albuquerque: Office of Contract Archeology, University of New Mexico, 1982.

———. *From the Rio to the Sierra: An Environmental History of the Middle Rio Grande Basin*. Fort Collins, Colo.: Rocky Mountain Research Station, Forest Service, U.S. Department of Agriculture, 1998.

Sigüenza y Góngora, Carlos de. *The Mercurio Volante of don Carlos de Sigüenza y Góngora, An Account of the First Expedition of don Diego de Vargas into New Mexico in 1692*. Edited and translated by Irving Albert Leonard. Los Angeles: The Quivira Society, 1932.

Simmons, Marc. "New Mexico's Smallpox Epidemic of 1780–1781." *New Mexico Historical Review* 41(1966): 319–26.

———. "New Mexico's Colonial Agriculture." *El Palacio* 89(1983): 3–10.

———. "Settlement Patterns and Village Plans in Colonial New Mexico." *Journal of the West* 8(1969): 7–21.

Smiley, Terah L., Stanley A. Stubbs, and Bryant Bannister. *A Foundation for Dating of Some Late Archeological Sites in the Rio Grande Area, New Mexico: Based on Studies in Tree-Ring Methods and Pottery Analysis*. Laboratory of Tree-Ring Research Bulletin 6. Tucson: University of Arizona, 1953.

Snow, David H. "The Identification of Puaray Pueblo." In *Collected Papers in Honor of Florence Hawley Ellis*. Edited by Theodore R. Frisbie. Papers of the Archeological Society of New Mexico 2: 463–80. Norman, Okla.: Hooper Publishing Company, 1975.

———. "Initial Entradas and Explorations: 1540–1593." In *The North Central Regional Overview*, volume 1 of *Historic Overview of North Central New Mexico*. Edited by Boyd C. Pratt and David H. Snow, 79–128. Santa Fe: New Mexico Historic Preservation Division, New Mexico Office of Cultural Affairs, 1988.

———. *Archeological Excavations at Pueblo del Encierro, LA 70*. Laboratory of Anthropology Note 78(2). Santa Fe: Museum of New Mexico, 1976.

———. "A Note on Encomienda Economics in Seventeenth-Century New Mexico." In *Hispanic Arts and Ethnohistory in the Southwest, Papers Inspired by the Work of E. Boyd*. Edited by Marta Weigle. Santa Fe, N.Mex.: Ancient City Press, 1983.

Spielmann, Katherine A. "Colonists, Hunters, and Farmers: Plains-Pueblo Interaction in the Seventeenth Century." In *Archeological and Historical Perspectives on the Spanish Borderlands West*. Edited by David Hurst Thomas. *Columbian Consequences* 1: 101–13. Washington, D.C.: Smithsonian Institution Press, 1989.

———. "Rio Abajo and Eastern Border Pueblos." In *The Prehistoric Pueblo World, A.D. 1150–1350*. Edited by Michael A. Adler. Tucson: University of Arizona Press, 1996.

Staley, David P. *Changes in the Morphology of the Rio Grande from Bernalillo to Isleta, New Mexico*. Ms. on file, Office of Contract Archeology. Albuquerque: University of New Mexico, 1981.

Stanislawski, Michael B. "Hopi-Tewa." In *Southwest*, volume 9 of *Handbook of North American Indians*. Edited by Alfonso Ortiz, 587–602. Washington, D.C.: Smithsonian Institution, 1979.

Steen, Charles R. *Pajarito Plateau Archeological Surveys and Excavations*. Los Alamos Scientific Laboratories Report No. 77–4. Los Alamos, N.Mex.: 1977.

Stodder, Ann L. W., and Debra L. Martin. "Health and Disease in the Southwest Before and After Spanish Contact." In *Disease and Demography in the Americas*. Edited by

John W. Verano and Douglas H. Ubelaker, 55–71. Washington, D.C.: Smithsonian Institution Press, 1992.

Strong, Pauline Turner. "Santa Ana Pueblo." In *Southwest,* volume 9 of *Handbook of North American Indians.* Edited by Alfonso Ortiz, 398–406. Washington, D.C.: Smithsonian Institution, 1979.

Stuart, David E., and Rory P. Gauthier. *Prehistoric New Mexico, Background for Survey.* Albuquerque: University of New Mexico Press, 1996.

Sundt, William M. "Pottery of Central New Mexico and Its Role as a Key to Both Time and Space." In *Secrets of a City: Papers on Albuquerque Area Archeology in Honor of Richard A. Bice.* Edited by Anne V. Poore and John L. Montgomery. Papers of the Archeological Society of New Mexico 13: 116–47. Santa Fe, N.Mex.: Ancient City Press, 1987.

Tainter, Joseph A. and David "A" Gillio. *Cultural Resources Overview, Mount Taylor Area, New Mexico.* Washington, D.C.: U.S. Government Printing Office, 1980.

Tainter, Joseph A. and Frances Levine. *Cultural Resources Overview, Central New Mexico.* Washington, D.C.: U.S. Government Printing Office, 1987.

Tamarón y Romeral, Pedro. *Bishop Tamarón's Visitation of New Mexico, 1760.* Publications in History 15. Edited by Eleanor B. Adams. Albuquerque: Historical Society of New Mexico, 1954.

Tello, Antonio. *Libro segundo de la crónica miscelanea, en que se trata de la conquista espiritual y temporal de la Santa provincia de Xalisco.* Guadalajara, Mexico, 1891.

Thomas, Alfred Barnaby, ed./trans. *Forgotten Frontiers: A Study of the Spanish Indian Policy of don Juan Bautista de Anza, Governor of New Mexico, 1777–1787; from the Original Documents in the Archives of Spain, Mexico, and New Mexico.* Norman: University of Oklahoma Press, 1932.

———. *After Coronado, Spanish Exploration Northeast of New Mexico, 1696–1727; Documents from the Archives of Spain, Mexico, and New Mexico.* Norman: University of Oklahoma Press, 1935.

———. *The Plains Indians and New Mexico, 1751–1778, A Collection of Documents Illustrative of the History of the Eastern Frontier of New Mexico.* Albuquerque: University of New Mexico Press, 1940.

Twitchell, Ralph E. *The Leading Facts of New Mexican History.* 5 vols. Cedar Rapids, Iowa: The Torch Press, 1911.

———, ed. and trans. *The Spanish Archives of New Mexico.* 2 vols. Cedar Rapids, Iowa: Torch Press, 1914.

Upham, Steadman. "Population and Spanish Contact in the Southwest." In *Disease and Demography in the Americas.* Edited by John W. Verano and Douglas H. Ubelaker, 223–36. Washington, D.C.: Smithsonian Institution Press, 1992.

———. "Smallpox and Climate in the American Southwest." *American Anthropologist* 88(1986): 115–28.

Usner, Donald J. *The Plaza del Cerro in Chimayó: Settlement and Function.* M.A. Thesis. Albuquerque: University of New Mexico, 1991.

———. *Sabino's Map, Life in Chimayó's Old Plaza.* Santa Fe: Museum of New Mexico Press, 1995.

Vargas, Diego de. *First Expedition of Vargas into New Mexico, 1692.* Edited and translated by J. Manuel Espinosa. Albuquerque: University of New Mexico Press, 1940.

———. *By Force of Arms, The Journals of don Diego de Vargas, 1691–1693.* Edited by John L. Kessell and Rick Hendricks. Albuquerque: University of New Mexico Press, 1992.

————. *To the Royal Crown Restored, The Journals of don Diego de Vargas, 1692–1694.* Edited by John L. Kessell, Rick Hendricks, and Meredith D. Dodge. Albuquerque: University of New Mexico Press, 1995.

————. *Blood on the Boulders, The Journals of don Diego de Vargas, New Mexico, 1694–1697.* 2 vols. Edited by John L. Kessell, Rick Hendricks, and Meredith D. Dodge. Albuquerque: University of New Mexico Press, 1998.

Vélez de Escalante, Fray Silvestre. "Carta del Padre Fray Silvestre Vélez de Escalante escrita en 2 de abril de 1778 años, Santa Fe." *Documentos para la historia de México* series 3, vol. 1: 113–26. Mexico, 1856.

Vetancurt, Fray Agustín de. *Teatro mexicano; descripción breve de los sucesos ejemplares, históricos, politicos, militares, y religiosos del nuevo mundo occidental de las Indias. Crónica de la provincia del Santo Evangelio de México.* Facsimile edition, Mexico, 1971.

Vierra, Bradley J. "The Tiguex Province: A Tale of Two Cities." In *Secrets of a City: Papers on Albuquerque Area Archeology in Honor of Richard A. Bice.* Edited by Anne V. Poore and John L. Montgomery. Papers of the Archeological Society of New Mexico 13: 70–86. Santa Fe, N.Mex.: Ancient City Press, 1987

Vierra, Bradley J., and Stanley M. Hordes. "Let the Dust Settle: A Review of the Coronado Campsite in the Tiguex Province." In *To Tierra Nueva: The Route of the Coronado Expedition in the Southwest.* Edited by Richard Flint and Shirley Cushing Flint. Niwot: University Press of Colorado, 1997.

Villagrá, Gaspar Pérez de. *History of New Mexico by Gaspar Pérez de Villagrá Acalá 1610.* Translated by Gilberto Espinosa. Los Angeles: Quivira Society, 1933.

Vivian, Gordon. *Restudy of the Province of Tiguex.* M.A. Thesis. Albuquerque: University of New Mexico, 1932.

Walz, Vina E. *History of the El Paso Area, 1680–1692.* Ph.D. Dissertation. Albuquerque: University of New Mexico, 1951.

Warren, A. Helene. "Glaze Paint Wares of the Upper Middle Rio Grande." In volume 4 of *Archeological Investigations in Cochiti Reservoir, New Mexico.* Edited by Jan V. Biella and Richard C. Chapman, 187–216. Albuquerque: Office of Contract Archeology, University of New Mexico, 1979.

————. "Indian and Spanish Mining in the Galisteo and Hagan Basins." *Special Publications* 8: 7–11. Socorro: New Mexico Geological Society, 1979.

————. *New Dimension in the Study of Prehistoric Pottery, A Preliminary Report Relating to the Excavation at Cochiti Dam, 1964–1966.* Laboratory of Anthropology Note 90. Santa Fe: Museum of New Mexico, 1973.

————. "Tonque." *El Palacio* 76 (1969): 36–42.

Warren, A. Helene, and Frances Joan Mathien. "Prehistoric and Historic Turquoise Mining in the Cerrillos District: Time and Place." *Southwestern Culture History: Collected Papers in Honor of Albert H. Schroeder.* Edited by Charles H. Lange, 93–127. Papers of the Archeological Society of New Mexico 10. Santa Fe, N.Mex.: Ancient City Press, 1985.

Wendorf, Fred, and Erik K. Reed. "An Alternative Reconstruction of Northern Rio Grande Prehistory." *El Palacio* 62(1955): 131–73.

Wheat, Carl I. *Mapping the Transmississippi West, 1540–1861.* 6 vols. San Francisco: Institute of Historical Cartography, 1957.

Wilcox, David R. "Changing Contexts of Pueblo Adaptations, A.D. 1250–1600." In *Farmers, Hunters, and Colonists: Interaction between the Southwest and the Southern Plains.* Edited by Katherine A. Spielmann, 128–54. Tucson: University of Arizona Press, 1991.

Wilson, John P. "Before the Pueblo Revolt: Population Trends, Apache Relations, and Pueblo Abandonments in Seventeenth Century New Mexico." In *Prehistory and History in the* Southwest. Edited by Nancy L. Fox. Papers of the Archeological Society of New Mexico 11: 113–20. Santa Fe, N.Mex.: Ancient City Press, 1985.

———. "Quarai, Living Mission to Monument." *El Palacio* 78(1973): 14–28.

Wimberly, Mark, and Peter Eidenbach. *Reconnaissance Study of the Archeological and Related Resources of the Lower Puerco and Salado Drainages, Central New Mexico.* Tularosa, N.Mex.: Human Systems Research, Inc., 1980.

Winship, George P., ed. *The Coronado Expedition, 1540–1542.* Fourteenth Annual Report of the U.S. Bureau of American Ethnology for the Years 1892–1893, Part 1: 329–637. Washington, D.C.: Smithsonian Institution, 1896.

Winter, Joseph C. "Life in Old Bernalillo in the Fifteenth Century." In *Excavations at Nuestra Señora de Dolores Pueblo (LA 677), A Prehistoric Settlement in the Tiguex Province.* Michael P. Marshall, et al., 183–99. Albuquerque: Office of Contract Archeology, University of New Mexico, 1982.

Woodhouse, Connie A., and Jonathan T. Overpeck. "2000 Years of Drought Variability in the Central United States." *Bulletin of the American Meteorological Society* 79(1998): 2693–2714.

Worcester, Donald E. "The Beginnings of the Apache Menace in the Southwest." *New Mexico Historical Review* 16(1941): 1–14.

Wozniak, Frank E. *The Ethnohistory of the Abiquiu Reservoir Area: A Study of the Native American Utilization of the Piedra Lumbre Valley (1500–1890).* Archeological and Historical Research at Abiquiu Reservoir, Rio Arriba County, New Mexico. vol. 3. Edited by Kenneth J. Lord and Nancy S. Sella. Albuquerque, N.Mex.: Chambers Consultants and Planners, 1987.

Zárate Salmerón, Fray Gerónimo de. *Relaciones: An Account of things seen and learned by Father Jerónimo de Zárate Salmerón from the Year 1538 to Year 1626.* Translated by Alicia Ronstadt Milich. Albuquerque, N.Mex.: Horn & Wallace Publishers, 1966.

Závala, Silvio A. *De encomiendas y propiedad territorial en algunas regiones de la América española.* Mexico, 1940.

Zoretich, Frank. "Paths Not Taken: Jonathan Haas Studies Pueblo Political Life Before the Spanish." Santa Fe Institute, *Bulletin* (summer 1997): 1–6.

Appendix Tables

Appendix Table A. Palmer Drought Severity Index Values for New Mexico,* 1500-1699

Year	Chup.	S. Fe	Cham	Rio G.	Year	Chup.	S. Fe	Cham.	Rio G.
1500	-2.512	-1.530	-.149	-3.412	1550	2.468	1.405	.103	.579
1501	.271	.026	-.587	.041	1551	-2.403	-1.517	-.591	-1.267
1502	-.086	.100	-2.381	.438	1552	.576	.269	-.659	1.057
1503	-1.316	.728	.019	-.174	1553	.443	3.078	2.941	2.045
1504	-1.293	.832	.200	.407	1554	.662	1.643	1.025	2.436
1505	.035	1.366	.280	.319	1555	1.778	2.085	1.973	1.184
1506	-3.225	-2.384	-1.337	-3.754	1556	.489	.473	2.507	4.810
1507	.225	1.075	2.688	-.388	1557	2.462	-.645	.044	1.845
1508	-5.002	-.060	.806	-.019	1558	-1.512	-.672	-.688	-1.426
1509	.512	-.364	.726	.579	1559	-.436	1.045	.137	-.564
1510	-.580	.776	.196	-1.369	1560	-2.909	-1.603	-2.671	-2.484
1511	.369	1.331	1.025	.758	1561	-.206	-.203	1.181	-1.721
1512	.518	-.624	-.756	-1.172	1562	-3.668	-2.470	1.640	-2.340
1513	3.204	1.743	.246	1.071	1563	.081	.819	-.554	.136
1514	1.093	1.864	.587	1.940	1564	-1.966	.039	-.528	.270
1515	1.599	1.249	1.067	-.233	1565	1.674	1.149	.166	1.261
1516	-6.802	-3.835	-2.697	-3.451	1566	-2.564	-.039	.461	-3.019
1517	-3.559	-.732	-1.648	-.782	1567	-2.604	.291	-.827	-1.011
1518	1.588	1.101	.369	2.267	1568	-1.782	1.253	.255	-1.855
1519	-.155	.963	1.013	1.089	1569	.731	1.604	-.065	.934
1520	1.335	1.097	1.556	.815	1570	2.508	-.151	-.655	1.022
1521	1.858	3.234	1.181	.677	1571	-.597	.091	-.928	-1.542
1522	-3.105	-.693	-3.084	-1.886	1572	1.421	-.108	-1.067	1.630
1523	-.603	-.659	-1.720	-.399	1573	-5.606	-2.717	-1.842	-2.628
1524	-2.639	-2.414	-3.071	-1.271	1574	-1.034	-.290	-.111	-1.995
1525	-.833	.711	-.280	-.131	1575	.029	.499	-.541	-.152
1526	.869	-.351	-.213	-.184	1576	-.097	-.208	-1.366	-.142
1527	-.741	.096	-.958	-.054	1577	1.335	1.292	1.139	.702
1528	.915	.941	-.406	-.444	1578	-2.593	.273	1.147	-1.243
1529	1.921	2.384	1.168	.087	1579	-5.158	-2.223	-.861	-3.880
1530	-.408	.811	1.278	.839	1580	-3.455	-1.755	-3.004	-2.822
1531	.415	.976	2.259	-2.101	1581	-1.282	-.277	-.217	-.736
1532	-3.461	-.693	.293	-1.260	1582	-1.857	-.229	-.709	-.666
1533	-1.679	.187	.107	-.395	1583	-2.972	-2.141	-2.861	-2.080
1534	-.097	1.422	2.777	.083	1584	-1.943	-.403	-.031	-2.389
1535	-3.415	-1.651	-1.021	-2.354	1585	-3.047	-1.564	-2.200	-2.495
1536	-.914	2.115	.221	.973	1586	.305	1.912	.503	-.061
1537	.415	.750	1.467	1.050	1587	-1.443	-0.910	-1.034	-1.046
1538	-2.783	.395	-.440	-1.197	1588	1.128	.169	2.899	-.582
1539	1.197	1.101	1.674	-.353	1589	3.256	1.318	1.918	-.634
1540	2.606	2.783	2.310	1.732	1590	-3.329	-.901	-3.602	-1.904
1541	-.080	1.318	1.674	.488	1591	.035	.113	2.528	-.993
1542	-5.710	-2.600	-.061	-3.602	1592	-.902	2.241	-.090	-.793
1543	1.542	1.998	2.608	-.328	1593	-5.560	-.932	-2.276	-2.526
1544	-2.098	.403	-1.067	-1.359	1594	4.912	3.888	1.366	-.008
1545	-2.346	-2.019	2.200	-2.336	1595	-.017	1.994	-.549	.829
1546	-.914	-1.829	-.394	-1.369	1596	2.117	2.466	2.394	-.342
1547	.898	.226	.339	-.701	1597	2.025	2.822	2.137	.192
1548	-1.782	-.130	1.072	-.624	1598	-4.238	-1.408	-.541	-3.043
1549	.254	-1.261	-2.212	.213	1599	-.431	.434	2.566	.129

Appendix Table A. Continued

Year	Chup.	S. Fe	Cham.	Rio G.	Year	Chup.	S. Fe	Cham.	Rio G.
1600	-4.031	-.932	-.743	-2.913	1650	-.678	-.632	-.095	-2.498
1601	-2.737	-2.388	-.259	-1.637	1651	3.871	1.379	1.905	3.551
1602	-1.880	.577	1.295	.044	1652	.616	.806	1.324	.523
1603	2.025	1.760	2.314	.403	1653	-1.057	-.407	-.145	-1.193
1604	2.163	.698	1.345	-1.193	1654	-3.358	-.940	-.621	-2.646
1605	2.433	.785	.116	.544	1655	3.313	.841	1.505	3.804
1606	-.051	-.624	.739	-.919	1656	-.321	-.329	-.023	.857
1607	-1.983	.512	.672	-.807	1657	-2.185	-.398	-2.221	-1.278
1608	2.663	-.619	.356	-.497	1658	-2.737	-.563	-1.930	-.835
1609	1.277	.481	-.208	-.040	1659	-1.713	-1.153	2.251	-.828
1610	3.900	2.492	3.425	2.137	1660	2.146	.897	-1.488	1.560
1611	3.261	1.985	2.183	.758	1661	1.657	1.426	-.781	-.325
1612	.616	1.561	1.362	.136	1662	1.007	2.406	1.501	2.527
1613	1.024	.993	-.600	1.163	1663	-.770	-.078	.920	.653
1614	.927	.065	-.250	-.560	1664	-5.232	-2.115	.301	-2.537
1615	-3.220	1,002	-.528	-1.538	1665	.035	.464	-.840	.927
1616	-2.915	-1.703	1.375	-2.456	1666	-2.558	-1.738	-.608	-2.343
1617	.127	.889	.347	1.718	1667	-2.144	-1.404	.082	-2.164
1618	1.490	2.280	1.063	.364	1668	-1.978	-.927	-.027	-.715
1619	.127	-.446	.209	-1.183	1669	-2.311	-.776	-.474	-.916
1620	.627	1.686	-1.025	1.205	1670	.058	-.802	-1.968	-1.760
1621	-.166	2.701	3.749	1.367	1671	-.563	.178	-1.185	-1.440
1622	.650	.026	1.223	-1.591	1672	.794	-.034	-.680	1.075
1623	-1.776	1.799	.061	.790	1673	.852	.611	-.031	-.378
1624	-1.541	-1.365	-1.985	-2.586	1674	.225	1.101	-.575	-.223
1625	-4.301	-1.772	.070	-2.639	1675	-1.144	-.052	.482	-1.039
1626	-.482	.035	-.735	-.606	1676	-3.662	-1.278	-1.105	-1.728
1627	1.674	.221	1.800	.340	1677	-.132	1.140	.802	.741
1628	-.758	-1.742	-3.202	-2.329	1678	-.540	-.533	.133	-.525
1629	2.525	2.336	1.897	.466	1679	-1.880	1.110	-.499	-.202
1630	1.663	,811	-.831	1.216	1680	2.755	2.579	.861	1.212
1631	-.218	.087	-.819	-1.109	1681	-,942	-.429	-.869	-.522
1632	-1.886	.711	-1.871	-1.334	1682	-1.253	.360	.836	-2.386
1633	-1.512	.551	.651	-1.513	1683	-,477	1.470	1,467	.864
1634	.823	1.812	.248	-1.531	1684	-3.030	-1.725	-.764	-3.310
1635	1.507	2.401	1.425	2.731	1685	-5.319	-3.060	-1.880	-3.409
1636	1.306	1.197	-2.166	-.332	1686	1.939	1.305	-.111	.097
1637	-2.041	2.237	.453	-.279	1687	-.264	1.244	-.040	-.473
1638	-4.094	-1.599	-.903	-1.809	1688	-1.575	.438	.689	-.420
1639	2.675	1.847	.166	1.455	1689	2.393	3.446	1.362	1.483
1640	1.674	1.409	-.482	2.995	1690	.518	.178	-.806	.459
1641	-2.576	-1.543	-1.059	-1.433	1691	-.810	-.481	.053	-1.932
1642	-1.483	-.082	-1.598	-.515	1692	1.065	3.498	.756	1.451
1643	.495	.542	-1.160	-.441	1693	.012	-.082	-.343	.319
1644	-1.109	-.550	-.154	.681	1694	-2.190	1.075	1.143	-.916
1645	-3.248	-1.543	-.756	-1.700	1695	-.850	.971	.571	-.480
1646	3.658	1.270	1.467	2,.492	1696	-4.215	-2.336	-1.939	-3.135
1647	3.549	.113	-.726	1.124	1697	-1.184	.967	1.232	-.673
1648	-.879	-1.421	-3.092	-1.774	1698	-1.241	-1.083	.764	-.726
1649	1.352	1.058	1.295	.973	1699	1.490	1.249	1.421	.417

Source: Southwest Paleoclimate Project, Laboratory of Tree-Ring Research, University of Arizona, Tucson, AZ (unpublished data).
*Palmer Drought Severity Index values, which integrate precipitation and temperature, are for June of each year for the four areas: Chupadera Mesa, Santa Fe, Chama Valley, and Northern Rio Grande (Taos). Values of less than 1.00 indicate increasing dryness.

Appendix Table B. Dendroclimatic Variability,* Rio Grande Region, NM, 1500-1699

Decade	Jemez Mountains	Chama Valley	Rio Grande Valley, No.	Santa Fe	Chupadera Mesa	Cebolleta Mesa
1500-09	-0.90	-1.60	0.30	-0.50	-0.20	-0.60
1510-19	1.40	1.00	0.80	0.50	-0.50	2.40
1520-29	-1.20	0.70	0.80	0.30	-1.90	-0.30
1530-39	0.70	-0.80	1.30	0.70	2.00	0.00
1540-49	0.50	-1.10	-0.60	-0.70	1.70	-0.50
1550-59	0.50	0.90	2.70	1.40	1.40	0.70
1560-69	-0.80	-2.80	-1.30	-1.20	-0.50	-0.30
1570-79	0.10	-1.70	-1.70	-1.20	-1.60	0.00
1580-89	-3.10	-2.00	-2.60	-2.00	-1.80	-3.50
1590-99	1.40	0.00	-0.20	1.90	0.80	0.10
1600-09	0.20	0.30	-0.20	-0.50	1.40	1.10
1610-19	2.50	3.40	1.50	1.90	2.00	-0.60
1620-29	0.20	-0.10	-0.50	0.40	0.20	-0.90
1630-39	-0.50	0.20	1.00	1.70	-1.20	-1.80
1640-49	0.20	1.40	1.00	-0.70	1.00	2.00
1650-59	1.20	0.90	-0.10	-0.80	0.50	0.80
1660-69	-0.80	-1.50	-1.30	-0.90	-0.70	-0.80
1670-79	-0.70	-1.40	0.40	-0.50	-0.20	-0.30
1680-89	-0.40	-0.90	-1.10	0.30	0.00	0.00
1690-99	0.50	-0.50	1.10	0.60	1.00	0.30

Source: Jeffrey S. Dean and William J. Robinson, *Dendroclimatic Variability in the American Southwest A.D. 680 to 1970,* Final Report of the National Park Service Project: Southwest Paleoclimate, Laboratory of Tree-Ring Research, (Tucson, AZ, 1977).

* Data are based on dendroclimatic variability, reflecting precipitation and temperature, expressed as standard deviations from a mean of zero. Positive departures from the mean indicate greater than normal rainfall and negative departures, the opposite.

Appendix Table C. Tree-Ring Index Values,* El Malpais, NM, 1500-1699

Year	Index	Year	Index	Year	Index	Year	Index	Year	Index
1500	.292	1540	1.567	1580	.006	1620	1.523	1660	1.267
1501	.653	1541	.945	1581	.532	1621	1.430	1661	.949
1502	1.087	1542	.415	1582	.434	1622	1.199	1662	.757
1503	.947	1543	1.057	1583	.379	1623	.696	1663	1.106
1504	.988	1544	.947	1584	.280	1624	.699	1664	.536
1505	1.165	1545	.753	1585	.068	1625	.446	1665	.987
1506	.407	1546	.511	1586	.635	1626	1.004	1666	.614
1507	1.421	1547	.704	1587	.443	1627	1.404	1667	1.018
1508	1.292	1548	.685	1588	.789	1628	.742	1668	.480
1509	1.151	1549	.952	1589	.378	1629	1.075	1669	.564
1510	.487	1550	1.371	1590	.297	1630	1.488	1670	.568
1511	1.505	1551	.757	1591	.819	1631	.989	1671	.705
1512	1.012	1552	.853	1592	.138	1632	.725	1672	.580
1513	1.276	1553	1.487	1593	.038	1633	1.401	1673	1.010
1514	1.338	1554	.897	1594	1.180	1634	1.915	1674	.578
1515	1.044	1555	1.913	1595	.880	1635	1.295	1675	1.334
1516	.446	1556	1.933	1596	.775	1636	1.171	1676	.375
1517	.342	1557	.939	1597	.681	1637	1.381	1677	1.113
1518	1.094	1558	.914	1598	.652	1638	1.069	1678	.518
1519	.894	1559	1.014	1599	.516	1639	1.263	1679	1.027
1520	1.368	1560	.652	1600	.374	1640	1.514	1680	1.137
1521	.922	1561	.359	1601	.558	1641	1.416	1681	1.090
1522	.928	1562	.727	1602	.671	1642	1.015	1682	.973
1523	.566	1563	.962	1603	.761	1643	1.239	1683	.930
1524	.731	1564	1.172	1604	1.164	1644	1.263	1684	.463
1525	.767	1565	1.064	1605	.892	1645	.399	1685	.331
1526	1.396	1566	.658	1606	.647	1646	1.564	1686	1.233
1527	1.081	1567	.564	1607	.804	1647	1.133	1687	.846
1528	.921	1568	.646	1608	.873	1648	.594	1688	.811
1529	1.401	1569	.891	1609	1.116	1649	1.783	1689	1.547
1530	1.214	1570	1.032	1610	1.669	1650	1.236	1690	1.566
1531	.899	1571	.458	1611	1.261	1651	1.923	1691	.812
1532	.719	1572	1.101	1612	1.464	1652	1.622	1692	1.708
1533	.801	1573	.186	1613	1.248	1653	1.121	1693	1.689
1534	1.187	1574	.661	1614	.567	1654	.654	1694	.816
1535	1.335	1575	.540	1615	1.219	1655	1.627	1695	.956
1536	1.208	1576	.317	1616	1.313	1656	1.210	1696	.604
1537	1.386	1577	.807	1617	.927	1657	.922	1697	1.168
1538	.514	1578	.754	1618	1.554	1658	.899	1698	.866
1539	1.206	1579	.259	1619	.893	1659	.449	1699	1.538

Source: Grissino-Mayer, H. "El Malpais Tree-Ring Record." In Grissino-Mayer and Fritts (eds.) *International Tree-Ring Data Bank*. IGBP Pages/World Data Center-A for Paleoclimatology. NOAA/NGDC Paleoclimarology Program, Boulder, CO, USA, 1998.

* Index of tree-ring growth corrected for effects of increasing tree age. Values of less than 1.00 indicate increasing dryness. See H.C. Fritts, *Tree-Rings and Climate* (London, New York, and San Francisco, 1979), 264-67.

Appendix Table D. Precipitation,* Southern Rio Grande Basin, NM, 1500-1699**

Year	Precip.	Year	Precip.	Year	Precip.	Year	Precip.	Year	Precip.
1500	10.97	1540	13.78	1580	8.51	1620	10.49	1660	9.64
1501	7.49	1541	10.62	1581	7.58	1621	12.43	1661	11.99
1502	6.31	1542	7.80	1582	9.39	1622	10.37	1662	10.86
1503	7.53	1543	10.79	1583	5.05	1623	8.71	1663	10.02
1504	9.07	1544	8.92	1584	7.62	1624	4.87	1664	8.39
1505	9.11	1545	9.81	1585	5.08	1625	7.78	1665	11.64
1506	6.28	1546	8.33	1586	9.73	1626	7.65	1666	8.08
1507	13.08	1547	7.80	1587	8.39	1627	12.36	1667	5.34
1508	12.09	1548	9.58	1588	11.21	1628	8.96	1668	4.10
1509	10.05	1549	6.59	1589	9.13	1629	14.34	1669	7.69
1510	11.44	1550	10.65	1590	8.54	1630	10.47	1670	5.86
1511	12.77	1551	7.03	1591	11.18	1631	7.10	1671	8.84
1512	9.55	1552	8.19	1592	9.24	1632	6.38	1672	7.69
1513	9.69	1553	13.51	1593	5.42	1633	9.48	1673	6.03
1514	8.00	1554	11.81	1594	11.25	1634	11.30	1674	8.96
1515	10.20	1555	13.34	1595	9.03	1635	10.22	1675	9.73
1516	6.66	1556	13.19	1596	9.76	1636	10.02	1676	9.35
1517	6.18	1557	9.70	1597	10.86	1637	12.16	1677	11.95
1518	9.66	1558	7.73	1598	8.62	1638	9.31	1678	10.72
1519	10.15	1559	10.61	1599	10.47	1639	11.61	1679	10.30
1520	10.27	1560	4.57	1600	8.35	1640	12.32	1680	12.10
1521	12.42	1561	9.08	1601	5.94	1641	11.28	1681	9.79
1522	6.27	1562	8.76	1602	9.36	1642	8.85	1682	12.96
1523	5.67	1563	7.27	1603	11.52	1643	8.35	1683	11.08
1524	4.11	1564	8.81	1604	10.33	1644	10.65	1684	8.21
1525	8.91	1565	9.98	1605	8.42	1645	10.52	1685	4.96
1526	10.49	1566	10.47	1606	9.55	1646	10.06	1686	11.56
1527	9.33	1567	7.85	1607	12.36	1647	10.94	1687	9.07
1528	8.15	1568	11.64	1608	10.94	1648	6.08	1688	8.35
1529	12.42	1569	8.98	1609	9.42	1649	9.47	1689	12.49
1530	12.57	1570	10.02	1610	11.39	1650	10.19	1690	9.98
1531	10.47	1571	7.44	1611	11.33	1651	12.53	1691	6.95
1532	6.60	1572	7.83	1612	13.23	1652	9.62	1692	13.13
1533	9.10	1573	6.09	1613	8.36	1653	8.81	1693	10.66
1534	11.80	1574	8.48	1614	6.77	1654	7.86	1694	10.79
1535	8.63	1575	7.69	1615	8.65	1655	11.00	1695	9.57
1536	12.48	1576	5.78	1616	9.38	1656	8.48	1696	6.56
1537	10.74	1577	8.75	1617	7.65	1657	6.87	1697	10.75
1538	6.70	1578	9.10	1618	11.53	1658	9.36	1698	9.60
1539	11.65	1579	6.77	1619	10.28	1659	8.87	1699	12.63

Source: Henri Grissino-Mayer, Christopher H. Baisan, and Thomas Swetnam. *A 1,373 Year Reconstruction of Annual Precipitation for the Southern Rio Grande Basin, Final Report.* Fort Bliss, TX: Department of the Army, Directorate of Environment, Natural Resources Division, 1997.

* Reconstructed values in inches.
** Data sites are in the Magdalena, San Mateo, and Organ Mountains, NM.

Appendix Table E. Precipitation,* Albuquerque, NM, 1602-1699

Year	Win	Spr	Sum	Fall	Ann	Year	Win	Spr	Sum	Fall	Ann
1602	0.76	2.69	3.06	2.11	8.62	1651	1.72.	2.68	3.38	2.81	10.59
1603	0.88	2.46	3.22	2.00	8.56	1652	1.04	1.30	2.95	2.69	7.99
1604	0.83	2.68	2.72.	2.22	8.45	1653	0.68	1.69	2.46	2.46	7.29
1605	0.63	2.93	2.74	1.89	8.18	1654	0.77	-.90	3.35	2.35	6.48
1606	0.76	1.73	2.92	2.35	7.75	1655	1.16	3.28	3.01	1.87	9.32
1607	0.87	1.85	2.97	2.72	8.40	1656	0.98	3.04	3.29	1.25	8.56
1608	1.26	1.44	2.76	2.44	7.91	1657	0.49	3.09	3.18	1.70	8.45
1609	1.18	1.32	3.15	2.68	8.35	1658	0.60	3.05	3.21	1.76	8.62
1610	1.14	2.49	3.18	2.22	9.02	1659	0.86	2.59	3.34	2.08	8.86
1611	1.30	0.86	3.04	3.13	8.32	1660	1.38	3.01.	3.39	1.91	9.67
1612	0.65	1.06	2.50	2.72	6.91	1661	0.97	3.40	3.27	2.00	9.64
1613	0.61	0.79	2.21	2.80	6.40	1662	0.73	2.07	3.75	2.32	8.86
1614	1.03	2.05	2.92	2.45	8.43	1663	0.84	2.54	3.13	2.16	8.67
1615	1.07	3.30	2.30	2.60	9.26	1664	0.14	2.37	2.85	2.58	7.94
1616	1.05	3.52	2.63	2.58	9.78	1665	0.99	1.97	3.05	1.66	7.67
1617	1.60	3.02	2.60	2.74	9.97	1666	0.68	1.42	3.21	1.72	7.02
1618	1.36	3.83	2.82	2.62	10.64	1667	0.46	0.75	2.66	1.86	5.73
1619	1.00	2.46	3.30	2.56	9.32	1668	0.20	-.09	2.57	1.78	4.54
1620	1.66	3.80	2.88	2.48	10.80	1669	0.65	1.44	2.89	1.48	6.48
1621	1.09	3.34	2.89	2.04	9.37	1670	0.71	0.64	3.06	1.72	6.13
1622	0.80	1.77	2.94	1.89	7.40	1671	0.74	2.74	2.93	1.93	8.35
1623	0.02	1.75	2.82	1.53	6.13	1672	0.78	0.29	3.32	1.94	6.32
1624	0.00	1.99	2.63	1.36	5.97	1673	1.14	2.90	2.76.	1.72	8.54
1625	0.16	1.66	3.17	1.58	6.56	1674	1.18	3.12	3.22	2.54	10.05
1626	0.00	2.35	3.24	1.99	7.59	1675	1.02	1.04	3.01	1.89	6.97
1627	0.74	2.86	3.15	1.71	8.45	1676	0.46	1.28	3.01	1.91	6.67
1628	0.36	1.81.	3.79	2.06	8.02	1677	0.94	3.00	3.28	1.87	9.08
1629	0.63	2.97	3.39	1.98	8.97	1678	0.84	2.45	2.98	2.11	8.37
1630	0.51	2.41	3.64	1.60	8.16	1679	0.89	2.30	3.05	2.12	8.37
1631	0.40	2.06	3.71	2.41	8.59	1680	1.16	3.32	3.01	2.05	9.99
1632	0.00	2.42	3.18	2.73	8.35	1681	1.03	2.29	3.11	2.39	8.83
1633	0.79	2.21	3.22	1.93	8.16	1682	1.51	1.79	3.33	1.93	8.56
1634	0.68	3.76	3.54	1.99	9.97	1683	1.54	2.82	3.17	1.83	9.37
1635	0.59	3.08	3.19	2.17	9.02	1684	0.43	0.25	3.01	1.02	4.73
1636	0.23	2.07	3.41	2.17	7.89	1685	-.06	0.59	3.60	2.14	6.32
1637	0.26	2.46	3.51	1.66	7.89	1686	0.36	2.10	3.18	1.94	7.59
1638	0.53	2.54	3.56	2.16	8.78	1687	0.69	2.78	3.11	2.06	8.64
1639	0.57	3.40	3.52	2.39	9.89	1688	0.56	1.60	2.89	2.73	7.78
1640	1.00	3.28	3.41	2.12	9.81	1689	1.37	2.49	3.28	2.79	9.94
1641	0.58	2.43	3.05	2.51	8.59	1690	1.43	1.47	3.01	2.08	7.99
1642	0.38	2.80	3.13	1.82	8.13	1691	1.05	1.19	3.77	2.45	8.45
1643	0.73	3.50	3.57	2.00	9.81	1692	1.61	2.38	2.98	2.33	9.29
1644	0.53	3.46	3.38	1.97	9.35	1693	0.92	2.15	3.21	1.81	8.08
1645	0.66	2.34	3.47	2.46	8.94	1694	1.27	1.66	3.65	1.98	8.56
1646	1.02	3.56	3.16	2.51	10.24	1695	0.97	2.66	3.11	1.40	8.13
1647	0.93	2.38.	2.65	2.09	8.05	1696	0.39	1.43	2.92	2.03	6.78
1648	0.66	1.28	2.81	2.86	7.62	1697	0.73	1.19	2.81	2.17	6.89
1649	1.05	3.57	2.95	2.48	10.05	1698	0.89	0.45	3.44	2.23	7.02
1650	1.17	2.31	3.04	2.66	9.18	1699	1.23	1.82	2.83	2.28	8.16
						Av.	0.81	2.22	3.11	2.15	8.29

Source: Harold C. Fritts, *Reconstructing Large-Scale Climatic Patterns from Tree-Ring Data, A Diagnostic Analysis.* Tucson, AZ: University of Arizona Press, 1991. Data are from the computer file related to this volume and made available through the courtesy of Louis A. Scuderi, Department of Georgraphy, University of New Mexico.

* Reconstructed values in inches.

Appendix Table F. Temperature,* Santa Fe, NM, 1602-1699

Year	Win	Spr	Sum	Fall	Ann	Year	Win	Spr	Sum	Fall	Ann
1602	34.06	50.95	68.51	50.52	49.55	1651	30.45	51.97	69.63	50.76	49.23
1603	32.80	51.55	67.95	50.52	49.33	1652	33.43	54.17	69.94	50.70	50.74
1604	34.28	51.62	68.58	50.28	49.78	1653	31.59	52.77	69.90	50.83	49.83
1605	31.86	51.85	67.72	50.36	49.12	1654	30.47	55.67	69.14	49.99	50.20
1606	32.32	53.53	68.14	50.59	49.93	1655	29.12	51.40	69.07	50.59	48.56
1607	30.69	52.70	67.98	50.78	49.26	1556	31.15	52.83	68.41	50.46	49.41
1608	33.65	52.67	67.81	50.59	49.91	1657	32.68	51.82	69.17	49.80	49.42
1609	32.66	51.72	66.82	50.76	49.23	1658	33.04	52.78	68.64	49.46	49.65
1610	34.79	51.03	67.22	51.53	49.80	1659	32.68	52.93	68.27	50.31	49.77
1611	35.52	52.23	67.94	50.63	50.27	1660	32.97	53.31	67.44	50.23	49.82
1612	31.71	51.27	67.94	51.00	49.10	1661	33.07	52.43	68.92	50.01	49.73
1613	33.14	52.34	69.55	51.24	50.12	1662	32.24	52.60	67.95	49.10	49.18
1614	30.93	52.83	67.88	51.96	49.64	1663	34.21	52.80	68.58	50.55	50.22
1615	35.81	50.07	69.55	51.85	50.20	1664	32.10	53.50	69.55	49.62	49.86
1616	33.14	50.21	68.34	52.12	49.44	1665	30.33	53.89	68.14	49.74	49.33
1617	37.58	50.22	69.18	51.98	50.67	1666	32.34	53.53	67.91	49.40	49.60
1618	33.04	49.71	68.81	51.39	49.13	1667	30.59	52.64	69.12	49.58	49.12
1619	34.47	49.72	68.98	51.55	49.57	1668	32.41	55.41	68.32	50.22	50.52
1620	33.82	50.91	68.24	51.42	49.65	1669	30.33	52.61	67.82	49.83	48.89
1621	34.86	49.45	68.55	51.55	49.52	1670	31.95	54.30	69.11	49.85	49.91
1622	31.86	51.56	68.15	50.92	49.25	1671	31.54	52.74	68.14	49.83	49.28
1623	33.60	51.75	69.11	51.02	49.93	1672	43.26	53.22	67.79	50.11	50.12
1624	33.31	52.02	68.54	51.03	49.86	1673	33.99	51.26	69.40	50.35	49.57
1625	33.77	51.46	69.10	50.84	49.82	1674	32.00	52.37	68.18	50.36	49.41
1626	32.46	51.08	68.98	50.99	49.39	1675	34.89	52.32	68.12	50.28	50.09
1627	33.33	52.23	69.14	51.05	50.04	1676	32.75	52.03	68.91	50.06	49.54
1628	34.26	51.67	68.31	50.68	49.83	1677	28.70	52.20	67.79	49.83	48.32
1629	33.72	50.80	69.67	50.03	49.48	1678	31.81	51.12	68.72	50.17	48.99
1630	32.61	52.81	69.15	50.36	49.88	1679	32.78	53.66	68.34	50.17	50.02
1631	35.20	52.75	68.75	49.98	50.35	1680	30.69	51.20	68.57	49.80	48.61
1632	35.11	52.39	68.27	51.16	50.41	1681	31.73	52.87	68.22	49.64	49.33
1633	34.77	52.98	68.25	50.81	50.43	1682	31.35	53.34	67.27	50.12	49.36
1634	31.64	51.62	67.74	50.43	49.01	1683	31.52	51.46	67.12	49.69	48.63
1635	33.33	51.08	68.97	51.16	49.64	1684	32.80	53.79	67.88	50.41	50.04
1636	34.06	52.42	69.37	49.87	50.02	1685	33.67	53.69	67.58	48.87	49.80
1637	31.06	52.67	69.34	50.31	49.46	1686	33.24	52.32	67.92	50.06	49.59
1638	32.83	53.57	68.10	49.93	49.89	1687	32.15	52.54	67.78	50.22	49.41
1639	32.20	50.77	67.78	50.22	48.83	1688	33.50	52.83	68.91	50.05	49.98
1640	32.56	51.27	67.88	49.85	49.01	1689	30.47	53.21	68.44	50.44	49.37
1641	34.94	51.56	68.00	50.09	49.78	1690	33.53	53.80	69.12	50.15	50.38
1642	32.95	51.46	67.98	51.02	49.48	1691	30.72	52.70	67.21	50.09	48.97
1643	32.78	50.89	67.65	50.44	49.05	1692	32.78	52.92	68.47	50.35	49.83
1644	35.08	49.81	68.64	50.38	49.41	1693	30.96	52.63	68.44	50.35	49.28
1645	32.78	52.40	68.52	50.39	49.68	1694	32.97	53.18	68.11	50.70	49.99
1646	31.47	50.79	68.51	50.46	48.83	1695	34.47	51.09	68.45	50.76	49.75
1647	32.70	52.58	68.25	50.19	49.62	1696	34.28	53.33	69.90	50.44	50.43
1648	31.03	53.83	68.80	50.25	49.73	1697	33.84	53.53	69.18	50.38	50.43
1649	31.90	51.15	68.37	50.79	49.12	1698	31.35	53.16	68.11	50.47	49.54
1650	32.80	53.51	68.12	50.71	50.07	1699	33.53	53.18	69.02	50.92	50.35
						Av.	32.76	52.27	68.43	49.93	49.63

Source: Harold C. Fritts, *Reconstructing Large-scale Climatic Patterns from Tree-Ring Data, A Diagnostic Analysis.* Tucson, AZ: University of Arizona Press, 1991. Data are from the computer file related to this volume and made available through the courtesy of Louis A. Scuderi, Department of Geography, University of New Mexico.

* Reconstructed values in degrees Fahrenheit.

Appendix Table G. Temperature Anomaly Data,* San Francisco Peaks, AZ, 1500-1699

Year	Temp.	Year	Temp.	Year	Temp.	Year	Temp.	Year	Temp.
1500	-0.12	1540	0.57	1580	0.34	1620	-0.81	1660	0.78
1501	0.39	1541	0.18	1581	-0.12	1621	-0.28	1661	-0.41
1502	-0.69	1542	0.20	1582	-0.37	1622	-0.44	1662	-0.54
1503	-0.32	1543	0.85	1583	-0.71	1623	-0.99	1663	0.30
1504	-0.35	1544	1.58	1584	-0.23	1624	-0.13	1664	-0.62
1505	-0.38	1545	0.53	1585	0.27	1625	-0.18	1665	-0.30
1506	0.14	1546	0.12	1586	0.60	1626	0.06	1666	-0.89
1507	-0.43	1547	0.92	1587	1.22	1627	0.91	1667	-0.69
1508	-0.14	1548	0.30	1588	0.93	1628	1.40	1668	-1.10
1509	0.13	1549	0.62	1589	1.00	1629	0.83	1669	-1.41
1510	-0.24	1550	-0.32	1590	1.14	1630	0.28	1670	-0.97
1511	-0.24	1551	-0.23	1591	1.39	1631	0.45	1671	-1.34
1512	-0.97	1552	-0.12	1592	1.18	1632	-0.14	1672	-0.90
1513	-0.75	1553	-0/23	1593	0.96	1633	0.64	1673	-0.96
1514	-0.93	1554	-0.72	1594	0.18	1634	0.20	1674	-0.27
1515	-1.14	1555	-0.13	1595	0.15	1635	-0.28	1675	-0.49
1516	-0.75	1556	-0.84	1596	0.39	1636	-0.42	1676	-1.01
1517	-1.82	1557	-0.83	1597	0.65	1637	-0.50	1677	-0.61
1518	-1.70	1558	-0.68	1598	-0.28	1638	-1.16	1678	-0.89
1519	-1.76	1559	0.17	1599	-1.21	1639	-0.94	1679	-1.62
1520	-2.35	1560	0.06	1600	-0.67	1640	-1.03	1680	-2.73
1521	-1.50	1561	0.08	1601	-1.00	1641	-1.57	1681	-0.61
1522	-1.06	1562	1.38	1602	-0.10	1642	-2.06	1682	-0.94
1523	-0.44	1563	1.02	1603	-0.51	1643	-2.69	1683	-0.40
1524	-0.58	1564	-0.19	1604	-0.96	1644	-2.45	1684	-0.09
1525	-0.58	1565	-0.74	1605	-1.61	1645	-2.38	1685	0.23
1526	-0.28	1566	-0.94	1606	-0.63	1646	-3.29	1686	-0.10
1527	-0.61	1567	-0.54	1607	-0.17	1647	-2.49	1687	-0.71
1528	-0.02	1568	-0.48	1608	-1.03	1648	-1.83	1688	0.59
1529	1.32	1569	0.06	1609	-1.35	1649	-1.77	1689	1.43
1530	1.11	1570	-0.83	1610	-0.94	1650	-1.19	1690	0.90
1531	2.79	1571	0.14	1611	-0.24	1651	-1.82	1691	1.21
1532	2.50	1572	-0.41	1612	-0.38	1652	-1.52	1692	1.12
1533	1.12	1573	0.07	1613	0.93	1653	-0.81	1693	2.24
1534	1.26	1574	-0.25	1614	0.06	1654	0.08	1694	2.46
1535	-0.16	1575	0.70	1615	0.20	1655	0.77	1695	1.06
1536	0.05	1576	-0.49	1616	-0.17	1656	0.49	1696	0.95
1537	-0.35	1577	-1.09	1617	-0.72	1657	0.89	1697	0.96
1538	1.22	1578	-0.95	1618	-0.75	1658	0.60	1698	0.35
1539	0.98	1579	-0.87	1619	0.30	1659	0.27	1699	-0.05

Source: Matthew W. Salzer, *Dendroclimatology in the San Francisco Peaks Region of Northern Arizona, USA,* Ph.D. Dissertation, University of Arizona, Tucson. Ann Arbor, MI: University Microfilms International, 2000.

* Values are derived from tree-ring data from bristlecone pine trees at the upper treeline (11,000+ feet above sea level) and are expressed as standard deviation units from a mean of zero, with negative numbers colder than the long-term average and positive numbers warmer.

INDEX